Houghton Mifflin

Math Expressions

Volume 2

Developed by
The Children's Math Worlds
Research Project

PROJECT DIRECTOR AND AUTHOR

Dr. Karen C. Fuson

This material is based upon work supported by the
National Science Foundation
under Grant Numbers
ESI-9816320, REC-9806020, and RED-935373.

Any opinions, findings, and conclusions or recommendations expressed in this material are those of the author and do not necessarily reflect the views of the National Science Foundation.

HOUGHTON MIFFLIN BOSTON

Teacher Reviewers

Kindergarten
Patricia Stroh Sugiyama
Wilmette, Illinois

Barbara Wahle
Evanston, Illinois

Grade 1
Sandra Budson
Newton, Massachusetts

Janet Pecci
Chicago, Illinois

Megan Rees
Chicago, Illinois

Grade 2
Molly Dunn
Danvers, Massachusetts

Agnes Lesnick
Hillside, Illinois

Rita Soto
Chicago, Illinois

Grade 3
Jane Curran
Honesdale, Pennsylvania

Sandra Tucker
Chicago, Illinois

Grade 4
Sara Stoneberg Llibre
Chicago, Illinois

Sheri Roedel
Chicago, Illinois

Grade 5
Todd Atler
Chicago, Illinois

Leah Barry
Norfolk, Massachusetts

Special Thanks
Special thanks to the many teachers, students, parents, principals, writers, researchers, and work-study students who participated in the Children's Math Worlds Research Project over the years.

Credits
Cover art: (tiger) © Juniors Bildarchiv/Alamy Images. (whale) © Francois Gohier/Photo Researchers, Inc. (grass) © Corel Stock Photo Library. (tape) © Eyewire.

Illustrative art: Robin Boyer/Deborah Wolfe, LTD
Technical art: Nesbitt Graphics, Inc.
Photos: Nesbitt Graphics, Inc.

Printed in the U.S.A.

ISBN-13: 978-0-618-50981-2
ISBN-10: 0-618-50981-X

8 9 1421 11 10 09

VOLUME 2 CONTENTS

Unit 4 Tables and Graphs

Mini Unit D Diagonals and Midpoints

Continued ▶

Unit 5 Subtracting 2-Digit Numbers

Mini Unit E Shapes and Patterns

* This lesson consists only of activities from the Teacher's Guide.

Unit 6 3-Digit Addition and Subtraction

Mini Unit F Metric Measurement and 3-D Shapes

Continued ▶

* This lesson consists only of activities from the Teacher's Guide.

Unit 7 Multiplication and Fractions

Mini Unit G Non-Standard and Standard Units of Measure

* This lesson consists only of activities from the Teacher's Guide.

Dear Family,

Your child is learning how to show information in various ways. In this unit, children will learn how to create and read picture graphs, bar graphs, circle graphs, and tables.

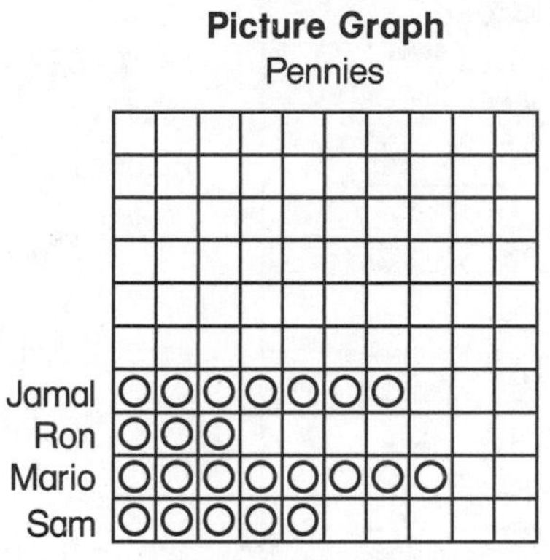

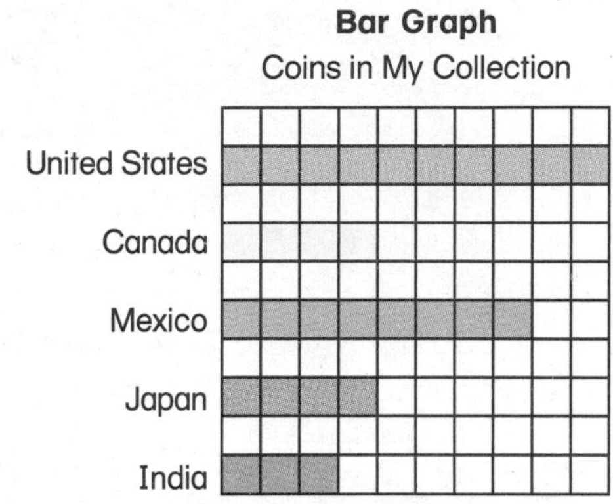

Circle Graph

Kacey's Babysitting Money

$4 Savings

$5 Clothes

$2 Snacks

$4 Games

$1 Movie Rental

Table

Seeds that Lara and Angelo Planted

	Bean	Corn	Total
Lara	67	79	146
Angelo	45	58	103
Total	112	137	249

An important feature of *Math Expressions* is its emphasis on real-world connections. In this unit, children will participate in a data collection project that lasts several days. Children will make a table to show the information they gathered during those days. They will then show the same information in a picture graph.

Children also explore the language of comparison by using such words as *same, more, less,* and *fewer.* The connection between pairs of terms is emphasized. For example: Carlos has 8 stickers. Maria has 3. Carlos has 5 *more* stickers than Maria. Maria has 5 *fewer* stickers than Carlos.

Please call if you have any questions or concerns. Thank you for helping your child learn how to create, read, and interpret graphs.

Sincerely,
Your child's teacher

Estimada familia:

Su niño está aprendiendo a mostrar información de varias maneras. En esta unidad los niños aprenderán a crear y a leer gráficas ilustradas, gráficas de barras, gráficas circulares y tablas.

Gráfica ilustrada

Monedas de 1 centavo

Gráfica de barras

Monedas de mi colección

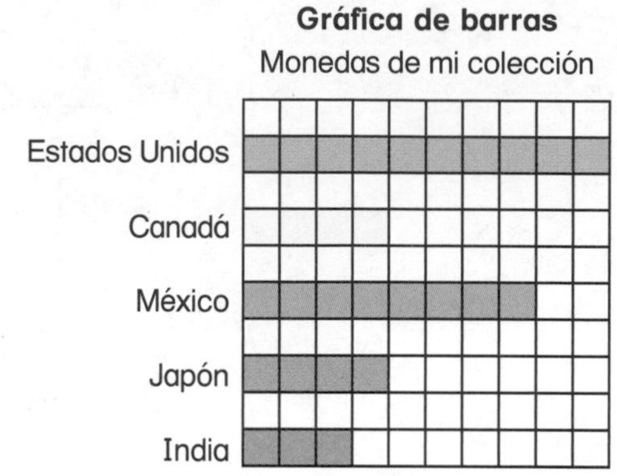

Gráfica circular

Dinero que ganó Kacey por cuidar niños

$4 Ahorros

$5 Ropa

$4 Juegos

$1 Alquiler de películas

$2 Comida

Tabla

Semillas que sembraron Lara y Angelo

	Frijol	Maíz	Total
Lara	67	79	146
Angelo	45	58	103
Total	112	137	249

Un aspecto importante de *Math Expressions* es el énfasis en las conexiones con el mundo real. En esta unidad, los niños participarán en un proyecto de recolección de datos que dura varios días. Los niños harán una tabla para mostrar los datos que obtuvieron en esos días. Luego mostrarán la misma información en una gráfica ilustrada.

Los niños también estudian el lenguaje de la comparación usando palabras como *igual, mismo, más* y *menos.* Se hace énfasis en la conexión entre los pares de términos. Por ejemplo: Carlos tiene 8 figuras adhesivas. María tiene 3. Carlos tiene 5 figuras adhesivas *más* que María. María tiene 5 figuras adhesivas *menos* que Carlos.

Si tiene alguna pregunta o comentario, por favor comuníquese conmigo. Gracias por ayudar a su niño a aprender a crear, leer e interpretar gráficas.

Atentamente,
El maestro de su niño

4–2 Class Activity

Name ____________________

► Use Picture Graphs to Compare Amounts

Write the number. Ring *more* or *fewer.*

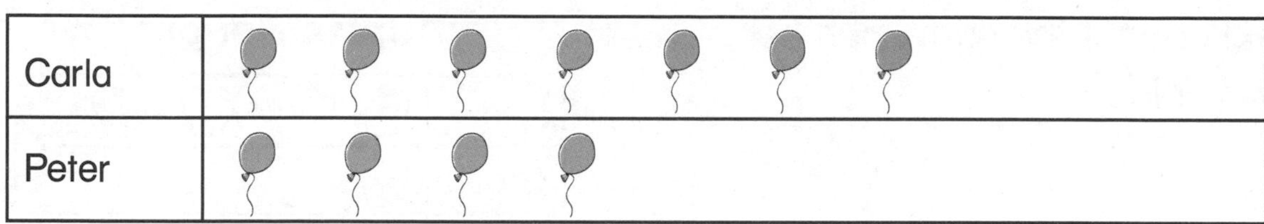

1. Carla has ☐ *more fewer* balloons than Peter.

2. Peter has ☐ *more fewer* balloons than Carla.

3. There are ☐ *more fewer* flowers than vases.

4. There are ☐ *more fewer* vases than flowers.

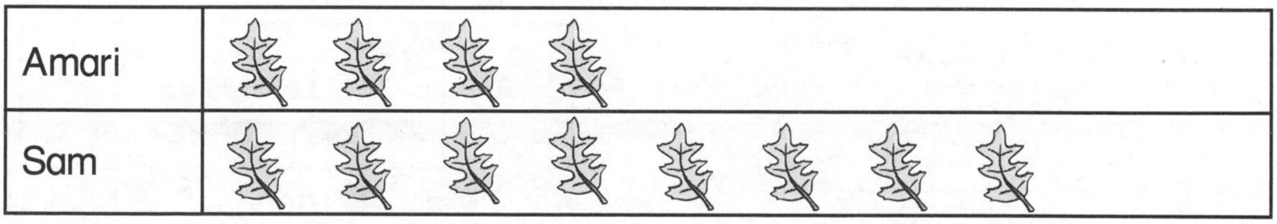

Amari	
Sam	

5. Amari has ☐ *more fewer* leaves than Sam.

6. Sam has ☐ *more fewer* leaves than Amari.

Name ______________________________

Vocabulary
pictograph

▶ Introduce Pictographs

This **pictograph** shows the number of apples Mrs. Reid bought at the store.

Apples Bought

Red	🍎 🍎 🍎 🍎
Green	🍎 🍎
Yellow	🍎 🍎

Key: Each 🍎 stands for 2 apples.

1. Mrs. Reid bought the same number of which two colors?

   __________ __________

2. How many red apples did she buy?

   ☐ __________ label

3. How many more red apples than green apples did she buy?

   ☐ __________ label

4. How many green and yellow apples did she buy?

   ☐ __________ label

This pictograph shows the number of books that four children read.

Books Read

Pablo	📕 📕 📕
Janis	📕 📕
Helen	📕
Ray	📕 📕 📕 📕

Key: Each 📕 stands for 5 books.

5. Who read the most books?

   ____

6. How many books did Pablo read?

   ☐ __________ label

7. How many more books did Janis read than Helen?

   ☐ __________ label

8. How many books did the children read altogether?

   ☐ __________ label

Name ______________________

► Use Comparison Language

Compare. Circle the extra amount. Write the number.
Then ring *more* or *fewer*.

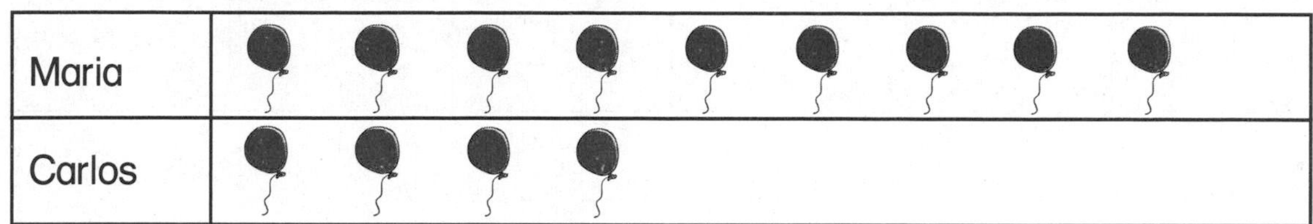

Maria	
Carlos	

1. Maria has ☐ *more* *fewer* balloons than Carlos.

2. Carlos has ☐ *more* *fewer* balloons than Maria.

3. Carlos needs ☐ balloons to have as many as Maria.

Jade	
Sean	

4. Jade has ☐ *more* *fewer* stars than Sean.

5. Sean has ☐ *more* *fewer* stars than Jade.

6. Sean must lose ☐ stars to have as many as Jade.

7. **On the Back** Draw a picture graph to show two children who have different amounts of flowers. Then write 3 sentences to describe the graph.

Name ______________________________

Name ______________________________

▶ Addition Sprint

5 + 7 =	9 + 6 =	7 + 6 =
4 + 8 =	7 + 8 =	4 + 6 =
3 + 9 =	9 + 7 =	0 + 7 =
7 + 5 =	9 + 2 =	4 + 9 =
4 + 5 =	5 + 2 =	6 + 8 =
8 + 4 =	6 + 4 =	8 + 5 =
8 + 6 =	8 + 7 =	6 + 1 =
6 + 9 =	5 + 5 =	5 + 4 =
9 + 9 =	1 + 9 =	7 + 4 =
6 + 3 =	7 + 9 =	3 + 6 =
9 + 0 =	4 + 7 =	9 + 4 =
7 + 7 =	8 + 8 =	5 + 8 =
9 + 1 =	6 + 6 =	3 + 4 =
8 + 9 =	3 + 5 =	6 + 7 =
2 + 5 =	9 + 3 =	1 + 6 =
3 + 9 =	2 + 9 =	5 + 6 =
2 + 7 =	2 + 6 =	5 + 5 =
9 + 4 =	5 + 9 =	6 + 8 =
2 + 8 =	8 + 2 =	4 + 4 =
0 + 8 =	9 + 8 =	1 + 8 =
8 + 3 =	6 + 5 =	6 + 7 =

Class Activity

Name ______________________

Vocabulary
comparison story problem

▶ Graph and Solve Comparison Story Problems

Make a drawing to solve each **comparison story problem**.

Show your work.

1. Carrie has 8 peaches. Dave has 7 more peaches than Carrie. How many peaches does Dave have?

☐ ______________ label

2. Sue has 11 markers. Tom has 4 fewer markers than Sue. How many markers does Tom have?

☐ ______________ label

3. Tony folded 12 sweaters. Janet folded 4 sweaters. How many more sweaters did Tony fold than Janet?

☐ ______________ label

4. Naheem swept the floor for 9 minutes. Sharon swept the floor for 5 minutes. How many fewer minutes did Sharon sweep the floor than Naheem?

☐ ______________ label

Name

Vocabulary
table

▶ More Comparisons

Use the **table**. Fill in the boxes with numbers. Ring *more* or *fewer*.

	Hamsters	Mice
Kendra	5	8
Scott	2	9
Ida	7	3

1. Scott has ☐ *more fewer* mice than Ida.

2. Kendra has ☐ *more fewer* hamsters than Scott.

3. Ida has ☐ *more fewer* mice than Scott.

4. The children have ☐ hamsters altogether.

5. Scott needs ☐ more hamsters to have as many as Kendra.

6. Ida must get ☐ more mice to have as many as Kendra.

7. Scott and Kendra have a total of ☐ mice.

8. **On the Back** Write two more sentences using the information in the table.

Name

Name ______________________

Class Activity

Vocabulary
table
picture graph

▶ From Table to Picture Graph

Lili has 5 turtles. Jason has 9 turtles.

1. Make a **table** to show this.

____

2. Turn the **table** into a **picture graph.**

Use a circle for each .

____

3. Use your own data to make a **table.**
Then turn it into a **picture graph.**

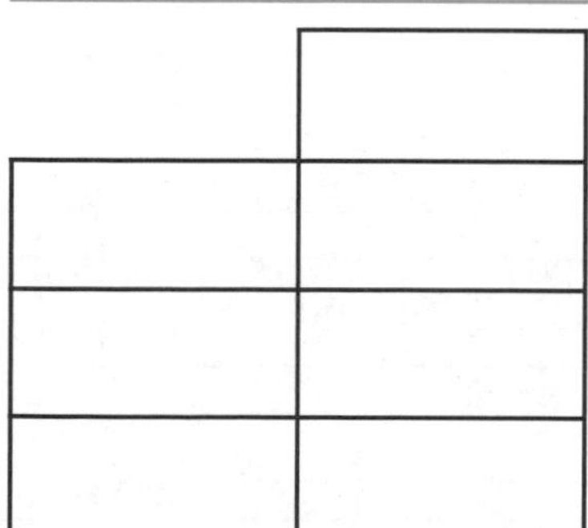

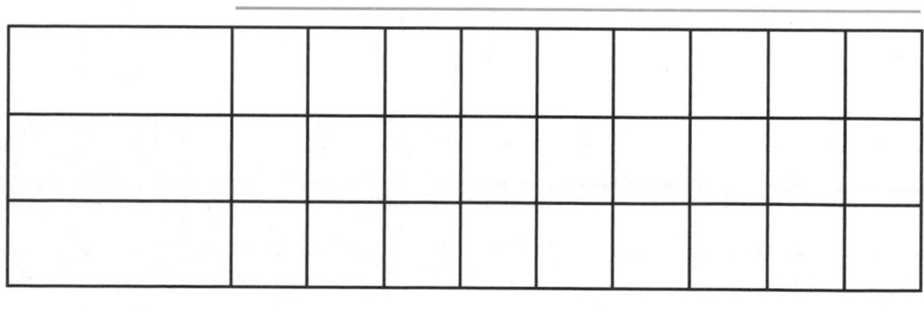

4. **On the Back** Write two questions that can be answered using your graph. Then give your questions to a classmate to answer.

Name

4–7 Class Activity

Name ______________________________

Vocabulary
table
picture graph
data

▶ Record the Collected Data

1. Fill in the **table**. Your teacher will help you.

____

	Number of Children

2. Fill in the **picture graph**. Your teacher will help you.

____

3. Write two questions about the **data** in the graph.

____

____

____

____

4-7 Going Further

Name ______________________

▶ Take a Survey and Record Results

1. What survey question will you ask? Choose a topic from the list or make up your own.

____

Possible Topics
Favorite pet
Favorite subject
Favorite book
Favorite game
Favorite sport

2. What are your four possible answer choices?

__________ __________

__________ __________

3. Take a survey. Use tally marks to record your data.

____

	Number of Children

4. Use your data to make a table.

____

	Number of Children

5. Use your table to make a picture graph.

____

Name

► Addition Sprint

5 + 7 =	9 + 6 =	7 + 6 =
4 + 8 =	7 + 8 =	4 + 6 =
3 + 9 =	9 + 7 =	0 + 7 =
7 + 5 =	9 + 2 =	4 + 9 =
4 + 5 =	5 + 2 =	6 + 8 =
8 + 4 =	6 + 4 =	8 + 5 =
8 + 6 =	8 + 7 =	6 + 1 =
6 + 9 =	5 + 5 =	5 + 4 =
9 + 9 =	1 + 9 =	7 + 4 =
6 + 3 =	7 + 9 =	3 + 6 =
9 + 0 =	4 + 7 =	9 + 4 =
7 + 7 =	8 + 8 =	5 + 8 =
9 + 1 =	6 + 6 =	3 + 4 =
8 + 9 =	3 + 5 =	6 + 7 =
2 + 5 =	9 + 3 =	1 + 6 =
3 + 9 =	2 + 9 =	5 + 6 =
2 + 7 =	2 + 6 =	5 + 5 =
9 + 4 =	5 + 9 =	6 + 8 =
2 + 8 =	8 + 2 =	4 + 4 =
0 + 8 =	9 + 8 =	1 + 8 =
8 + 3 =	6 + 5 =	6 + 7 =

4–8

Class Activity

Name ______________________________

Vocabulary
picture graph
bar graph

▶ Make a Picture Graph

Title: ______________________________

▶ Make a Bar Graph

Title: ______________________________

Number of Children

Name

Vocabulary
bar graphs

▶ Read a Horizontal Bar Graph

Talk about these **bar graphs** with your classmates.

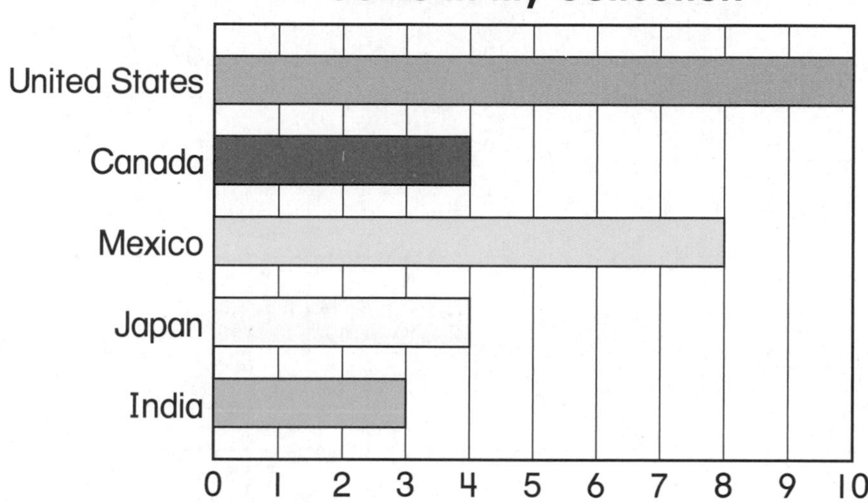

▶ Read a Vertical Bar Graph

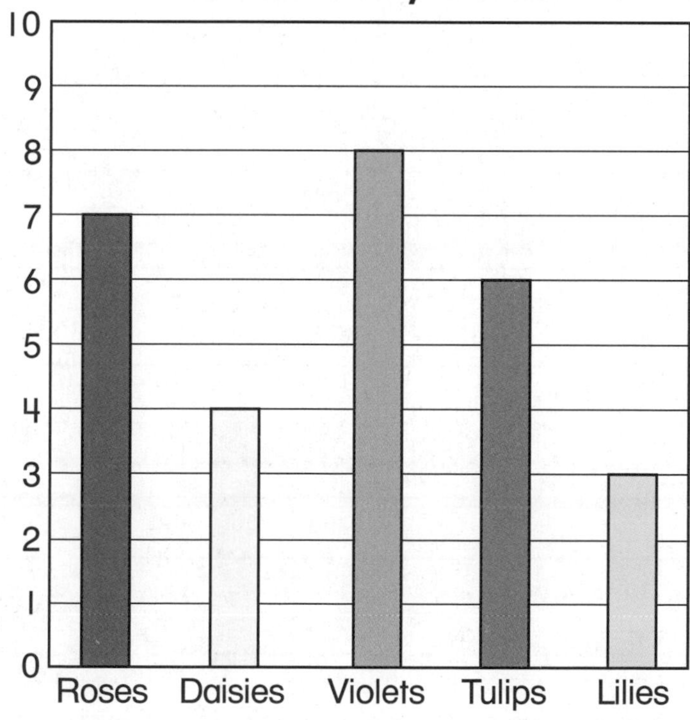

On the Back Write two questions you can answer using these bar graphs.

Name

Name ______________________________

Vocabulary
bar graph

▶ Read a Horizontal Bar Graph

Use the **bar graph** to complete the sentences.
Write the number. Ring *more* or *fewer.*

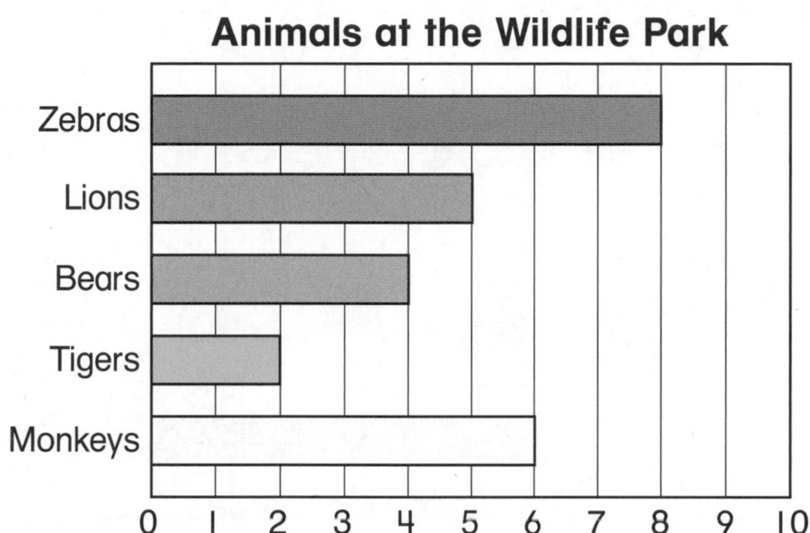

1. There are ☐ *more* *fewer* tigers than bears.
2. There are ☐ *more* *fewer* monkeys than tigers.
3. There are ☐ *more* *fewer* lions than tigers.
4. There are ☐ *more* *fewer* tigers than zebras.
5. There are ☐ lions, tigers, and bears combined.
6. There are ☐ zebras and monkeys in all.
7. There are 2 more monkeys than ______________.

Name ______________________

▶ Organize and Graph Information

Here are some shapes for you to graph.

First make a table.

Then make a bar graph.

____

	How Many?

Name ______________________________

Vocabulary
bar graph
circle graph

► Compare Bar Graphs and Circle Graphs

Fill in the **bar graph** from the information given.

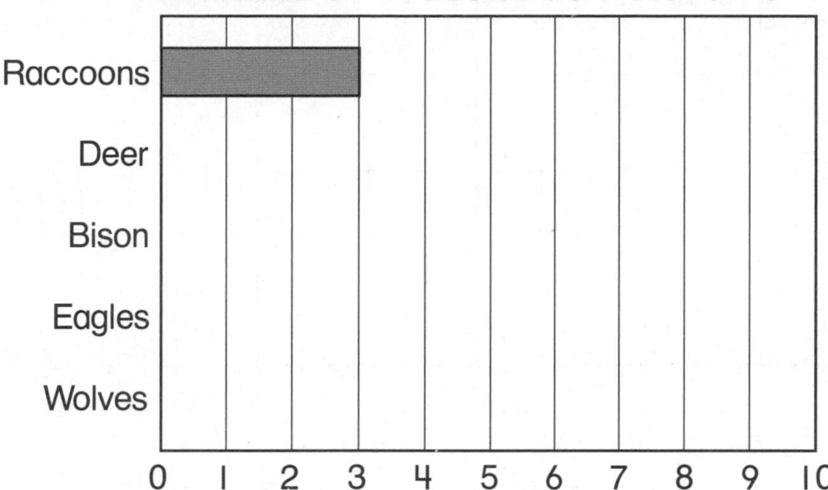

1. There are 3 more deer than raccoons. There are ______ deer.
2. There are 2 more bison than deer. There are ______ bison.
3. There are 4 fewer wolves than bison. There are ______ wolves.
4. The park needs 4 more eagles to have as many eagles as deer.

   There are ______ eagles.

5. Use the information from the bar graph to fill in the **circle graph.**

Title: ______________________________

____

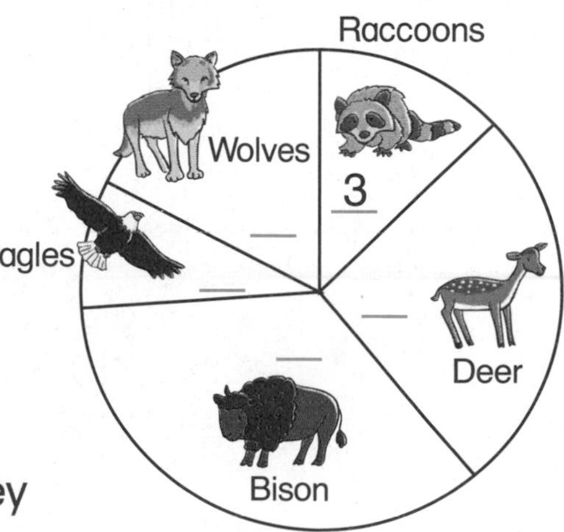

6. **On the Back** Ask 8 friends which subject they like most: Reading, Math, Science, or Social Studies. Make a tally chart and a circle graph to show your results.

Name ______________________________

Favorite Subject

	Tally Marks	Number of Children
Reading		
Math		
Science		
Social Studies		

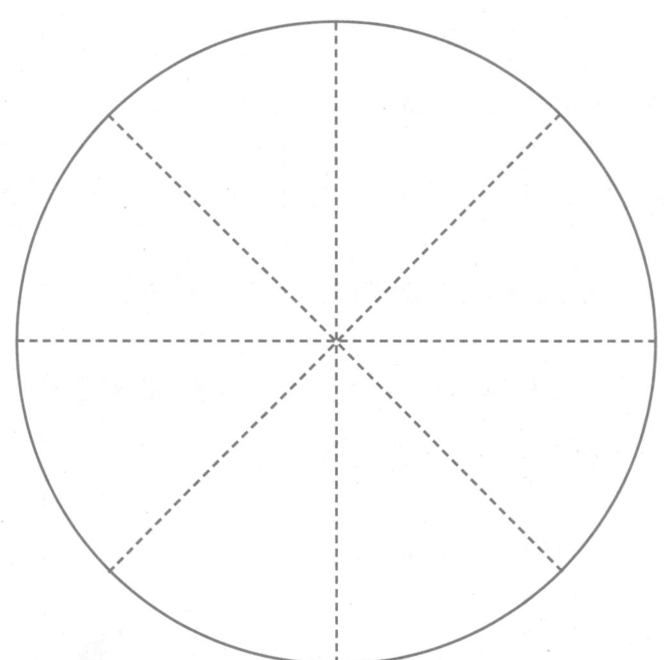

Name

▶ Addition Sprint

5 + 7 =	9 + 6 =	7 + 6 =
4 + 8 =	7 + 8 =	4 + 6 =
3 + 9 =	9 + 7 =	0 + 7 =
7 + 5 =	9 + 2 =	4 + 9 =
4 + 5 =	5 + 2 =	6 + 8 =
8 + 4 =	6 + 4 =	8 + 5 =
8 + 6 =	8 + 7 =	6 + 1 =
6 + 9 =	5 + 5 =	5 + 4 =
9 + 9 =	1 + 9 =	7 + 4 =
6 + 3 =	7 + 9 =	3 + 6 =
9 + 0 =	4 + 7 =	9 + 4 =
7 + 7 =	8 + 8 =	5 + 8 =
9 + 1 =	6 + 6 =	3 + 4 =
8 + 9 =	3 + 5 =	6 + 7 =
2 + 5 =	9 + 3 =	1 + 6 =
3 + 9 =	2 + 9 =	5 + 6 =
2 + 7 =	2 + 6 =	5 + 5 =
9 + 4 =	5 + 9 =	6 + 8 =
2 + 8 =	8 + 2 =	4 + 4 =
0 + 8 =	9 + 8 =	1 + 8 =
8 + 3 =	6 + 5 =	6 + 7 =

4-12 Class Activity

Name ______________________

Vocabulary
circle graph

▶ Explore Circle Graphs

Here is a **circle graph.**

1. Tell two things the graph shows.

How Kacey Spent Her Babysitting Money

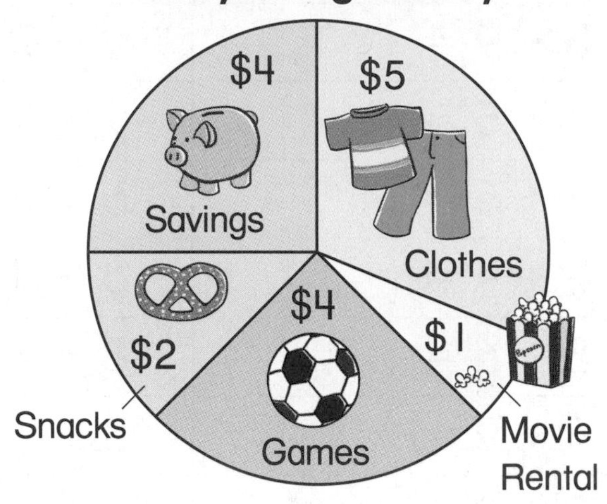

2. How many hours did Rufus spend traveling and meeting fans?

How Rufus Spends His Day (in hours)

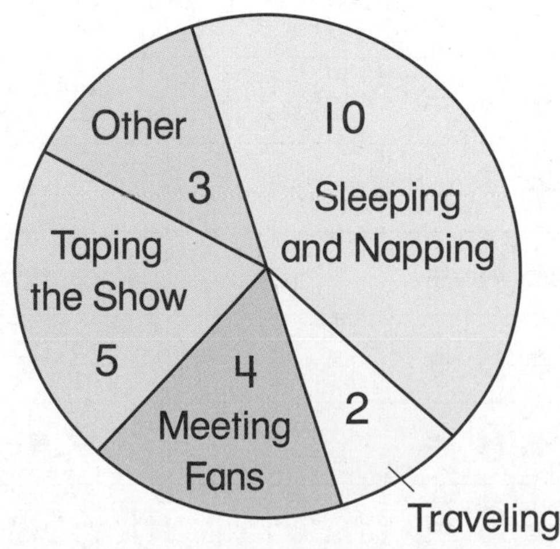

Name ______________________________

Vocabulary
ordered pair
coordinate grid

▶ Graph on a Coordinate Grid

You can use **ordered pairs** to find and name points on a **coordinate grid.**

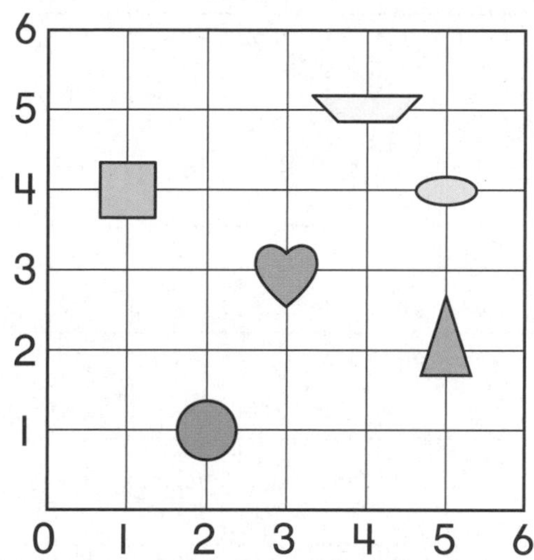

- The *first* number tells you how many spaces to move to the *right*.
- The *second* number tells you how many spaces to move *up*.

What shape is at (1, 4)?

Start at 0.
Count 1 space to the right.
Go up 4 spaces.

The square is at (1, 4).

Use the **ordered pair.** Draw the shape you find.

1. (5, 2) ________
2. (4, 5) ________
3. (3, 3) ________
4. (1, 4) ________
5. (2, 1) ________
6. (5, 4) ________

Write the **ordered pair** for each shape.

7. ____________________
8. ____________________
9. ____________________
10. ____________________

11. Draw a rectangle at (2, 5).

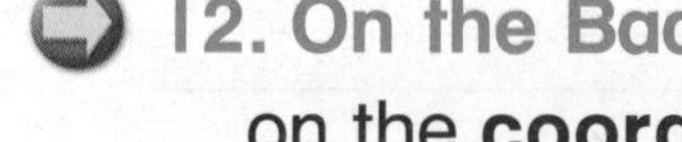

12. **On the Back** Explain how you can find the circle on the **coordinate grid.**

Name

4-13 Class Activity

Name ______________________

Vocabulary
horizontal bar graph
vertical bar graph

▶ Write Comparison Statements

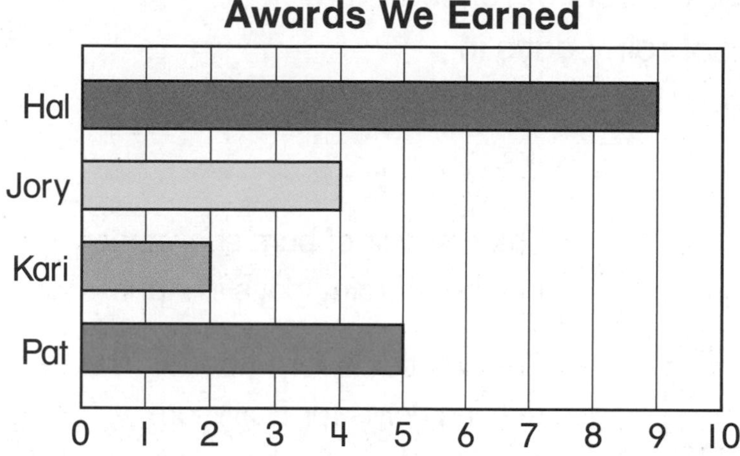

1. Use the **horizontal bar graph**. Write an *is greater than* statement.

____

____

▶ Make a Vertical Bar Graph

2. Create a **vertical bar graph** from the horizontal bar graph above.

4-13 Going Further

Name ______________________________

▶ Introduce Double Bar Graphs

A double bar graph compares two sets of related data. This graph shows the number of rainy days in Phoenix, Arizona and Baltimore, Maryland.

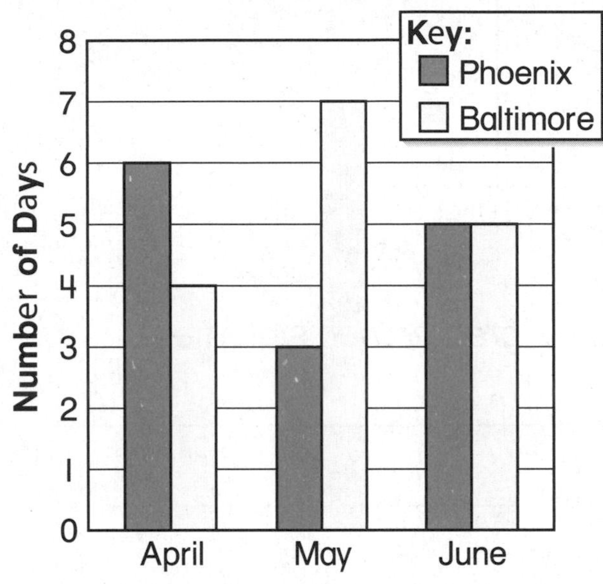

The first pair of bars shows the number of rainy days in April.

The first bar is for Phoenix. The second bar is for Baltimore.

1. How many fewer days did it rain in Phoenix than in Baltimore in May?

____

2. How many more days did it rain in May than in June in Baltimore?

____

3. How many days total did it rain in Phoenix in the three months?

____

4. **Write Your Own** Write and answer your own question comparing the data for Phoenix with the data for Baltimore.

____

____

4-14 Class Activity

Name ______________________

Vocabulary
table

► Read and Complete Tables

This **table** shows information about seeds that Lara and Angelo planted. Follow the directions to complete the **table.**

Seeds Planted

	Bean	Corn	Total
Lara	67	79	
Angelo	45	58	
Total			

1. How many seeds did Lara plant in all? ______ seeds
   Put this number in the table.

2. How many seeds did Angelo plant in all? ______ seeds
   Put this number in the table.

3. How many bean seeds did the children plant? ______ bean seeds
   Put this number in the table.

4. How many seeds did the children plant altogether? ______ seeds
   Put this number in the table.

► Partners and Totals in a Table

Answer these questions about the table.

5. Find the total number of corn seeds planted. ______ corn seeds

   The partners are ______ and ______.

6. Find the total number of seeds Lara planted. ______ seeds

   The partners are ______ and ______.

Name ____________________

Vocabulary
bar graph
circle graph

▶ Read Two Kinds of Graphs

Use the **bar graph**.

7. Which two rides together are as tall as the Towering Tower?

____

____

8. Which three rides are shorter than Towering Tower?

____

____

9. If Super Slide were put on top of Crazy Coaster, how tall would they be together?

____

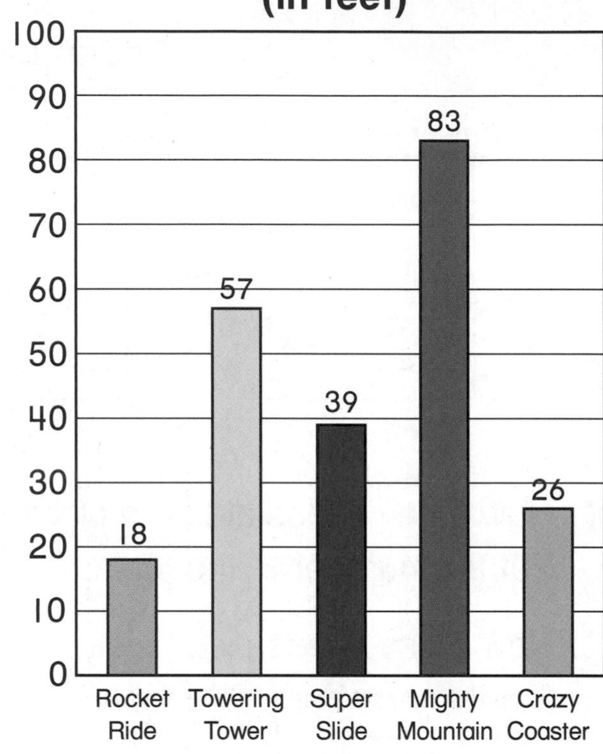

Use the **circle graph**.

10. How many pear trees and apple trees are there altogether?

____

11. There are as many lemon and peach trees together as there are what kind of tree?

____

12. How many trees are there altogether whose names start with the letter *P*?

____

Name ______________________

Use the picture graph. Write the number.
Ring *more* or *fewer*.

Paula	🍓	🍓	🍓	🍓						
Reynaldo	🍓	🍓	🍓	🍓	🍓	🍓	🍓			

1. Paula has ☐ *more* *fewer* strawberries than Reynaldo.

Solve the comparison story problems.	**Show your work.**
2. Ray has 9 peaches in his basket. Maria has 4 peaches in her basket. How many more peaches does Ray have than Maria? ☐ ______________ label	
3. Michelle picked 4 apples. Michelle picked 2 fewer than Hakim. How many apples did Hakim pick? ☐ ______________ label	

Name ______________________________

Use the table to answer the questions. Fill in the boxes with the answers. Ring *more* or *fewer*.

Number of Roses

	Roses
Brad	5
Mark	9
Pam	8

4. Mark has ☐ *more* *fewer* roses than Brad.

5. Brad needs ☐ more roses to have as many as Pam.

Turn the above table into a picture graph.
Use a circle for each rose.

6. ______________________________

Name

Use the bar graph. Write the numbers.
Ring *more* or *fewer*.

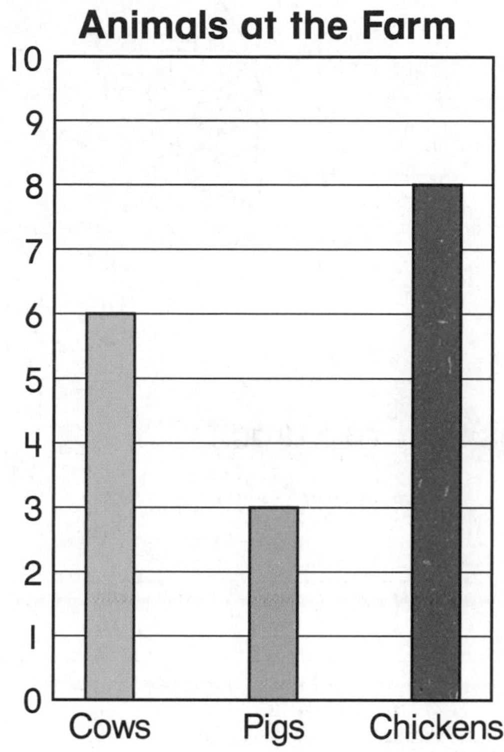

7. There are ☐ *more* *fewer* chickens than pigs.

8. There are ☐ animals at the farm in all.

Name ____________________

Use the circle graph to answer the question.

Vegetables in the Garden

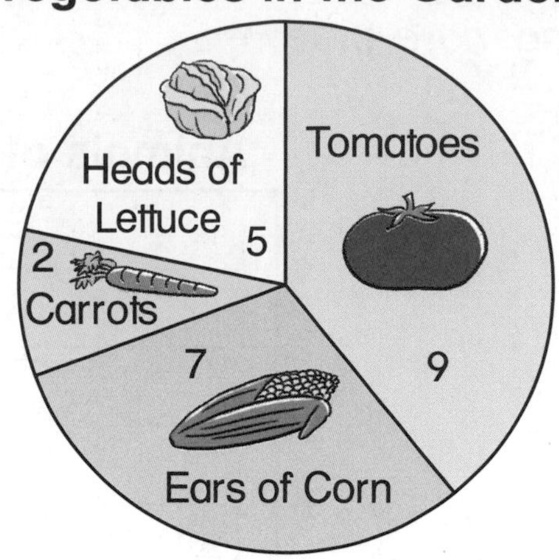

9. How many more tomatoes than carrots are in the vegetable garden?

____

____

10. Write Your Own Tell two things the circle graph in exercise 9 shows.

____

____

____

____

____

____

____

D–1

Class Activity

Name

Vocabulary

square
rectangle
parallelogram
quadrilateral

▶ Name Quadrilaterals

	Is it a **square**? Explain.	Is it a **rectangle**? Explain.	Is it a **parallelogram**? Explain.	Is it a **quadrilateral**? Explain.
1.	Yes. It has 4 equal sides and the corners are square.			
2.				
3.				
4.				

Name ____________________

Vocabulary
diagonal

▶ Draw Diagonals

A line segment that connects opposite corners of a quadrilateral is called a **diagonal**.

5. Draw a diagonal in this square.

6. What shapes are formed by drawing a diagonal in a square?

____

7. What are your observations about the two shapes that are formed?

____

____

8. Draw a diagonal in this rectangle.

9. What shapes are formed by drawing a diagonal in a rectangle?

____

Dear Family,

Your child is working on a geometry unit about dividing quadrilaterals into smaller shapes by drawing diagonals and line segments that connect the midpoints of opposite sides. The main goal of this unit is to help children develop their spatial abilities.

Diagonals are line segments that join opposite corners of a quadrilateral.

A midpoint divides a line segment into two equal parts.

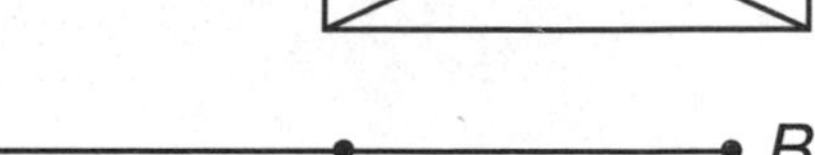

When you join the midpoints of opposite sides, you divide a quadrilateral into four parts.

Encourage your child to look for quadrilaterals in your home and neighborhood. Ask your child to predict what shapes will be formed by drawing diagonals in the quadrilaterals or by connecting the midpoints of opposite sides.

For example, ask your child to describe the shape of a sandwich before you cut it. Ask your child to then predict what shapes will be formed if you cut the sandwich along the diagonals or along the line segments made by joining the midpoints on opposite sides.

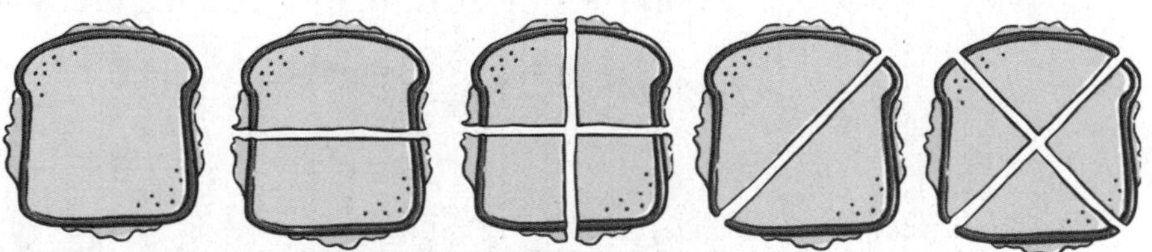

In this unit, your child will be asked to draw diagonals on three identical shapes. Your child will draw a different diagonal in each of the first two shapes and draw both diagonals in the third shape.

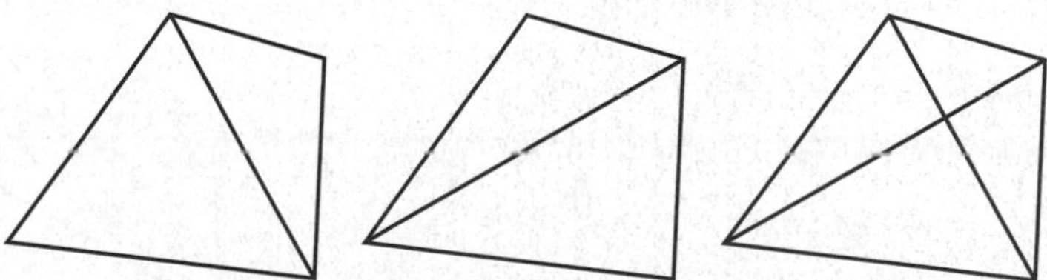

If you have any questions or comments, please call or write to me.

Sincerely,
Your child's teacher

Estimada familia:

Su niño está trabajando en una unidad de geometría. Aprenderá a dividir cuadriláteros en figuras más pequeñas dibujando diagonales y segmentos que unen los puntos medios de lados opuestos. El objetivo principal de esta unidad es ayudar a los niños a desarrollar su sentido espacial.

Las diagonales son segmentos que unen vértices opuestos de un cuadrilátero.

Los puntos medios dividen un segmento en dos partes iguales.

Cuando se unen los puntos medios de lados opuestos se divide el cuadrilátero en cuatro partes.

Anime a su niño a buscar cuadriláteros en la casa y en el vecindario. Pídale que prediga qué figuras se formarán al dibujar diagonales en los cuadriláteros o al unir los puntos medios de lados opuestos.

Por ejemplo, pida a su niño que describa la figura de un sándwich antes de cortarlo. Pídale que prediga qué figuras se formarán si corta el sándwich por las diagonales o por los segmentos formados al unir los puntos medios con los lados opuestos.

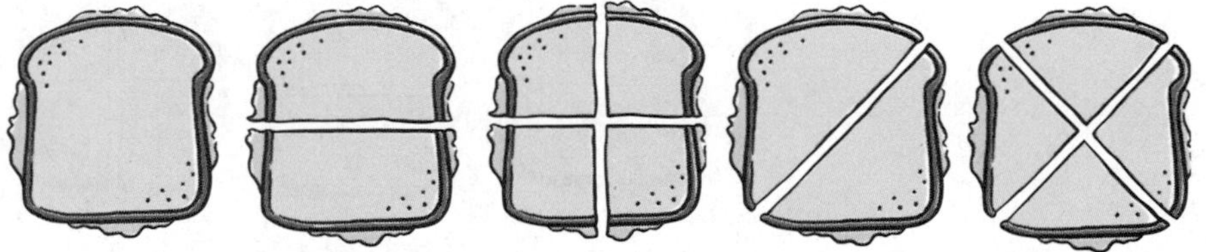

En esta unidad su niño deberá dibujar diagonales en tres figuras idénticas. Se le pedirá que dibuje una diagonal diferente en cada una de las primeras dos figuras y que dibuje ambas diagonales en la tercera figura.

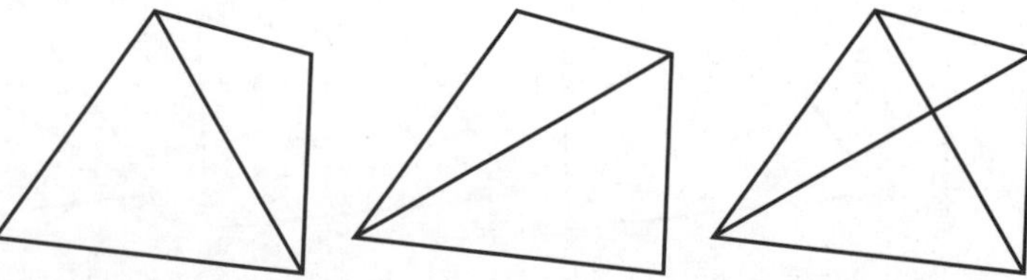

Si tiene alguna pregunta o comentario, por favor comuníquese conmigo.

Atentamente,
El maestro de su niño

D-2 Class Activity

Name ______________________

Vocabulary
midpoint

▶ Explore Methods of Finding Midpoints

The **midpoint** of a line segment divides the line segment into two equal parts.

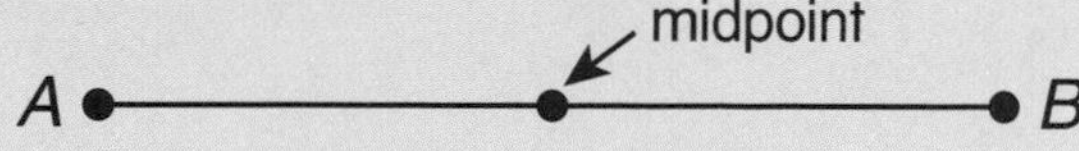

Use at least two different ways to find the midpoint of each line segment and draw a dot at that point.

1. J ——— K

2. C ——— D

3. E ——— F

4. P ——— Q

5. **Explain Your Thinking** Describe two of the ways you used to find the midpoints of the line segments above.

____

____

____

____

____

____

D–2

Class Activity

Name ______________________________

Vocabulary
opposite sides

► Connect Midpoints

6. Mark the midpoints of two **opposite sides**.

7. What shapes do you think you will see when you connect the midpoints?

____

8. Connect the midpoints. Describe the shapes you see.

____

9. Mark the midpoints of the other two opposite sides.

10. Connect the midpoints. What shapes do you see?

____

11. How are these shapes like the shapes in the first square? How are they different?

____

____

Class Activity

Name ____________________

► Add Line Segments to Shapes

	Draw one diagonal.	Draw the other diagonal.	Draw both diagonals.
1.			
2.			
3.			
4.			

D–3

Class Activity

Name

▶ Add Line Segments to Shapes

	Connect the midpoints of two opposite sides.	Connect the midpoints of the other two sides.	Draw both line segments.
5.			
6.			
7.			
8.			

Name ______________________

	Draw one diagonal.	Draw the other diagonal.	Draw both diagonals.
1.			
2.			

3. Find the midpoint of the line segment and draw a dot at that point.

H • ———————————————— • *I*

D

Unit Test

Name ______________________________

4. Draw one diagonal in the square.

Describe the new shapes.

____

____

5. Draw two diagonals in the parallelogram.

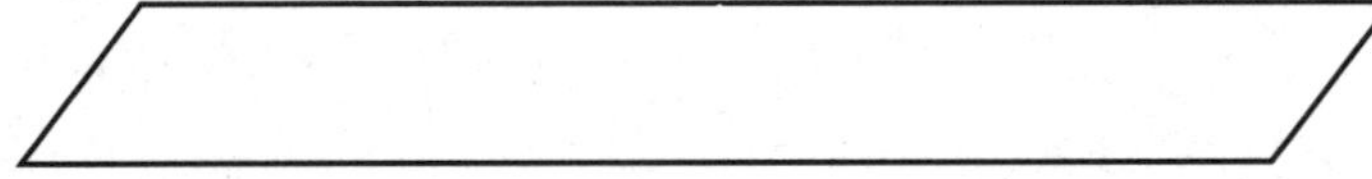

Describe the new shapes.

____

____

6. Draw two diagonals in this quadrilateral.

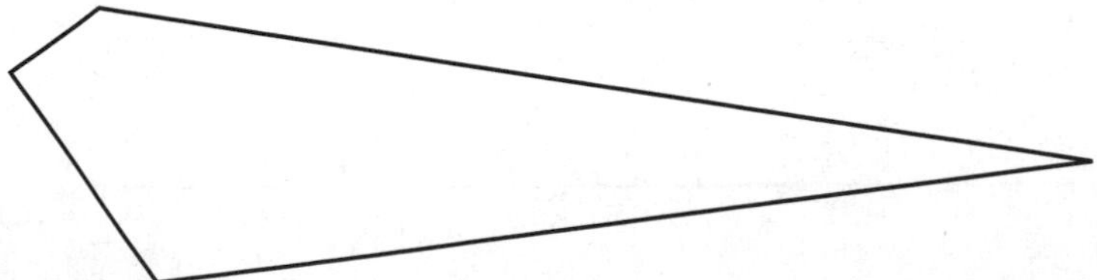

Describe the new shapes.

____

____

Name ______________________________

7. Connect the midpoints of two opposite sides.

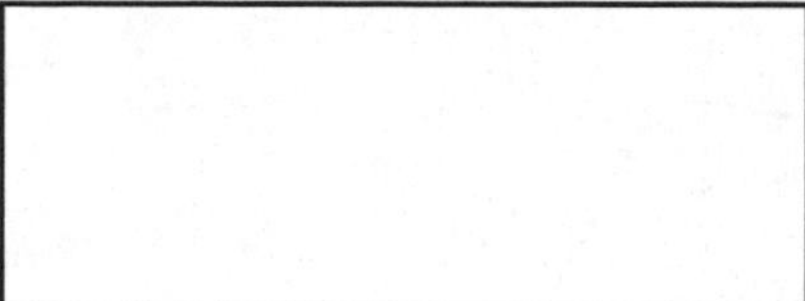

Describe the new shapes.

____

____

8. Connect the midpoints of two opposite sides. Then connect the midpoints of the other two sides.

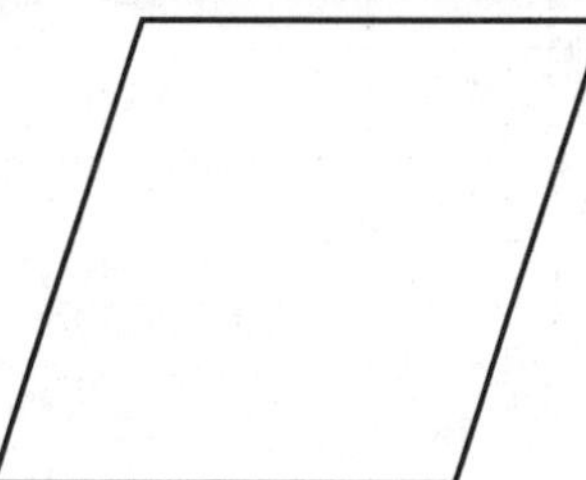

Describe the new shapes.

____

____

Name ______________________________

9. Connect the midpoints of two opposite sides. Then connect the midpoints of the other two sides.

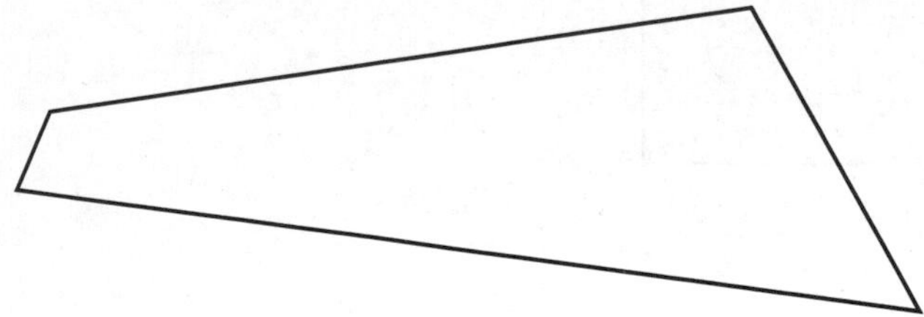

Describe the new shapes.

____

____

10. **Extended Response** Use two different methods to find the midpoint of this line segment.

S •———————• *T*

Describe both methods.

____

____

____

____

____

____

____

____

____

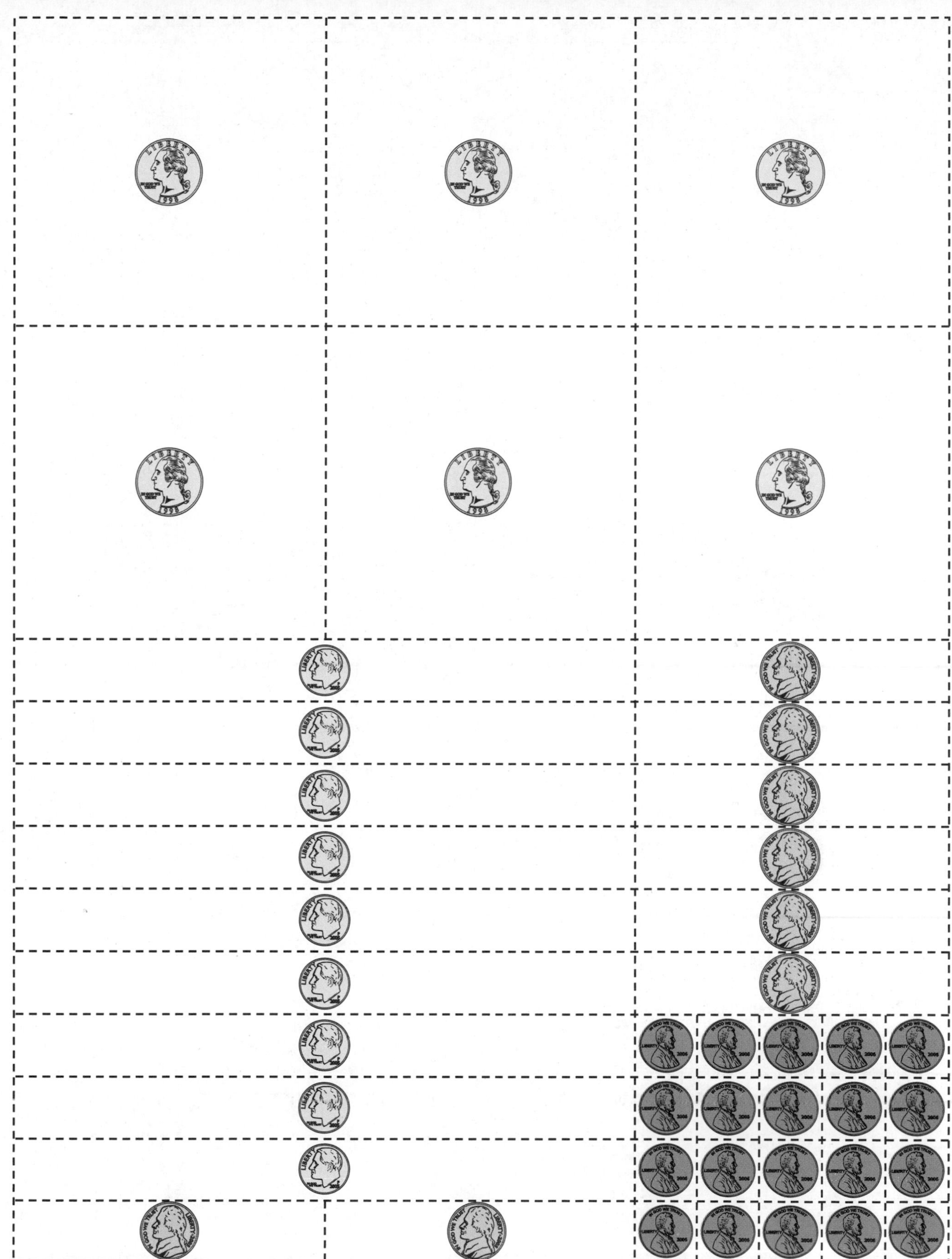

Cut on dashed lines.

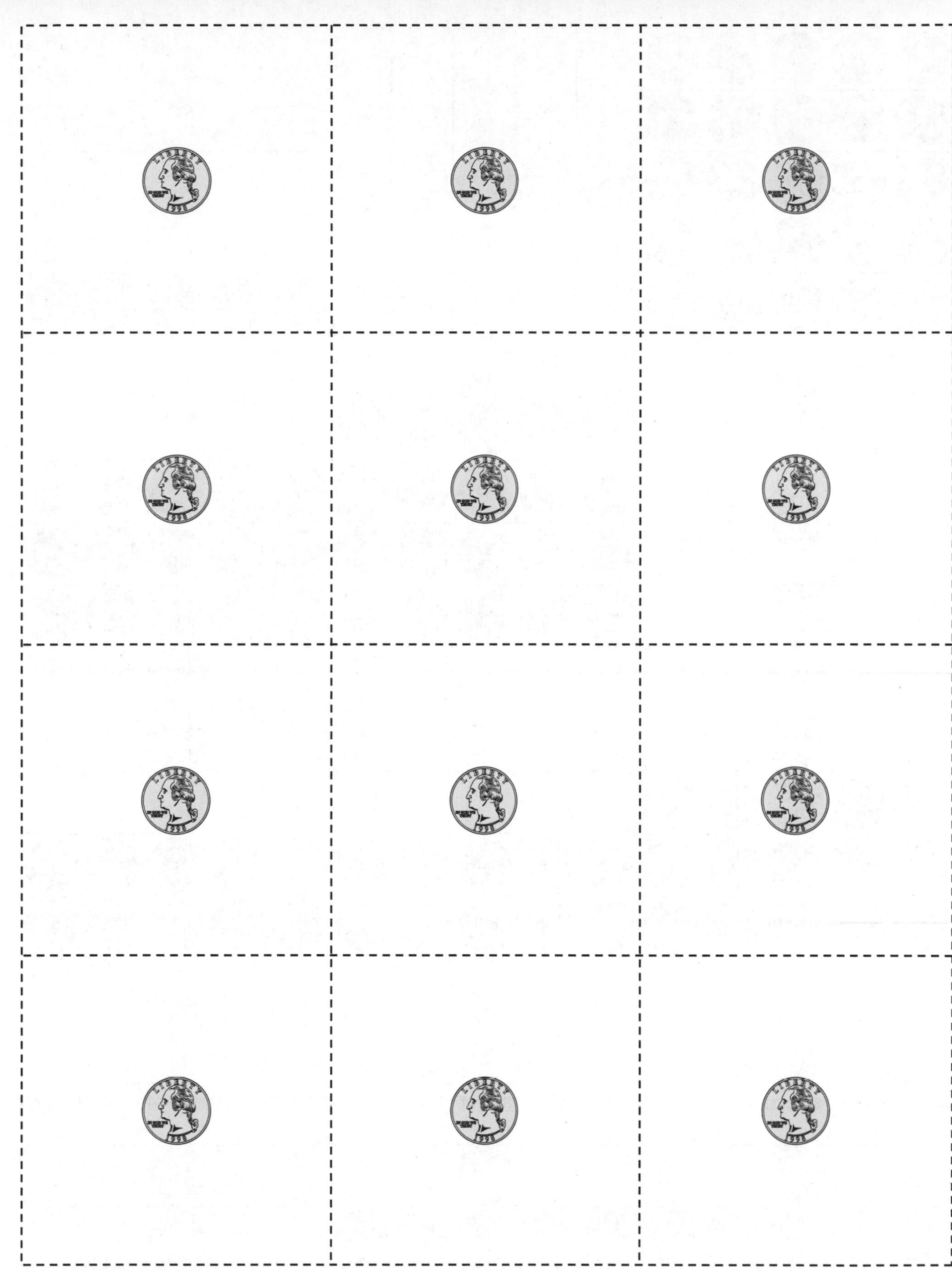

Cut on dashed lines.

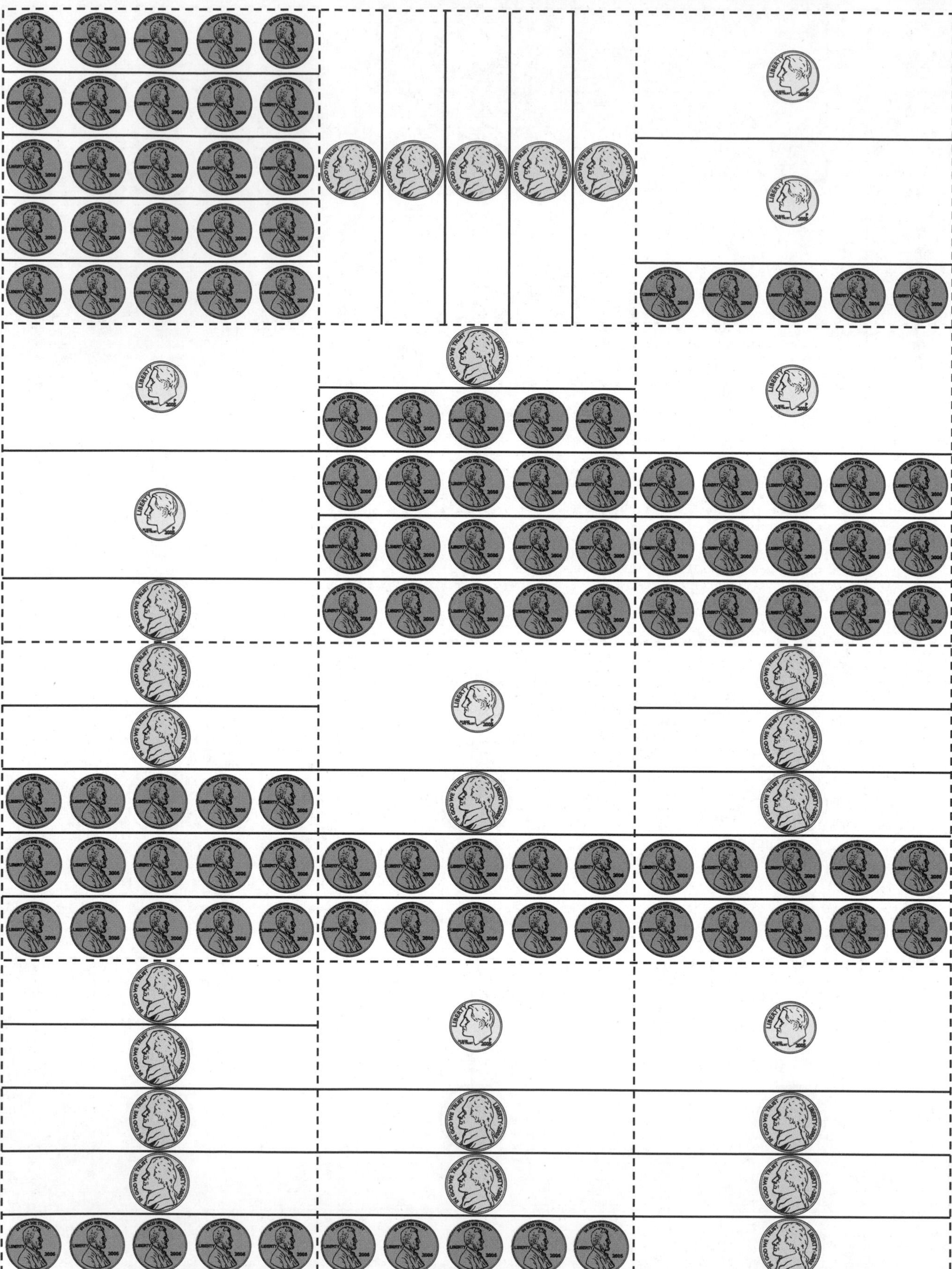

Cut only on dashed lines.

Dear Family,

In this unit, your child will explore and count coins and various coin combinations. Children will also explore dollars and combine different coins to equal one dollar.

25¢ + 25¢ + 10¢ + 10¢ + 10¢ + 10¢ + 10¢ = 100¢

Then your child will count both dollars and coins.

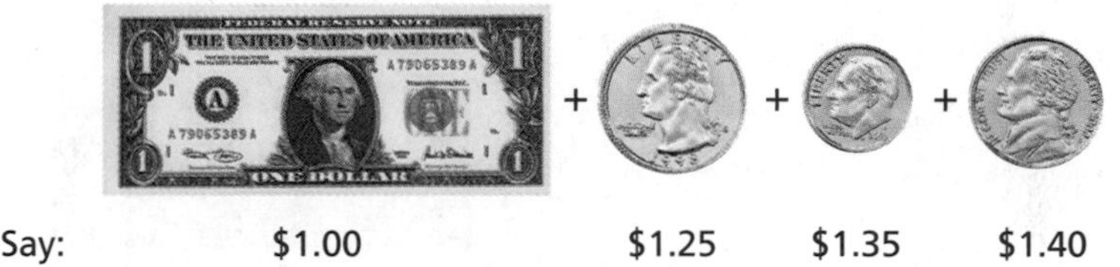

Say: $1.00 $1.25 $1.35 $1.40

You can help at home by providing opportunities for your child to practice counting money. Begin with amounts less than $1.00.

Please call if you have any questions or concerns. Thank you for helping your child to learn mathematics.

Sincerely,
Your child's teacher

Estimada familia:

En esta unidad su niño va a contar monedas y diversas combinaciones de monedas. Los niños también trabajarán con dólares y combinarán diferentes monedas para igualar el valor de un dólar.

25¢ + 25¢ + 10¢ + 10¢ + 10¢ + 10¢ + 10¢ = 100¢

Luego su niño contará tanto billetes de dólares como monedas.

Se dice: $1.00 $1.25 $1.35 $1.40

Usted puede ayudar en su casa ofreciéndole al niño oportunidades de practicar contando dinero. Empiece con cantidades menores que $1.00.

Si tiene alguna duda o comentario, por favor comuníquese conmigo. Gracias por ayudar a su niño a aprender matemáticas.

Atentamente,
El maestro de su niño

Cut on dashed lines.

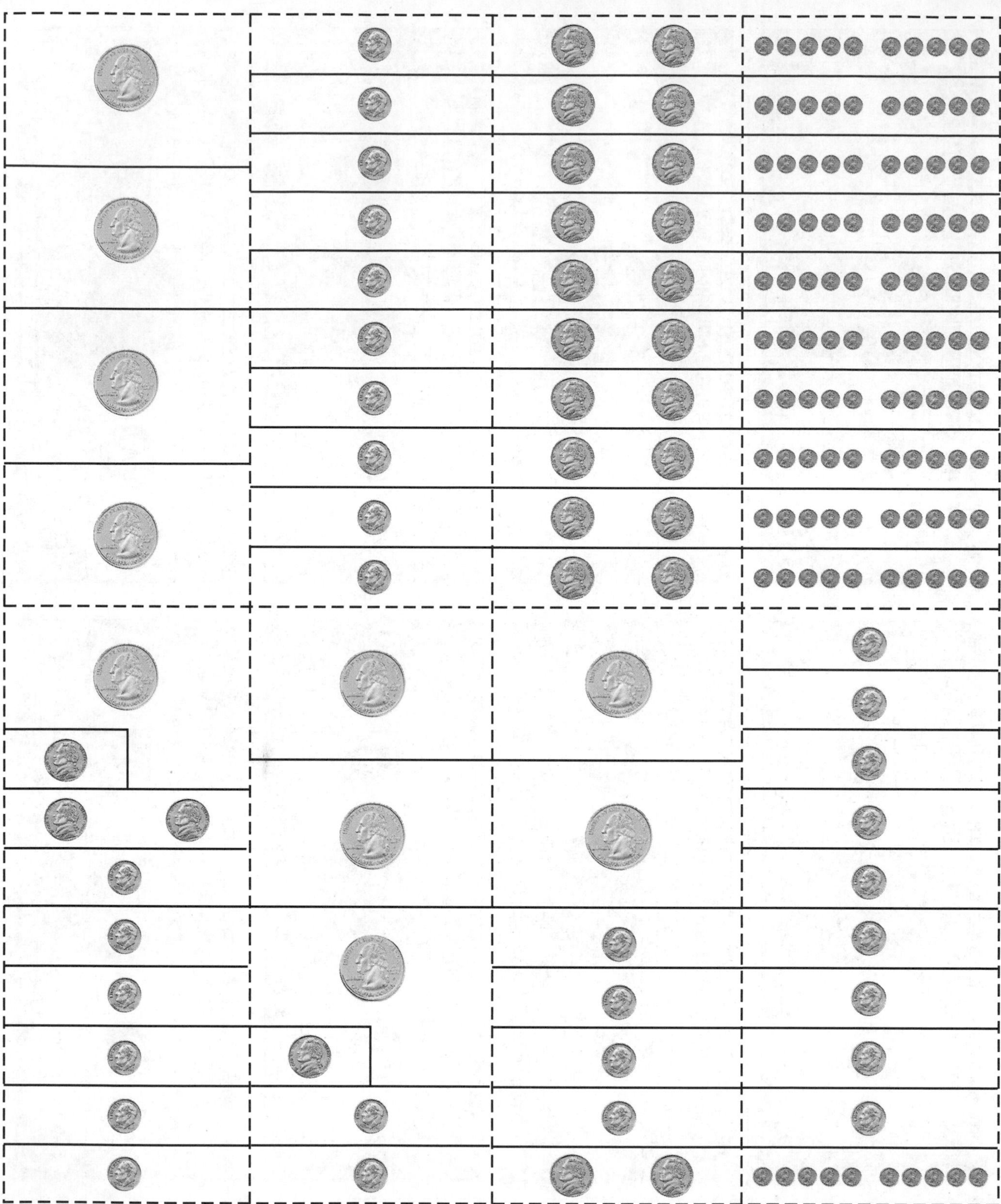

Cut only on dashed lines.

Name ____________________

▶ Problems Using 100-Partners

When you subtract, you can use the following drawings to help you ungroup.

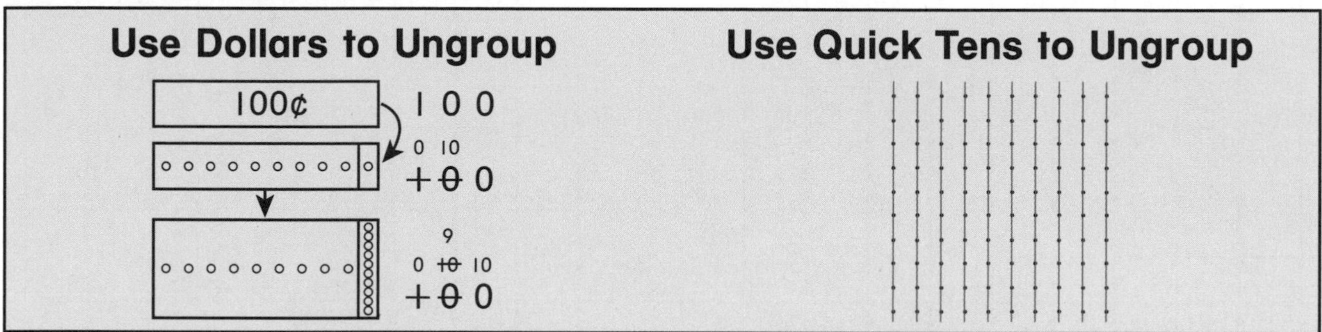

Solve the story problems.

1. The baker baked 100 loaves of bread. He sold 73 loaves. How many loaves are left?

   ☐ ____________________ label

2. I had 100 flowers in my garden. I gave 26 of them away. How many flowers are left in my garden?

   ☐ ____________________ label

3. The letter carrier had 100 letters in his bag. He delivered 52 letters. How many letters are left in his bag?

   ☐ ____________________ label

4. **On the Back** Use the drawings to help you solve the exercises your teacher gives you.

Name

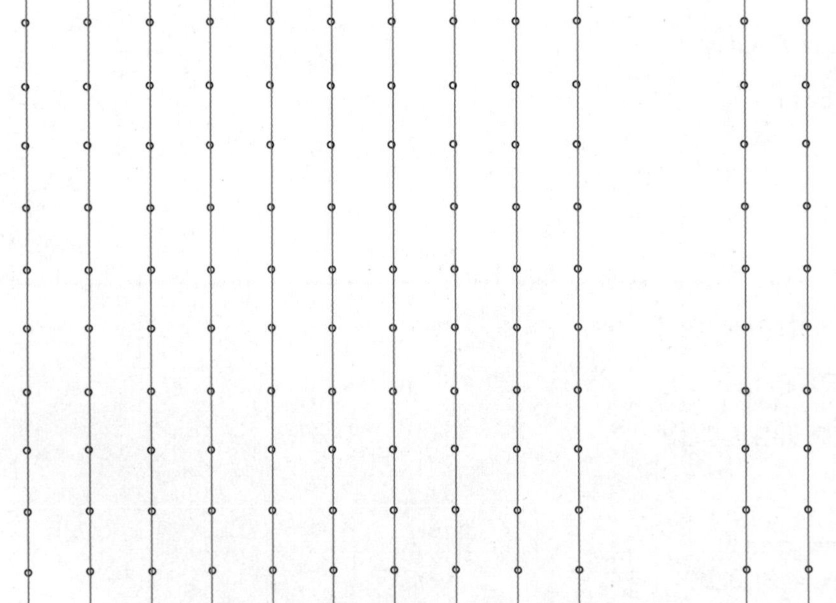

Name

▶ Subtraction Sprint

7 − 4 =	10 − 6 =	17 − 9 =
13 − 5 =	15 − 9 =	6 − 4 =
9 − 3 =	11 − 3 =	10 − 7 =
11 − 2 =	18 − 9 =	13 − 9 =
8 − 6 =	8 − 4 =	12 − 5 =
12 − 9 =	9 − 7 =	16 − 8 =
6 − 3 =	13 − 6 =	14 − 7 =
15 − 7 =	12 − 3 =	10 − 6 =
10 − 8 =	16 − 7 =	8 − 5 =
8 − 3 =	7 − 5 =	11 − 9 =
14 − 5 =	12 − 4 =	13 − 7 =
11 − 7 =	17 − 8 =	14 − 8 =
10 − 4 =	9 − 4 =	10 − 5 =
12 − 8 =	14 − 8 =	12 − 6 =
16 − 9 =	11 − 4 =	15 − 7 =
14 − 6 =	9 − 6 =	13 − 6 =
9 − 5 =	12 − 7 =	11 − 8 =
13 − 9 =	14 − 9 =	12 − 3 =
10 − 3 =	13 − 4 =	13 − 5 =
15 − 8 =	7 − 3 =	15 − 6 =
11 − 5 =	11 − 6 =	13 − 8 =

Dive the Deep

11 − 6 = 5	12 − 6 = 6	13 − 8 = 5
12 − 7 = 5	17 − 8 = 9	15 − 6 = 9
12 − 9 = 3	13 − 5 = 8	11 − 9 = 2
13 − 4 = 9	14 − 6 = 8	13 − 9 = 4
11 − 5 = 6	17 − 9 = 8	15 − 7 = 8
14 − 9 = 5	11 − 8 = 3	14 − 8 = 6
14 − 7 = 7	12 − 4 = 8	12 − 5 = 7
16 − 7 = 9	16 − 8 = 8	11 − 3 = 8
11 − 7 = 4	15 − 7 = 8	13 − 6 = 7
12 − 3 = 9	16 − 9 = 7	18 − 9 = 9
13 − 7 = 6	11 − 4 = 7	12 − 8 = 4

Name ______________________

Vocabulary
Expanded Method

▶ Explain the Expanded Method

Mr. Green likes this method. Explain what he does.

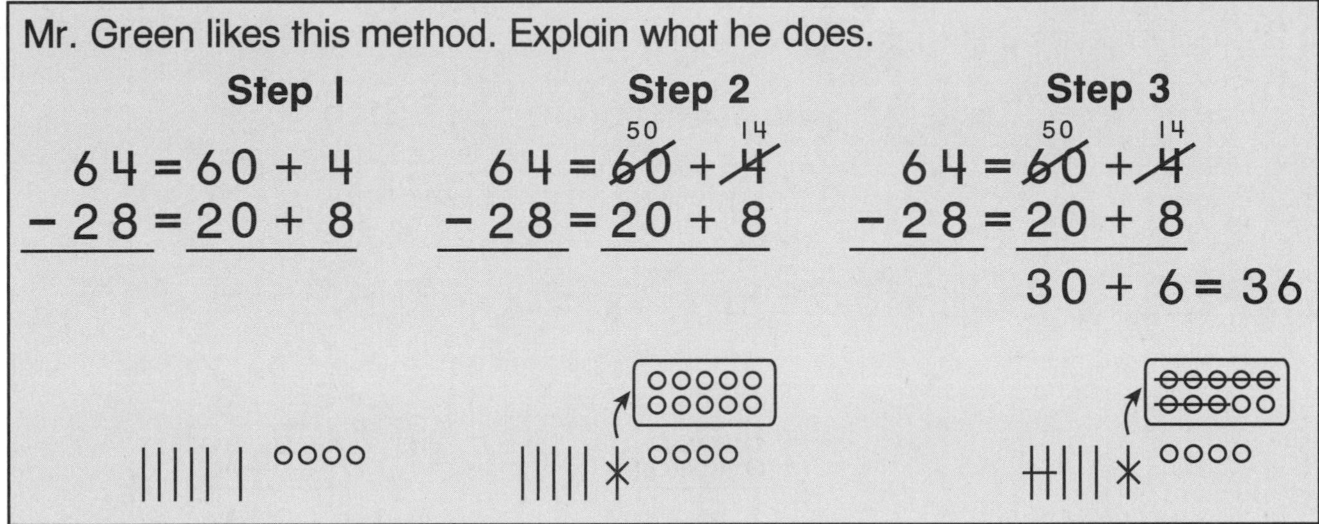

▶ Try the Expanded Method

Show your work numerically and with a Proof Drawing.

1. $\begin{array}{r} 42 \\ -\ 19 \\ \hline \end{array}$

2. $\begin{array}{r} 75 \\ -\ 46 \\ \hline \end{array}$

3. $\begin{array}{r} 81 \\ -\ 37 \\ \hline \end{array}$

5–5 Class Activity

Name

Vocabulary
Ungroup First Method

▶ Explain the Ungroup First Method

Mrs. Green likes this method. Explain what she does.

Step 1	Step 2	Step 3
64 − 28	 − 28	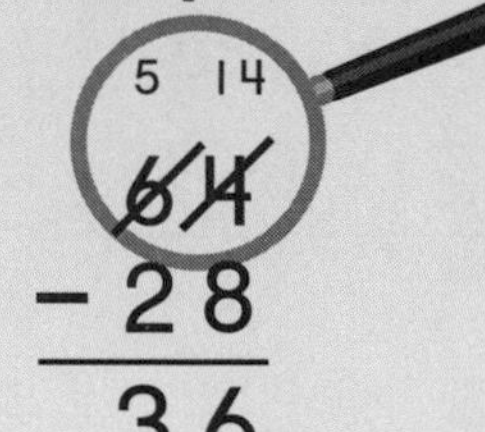 − 28 36
||||| | oooo	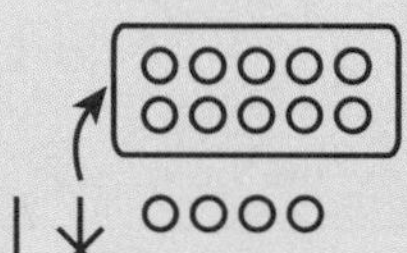	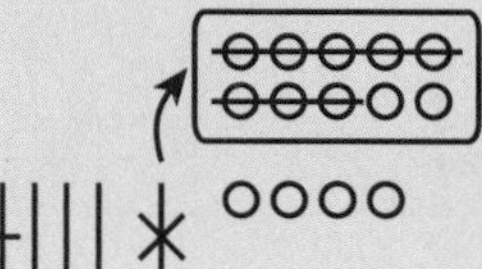

▶ Try the Ungroup First Method

Show your work numerically and with a Proof Drawing.

4. 42 − 19

5. 75 − 46

6. 81 − 37

Dear Family,

Your child is now learning how to subtract 2-digit numbers. The big mystery is how to get enough ones in order to subtract. As with addition, children first use methods they invent themselves. We have found that children take pride in using their own methods.

In this program, children learn two methods for 2-digit subtraction, but children may use any method that they understand, can explain, and can do fairly quickly.

Expanded Method	Ungroup First Method
Step 1 "Expand" each number to show that it is made up of tens and ones. $64 = 60 + 4$ $-28 = 20 + 8$	**Step 1** Check to see if there are enough ones to subtract from. If not, ungroup by opening up 1 of the 6 tens in 64 to be 10 ones. 4 ones plus these new 10 ones make 14 ones. We draw a "magnifying glass" around the top number to focus children on whether they need to ungroup before subtraction. 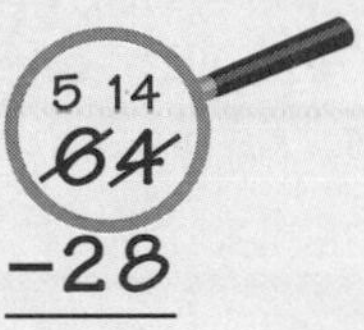 -28
Step 2 Check to see if there are enough ones to subtract from. If not, ungroup a ten into 10 ones and add it to the existing ones. $64 = \overset{50}{\cancel{60}} + \overset{14}{\cancel{4}}$ $-28 = 20 + 8$	
Step 3 Subtract to find the answer. Children may subtract from left to right or right to left. $64 = \overset{50}{\cancel{60}} + \overset{14}{\cancel{4}}$ $-28 = 20 + 8$ $30 + 6 = 36$	**Step 2** Subtract to find the answer. Children may subtract from left to right or right to left.  -28 36

In explaining any method they use, children are expected to use "tens and ones" language. This shows that they understand they are subtracting 2 tens from 5 tens (not 2 from 5) and 8 ones from 14 ones.

Please call if you have any questions or comments.

Sincerely,
Your child's teacher

Estimada familia:

Su niño está aprendiendo a restar números de 2 dígitos. El misterio es cómo obtener suficientes unidades para poder restar. Iqual que en la suma, los niños primero usan métodos que ellos mismos inventan. Hemos notado que los niños se sienten orgullosos de usar sus propios métodos.

En este programa, los niños aprenden dos métodos para la resta con números de 2 dígitos, pero pueden usar cualquier método que comprendan, puedan explicar y puedan hacer relativamente rápido.

Método extendido

Paso 1 "Extender" cada número para mostrar que tiene decenas y unidades.

$$\begin{array}{r} 64 = 60 + 4 \\ -28 = 20 + 8 \\ \hline \end{array}$$

Paso 2 Observar si hay suficientes unidades para restar. Si no las hay, desagrupar una decena para formar 10 unidades y sumarla a las unidades existentes.

$$\begin{array}{r} 50 \quad + \ 14 \\ 64 = \cancel{60} + \cancel{4} \\ -28 = 20 + 8 \\ \hline \end{array}$$

Paso 3 Restar para hallar la respuesta. Los niños pueden restar de izquierda a derecha o de derecha a izquierda.

$$\begin{array}{r} 50 \quad + \ 14 \\ 64 = \cancel{60} + \cancel{4} \\ -28 = 20 + 8 \\ \hline 30 + 6 = 36 \end{array}$$

Método de desagrupar primero

Paso 1 Observar si hay suficientes unidades para restar. Si no las hay, pueden desagrupar una de las 6 decenas en 64 para obtener 10 unidades. 4 unidades más las 10 unidades nuevas hacen 14 unidades. Dibujamos una "lupa" alrededor del número superior para que los niños piensen si necesitan desagrupar antes de restar.

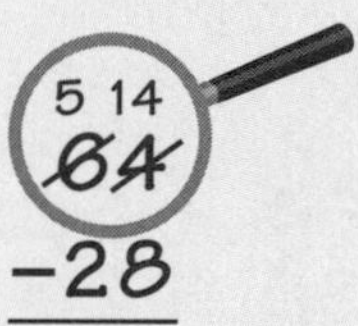

Paso 2 Restar para hallar la respuesta. Los niños pueden restar de izquierda a derecha o de derecha a izquierda.

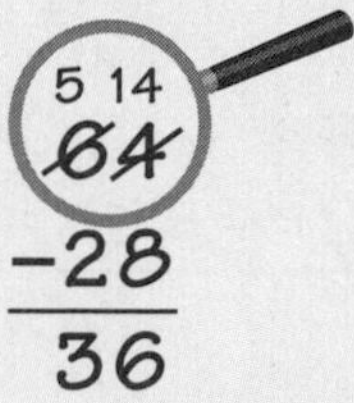

Cuando los niños explican el método que usan, deben usar un lenguaje relacionado con "decenas y unidades". Esto mostrará que comprenden que están restando 2 decenas de 5 decenas (no 2 de 5) y 8 unidades de 14 unidades.

Si tiene alguna duda o comentario, por favor comuníquese conmigo.

Atentamente,
El maestro de su niño

5–6 Class Activity

Name ______________________________

▶ Solve and Discuss

Subtract.

1. $\begin{array}{r} 75 \\ -47 \\ \hline \end{array}$

2. $\begin{array}{r} 54 \\ -18 \\ \hline \end{array}$

3. $\begin{array}{r} 94 \\ -36 \\ \hline \end{array}$

4. $\begin{array}{r} 66 \\ -34 \\ \hline \end{array}$

5. $\begin{array}{r} 85 \\ -58 \\ \hline \end{array}$

6. $\begin{array}{r} 89 \\ -69 \\ \hline \end{array}$

7. $\begin{array}{r} 82 \\ -59 \\ \hline \end{array}$

8. $\begin{array}{r} 97 \\ -78 \\ \hline \end{array}$

9. $\begin{array}{r} 65 \\ -28 \\ \hline \end{array}$

10. $\begin{array}{r} 78 \\ -19 \\ \hline \end{array}$

11. $\begin{array}{r} 53 \\ -26 \\ \hline \end{array}$

12. $\begin{array}{r} 91 \\ -46 \\ \hline \end{array}$

5–6

Going Further

Name ________________________________

Vocabulary
estimate
difference

▶ Introduce Estimating Differences

Estimate the **difference**.

78 − 42

You can use number lines and rounding to estimate a difference.

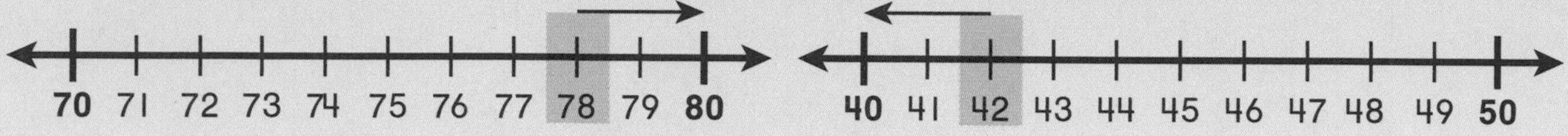

78 is closer to 80 than 70. Round up to 80.
42 is closer to 40 than 50. Round down to 40.

80 − 40 = 40

▶ Practice Estimating Differences

Round each number to the nearest ten. Estimate the difference.

1. 67 − 43

   ______ − ______ = ______

2. 72 − 58

   ______ − ______ = ______

3. 87 − 52

   ______ − ______ = ______

4. 61 − 49

   ______ − ______ = ______

5. There were 74 plants in Mr. Codero's greenhouse. Then Mr. Codero sold 37 plants. About how many plants did Mr. Codero have in his greenhouse then? Estimate to find the answer.

   ____

6. **Write Your Own** On a separate sheet of paper, write a subtraction story problem that can be solved by using an estimate.

Name ______________________

Vocabulary
Expanded Method
Ungroup First Method

▶ Explain Ungrouping 200

Explain why 200 = 100 + 90 + 10.

▶ Explain the Expanded Method

Explain how ungrouping and subtraction work.
Relate steps here to steps in the drawing above.

Expanded Method

```
                      90  +  10
           100  +  100 (crossed out)                      100  +  90  +  10
  200  =  200 (crossed out)  +  0  +  0      or    200 (crossed out)  +  0  +  0
-  68  =                 60  +  8
-----     -----------------------
           100  +  30  +  2  = 132
```

▶ Explain the Ungroup First Method

Explain how ungrouping and subtraction work.
Relate steps here to steps in the drawing above.

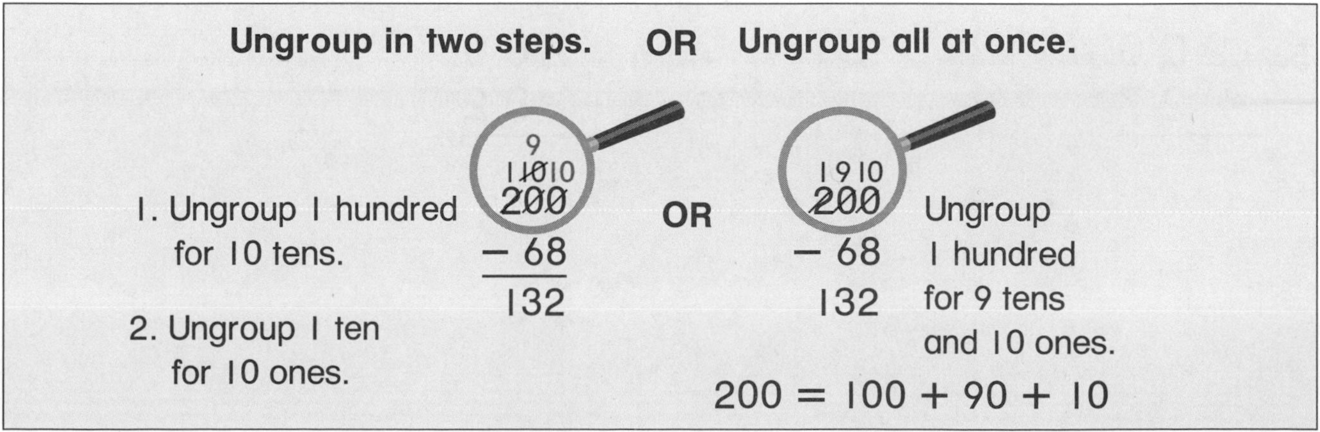

Name

▶ Practice Both Methods

Use the Ungroup First Method or the Expanded Method to find each difference.

1. $\begin{array}{r} 200 \\ -\ 87 \\ \hline \end{array}$

2. $\begin{array}{r} 200 \\ -\ 89 \\ \hline \end{array}$

3. $\begin{array}{r} 200 \\ -\ 46 \\ \hline \end{array}$

4. $\begin{array}{r} 200 \\ -\ 38 \\ \hline \end{array}$

5. $\begin{array}{r} 200 \\ -\ 27 \\ \hline \end{array}$

6. $\begin{array}{r} 200 \\ -\ 82 \\ \hline \end{array}$

5-8 Class Activity

Name

▶ **Subtraction Sprint**

7 − 4 =	10 − 6 =	17 − 9 =
13 − 5 =	15 − 9 =	6 − 4 =
9 − 3 =	11 − 3 =	10 − 7 =
11 − 2 =	18 − 9 =	13 − 9 =
8 − 6 =	8 − 4 =	12 − 5 =
12 − 9 =	9 − 7 =	16 − 8 =
6 − 3 =	13 − 6 =	14 − 7 =
15 − 7 =	12 − 3 =	10 − 6 =
10 − 8 =	16 − 7 =	8 − 5 =
8 − 3 =	7 − 5 =	11 − 9 =
14 − 5 =	12 − 4 =	13 − 7 =
11 − 7 =	17 − 8 =	14 − 8 =
10 − 4 =	9 − 4 =	10 − 5 =
12 − 8 =	14 − 8 =	12 − 6 =
16 − 9 =	11 − 4 =	15 − 7 =
14 − 6 =	9 − 6 =	13 − 6 =
9 − 5 =	12 − 7 =	11 − 8 =
13 − 9 =	14 − 9 =	12 − 3 =
10 − 3 =	13 − 4 =	13 − 5 =
15 − 8 =	7 − 3 =	15 − 6 =
11 − 5 =	11 − 6 =	13 − 8 =

5–8 Name ______

Class Activity

▶ Decide When to Ungroup

Decide if you need to ungroup. Then subtract.

1. $\begin{array}{r} 134 \\ -\ 78 \\ \hline \end{array}$

Did you ungroup a ten to get more ones? ______

Did you ungroup a hundred to get more tens? ______

2. $\begin{array}{r} 134 \\ -\ 73 \\ \hline \end{array}$

Did you ungroup a ten to get more ones? ______

Did you ungroup a hundred to get more tens? ______

3. $\begin{array}{r} 158 \\ -\ 37 \\ \hline \end{array}$

Did you ungroup a ten to get more ones? ______

Did you ungroup a hundred to get more tens? ______

4. $\begin{array}{r} 158 \\ -\ 39 \\ \hline \end{array}$

Did you ungroup a ten to get more ones? ______

Did you ungroup a hundred to get more tens? ______

5. $\begin{array}{r} 146 \\ -\ 57 \\ \hline \end{array}$

Did you ungroup a ten to get more ones? ______

Did you ungroup a hundred to get more tens? ______

6. $\begin{array}{r} 146 \\ -\ 35 \\ \hline \end{array}$

Did you ungroup a ten to get more ones? ______

Did you ungroup a hundred to get more tens? ______

Name ____________________

▶ Subtract with Zeroes

Decide if you need to ungroup. Then subtract.

1. $\begin{array}{r} 108 \\ -\ 46 \\ \hline \end{array}$

2. $\begin{array}{r} 103 \\ -\ 65 \\ \hline \end{array}$

3. $\begin{array}{r} 150 \\ -\ 79 \\ \hline \end{array}$

4. $\begin{array}{r} 102 \\ -\ 83 \\ \hline \end{array}$

5. $\begin{array}{r} 160 \\ -\ 92 \\ \hline \end{array}$

6. $\begin{array}{r} 107 \\ -\ 61 \\ \hline \end{array}$

7. $\begin{array}{r} 106 \\ -\ 38 \\ \hline \end{array}$

8. $\begin{array}{r} 170 \\ -\ 40 \\ \hline \end{array}$

9. $\begin{array}{r} 180 \\ -\ 93 \\ \hline \end{array}$

10. $\begin{array}{r} 140 \\ -\ 57 \\ \hline \end{array}$

11. $\begin{array}{r} 150 \\ -\ 84 \\ \hline \end{array}$

12. $\begin{array}{r} 106 \\ -\ 43 \\ \hline \end{array}$

5–9

Name ______________________________

Class Activity

▶ Solve and Discuss

Decide if you need to ungroup. Then subtract.

13. $\begin{array}{r} 106 \\ -\ 81 \\ \hline \end{array}$

14. $\begin{array}{r} 110 \\ -\ 18 \\ \hline \end{array}$

15. $\begin{array}{r} 190 \\ -\ 72 \\ \hline \end{array}$

16. $\begin{array}{r} 107 \\ -\ 38 \\ \hline \end{array}$

17. $\begin{array}{r} 130 \\ -\ 22 \\ \hline \end{array}$

18. $\begin{array}{r} 120 \\ -\ 63 \\ \hline \end{array}$

Solve the story problems.	**Show your work.**
19. Larry sells cars. He wants to sell 109 cars this month. So far he has sold 34. How many more cars does he need to sell? ☐ ____________ label	
20. Abbie grilled 110 burgers for the school picnic. 79 were eaten. How many are left? ☐ ____________ label	

5-10 Class Activity

Name ____________________

Vocabulary
exact change

▶ Use Exact Change

First, see how much money you have. Then decide what to buy. Pay for the item with **exact change**. Then write how much money you have left.

Yard Sale

Cork Board	Toy Rabbit	Toy Guitar	Perfume	Knit Cap
78¢	84¢	75¢	89¢	99¢

1. I have 162¢ in my pocket.

   I bought the ____________________.

   $$\begin{array}{r} 162¢ \\ -\quad\;\; ¢ \\ \hline \end{array}$$

   I have ____________ ¢ left.

2. I have 143¢ in my pocket.

   I bought the ____________________.

   $$\begin{array}{r} 143¢ \\ -\quad\;\; ¢ \\ \hline \end{array}$$

   I have ____________ ¢ left.

3. I have 154¢ in my pocket.

   I bought the ____________________.

   $$\begin{array}{r} 154¢ \\ -\quad\;\; ¢ \\ \hline \end{array}$$

   I have ____________ ¢ left.

4. I have 126¢ in my pocket.

   I bought the ____________________.

   $$\begin{array}{r} 126¢ \\ -\quad\;\; ¢ \\ \hline \end{array}$$

   I have ____________ ¢ left.

Name ______________________

Vocabulary
decimal notation

▶ Use Decimal Notation for Money

Write the money amount.

1. 134¢ = 1 dollar 3 dimes 4 pennies = $ 1 . 3 4

2. 76¢ = ______ dollar ______ dimes ______ pennies = $ ______ . ______ ______

3. 179¢ = ______ dollar ______ dimes ______ pennies = $ ______ . ______ ______

4. 58¢ = ______ dollar ______ dimes ______ pennies = $ ______ . ______ ______

Find the difference. Use play money to help you ungroup, if you wish.

5.
$$\begin{array}{r} \$1.44 \\ -\ \ .23 \\ \hline \end{array}$$

6.
$$\begin{array}{r} \$1.25 \\ -\ \ .95 \\ \hline \end{array}$$

7.
$$\begin{array}{r} \$1.63 \\ -\ \ .95 \\ \hline \end{array}$$

8.
$$\begin{array}{r} \$1.58 \\ -\ \ .45 \\ \hline \end{array}$$

9.
$$\begin{array}{r} \$1.36 \\ -\ \ .75 \\ \hline \end{array}$$

10.
$$\begin{array}{r} \$1.92 \\ -\ \ .95 \\ \hline \end{array}$$

Name ______________________

► Addition and Subtraction Story Problems

Draw a Math Mountain to solve each story problem. Show how you add or subtract.

Show your work.

1. Teresa had 85 blocks. Then she found 47 more under the couch. How many blocks does Teresa have now?

   [ ] ______________ label

2. Krina's class made 163 masks. They hung 96 of them in the library. How many masks do they have left?

   [ ] ______________ label

3. Andy's plant was 138 inches tall. It grew 27 inches. How many inches tall is his plant now?

   [ ] ______________ label

4. The school store had 144 glue sticks. They sold 79 so far this year. How many glue sticks do they have left?

   [ ] ______________ label

Name ____________________

Vocabulary
estimate

▶ Estimate to Find the Answer

Use any method to **estimate** the solutions to exercises 1–4. Write the estimate on the line. Then use the estimate to help you match the exercise to its answer.

Exercise	Estimate	Problem	Answer
1.	____________	92 − 17	9
2.	____________	72 + 52	93
3.	____________	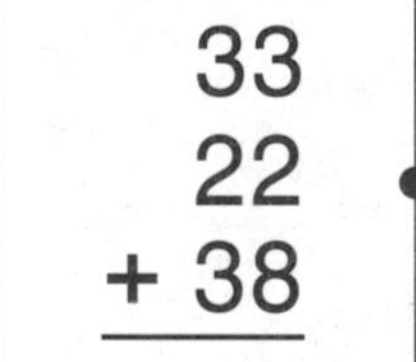	124
4.	____________	48 − 39	75

Jason has 38 cartoon videos and 19 movie videos. He wants to buy a cabinet that will hold 70 videos.

5. About how many videos does he have in all? ____________

6. Will they all fit in the cabinet? ____________

Name ______________________

► Find Equations for Math Mountains

1. Write all of the equations for 83, 59, and 24.

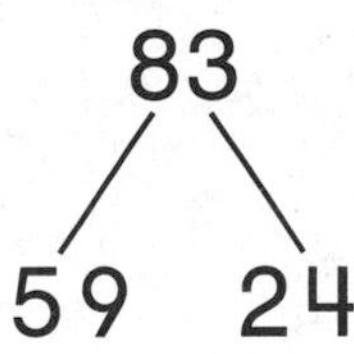

59 + 24 = 83 ______________________

83 = 59 + 24 ______________________

____

____

____

____

____

____

2. Write all of the equations for 142, 96, and 46.

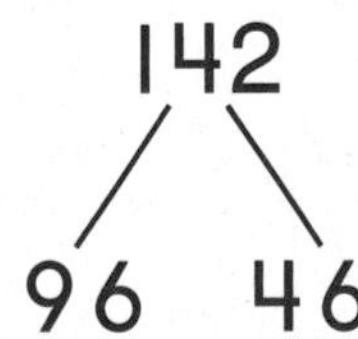

96 + 46 = 142 ______________________

142 = 96 + 46 ______________________

____

____

____

____

____

____

3. **On the Back** Show how you can subtract to find the unknown partner for 96 + ☐ = 142.

Name

5–13

Class Activity

Name ______________________________

▶ Practice Preferred Methods

Add or subtract. Watch the sign!

1. $\begin{array}{r} 151 \\ -\ 63 \\ \hline \end{array}$

2. $\begin{array}{r} 46 \\ +\ 72 \\ \hline \end{array}$

3. $\begin{array}{r} 105 \\ -\ 74 \\ \hline \end{array}$

4. $\begin{array}{r} 97 \\ +\ 88 \\ \hline \end{array}$

5. $\begin{array}{r} 64 \\ -\ 23 \\ \hline \end{array}$

6. $\begin{array}{r} 73 \\ +\ 66 \\ \hline \end{array}$

7. $\begin{array}{r} 180 \\ -\ 56 \\ \hline \end{array}$

8. $\begin{array}{r} 94 \\ +\ 38 \\ \hline \end{array}$

9. $\begin{array}{r} 147 \\ -\ 89 \\ \hline \end{array}$

10. $\begin{array}{r} 43 \\ +\ 67 \\ \hline \end{array}$

11. $\begin{array}{r} 176 \\ -\ 78 \\ \hline \end{array}$

12. $\begin{array}{r} 83 \\ +\ 79 \\ \hline \end{array}$

13. **On the Back** Explain each step you do to subtract 63 from 155. Use tens and ones language.

Name

5-14

Class Activity

Name

▶ **Introduce the Juice Bar**

Grapefruit Juice 68¢	Red Apple Juice 59¢	Lemon Juice 77¢	Pear Juice 78¢
Green Apple Juice 89¢	Peach Juice 88¢	Orange Juice 97¢	Cantaloupe Juice 87¢
Pineapple Juice 98¢	Raspberry Juice 65¢	Banana Juice 76¢	Watermelon Juice 56¢
Grape Juice 67¢	Celery Juice 58¢	Tomato Juice 96¢	Carrot Juice 79¢

Name ______________________

▶ Continue Buying and Selling

Choose two juices from the Juice Bar you would like to mix together. Find the total cost. Then find the change from two dollars.

1. I pick ______________________

and ______________________.

Juice #1 price: ______¢

Juice #2 price: + ______¢

Total: ______

200¢ − ______ = ______

My change is ______¢.

2. I pick ______________________

and ______________________.

Juice #1 price: ______¢

Juice #2 price: + ______¢

Total: ______

200¢ − ______ = ______

My change is ______¢.

3. I pick ______________________

and ______________________.

Juice #1 price: ______¢

Juice #2 price: + ______¢

Total: ______

200¢ − ______ = ______

My change is ______¢.

4. I pick ______________________

and ______________________.

Juice #1 price: ______¢

Juice #2 price: + ______¢

Total: ______

200¢ − ______ = ______

My change is ______¢.

Class Activity

Name ______________________

▶ Practice the Adding Up Method

Add up to solve the story problems.

Show your work.

1. Doug has 92 baseball cards. After he goes shopping today, he will have 175 baseball cards. How many baseball cards is Doug going to buy?

☐ ______________________
label

2. Myra had 87 dollars. After she bought some gifts, she had 68 dollars. How much money did Myra spend on gifts?

☐ ______________________
label

3. There were 151 tons of corn in a silo in May. In June there were 213 tons of corn. How many tons of corn were added to the silo?

☐ ______________________
label

4. Azim found 113 golf balls. After he gave some of them to Max, he had 54 golf balls left. How many golf balls did Azim give to Max?

☐ ______________________
label

Name

▶ Choose a Reasonable Answer

Each picture shows an item Ella wants to buy and the amount of money she has. Circle the most reasonable estimate of how much more money Ella needs to buy the item.

1. 80¢

   3¢

   30¢

   300¢

   3,000¢

2. 

   20¢

   40¢

   60¢

   80¢

3. 

   8¢

   80¢

   800¢

   8,000¢

4. WATER 109¢

   1¢

   10¢

   100¢

   1,000¢

Name ______________________________

▶ Practice the Adding Up Method

Solve the story problems.	Show your work.
1. Justin read 162 comics. Trina read 93 comics. How many more comics did Justin read than Trina? ☐ ____________ label	
2. Maya made 64 drawings. Philip made 132 drawings. How many fewer drawings did Maya make than Philip? ☐ ____________ label	
3. There were 187 birds in the zoo. The zoo received some more birds, and now they have 246 birds. How many birds did the zoo receive? ☐ ____________ label	
4. Rita had 121 pens. She gave some pens to her friends. Now she has 75 pens. How many pens did Rita give away? ☐ ____________ label	

5–16

Name ______________________

Extra Practice

▶ Alphabet Math Puzzle

Add or subtract. Then, solve the alphabet puzzle by using the answer for the exercise to find the next letter in the puzzle.

A = $42 + 79$

O = $142 - 17$

H = $137 - 76$

M = $125 + 38$

C = $126 - 84$

N = $121 - 37$

D = $84 + 58$

A = $163 - 75$

T = $88 + 49$

I ___   ___ ___ ___   ___ ___   ___ ___ ___ ___ !

42 121 84   142 125   163 88 137 61

Name ______________________

Count the money.

1.           

25¢ 50¢ 75¢ 85¢ ____ ____ ____ ____ ____

2.         

____ ____ ____ ____ ____ ____ ____ ____ ____

3.         

____ ____ ____ ____ ____ ____ ____ ____ ____

Subtract. Ungroup if you need to.

4. $\begin{array}{r} 63 \\ -27 \\ \hline \end{array}$

5. $\begin{array}{r} 84 \\ -19 \\ \hline \end{array}$

6. $\begin{array}{r} 92 \\ -46 \\ \hline \end{array}$

7. $\begin{array}{r} 57 \\ -25 \\ \hline \end{array}$

Name ______________________

Subtract.

8.
$$\begin{array}{r} 100 \\ -\ 18 \\ \hline \end{array}$$

9.
$$\begin{array}{r} 200 \\ -\ 43 \\ \hline \end{array}$$

10.
$$\begin{array}{r} 179 \\ -\ 81 \\ \hline \end{array}$$

11.
$$\begin{array}{r} 198 \\ -\ 56 \\ \hline \end{array}$$

12.
$$\begin{array}{r} 130 \\ -\ 67 \\ \hline \end{array}$$

13.
$$\begin{array}{r} 104 \\ -\ 13 \\ \hline \end{array}$$

14.
$$\begin{array}{r} 156 \\ -\ 39 \\ \hline \end{array}$$

15.
$$\begin{array}{r} 143 \\ -\ 84 \\ \hline \end{array}$$

Name ______________________________

Solve the story problems.	Show your work.
16. Vince has 89 purple bicycles and 47 red bicycles in his store. How many bicycles does he have altogether? [ ] ______ label	
17. Bonita had 97 raisins. She ate 58 of them. How many raisins are left? [ ] ______ label	
18. There are 42 birds at the feeder in our tree. There are 35 more at the feeder on the fence. How many birds are at both feeders in all? [ ] ______ label	
19. Jeffrey bought 200 paper cups for his party. 79 cups were used. How many paper cups does Jeffrey have left? [ ] ______ label	

5 Unit Test

Name ______________________________

20. Extended Response Explain all the steps you do to subtract 59 from 148.

____

____

____

____

____

____

Name ____________________

Vocabulary
congruent

▶ Congruent Figures

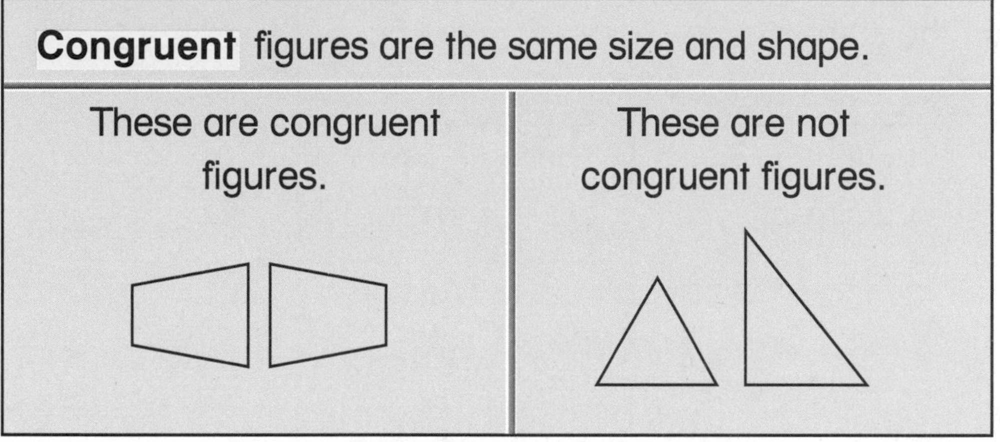

Which two figures are congruent?

1. Figures ______ and ______ are congruent.

2. Figures ______ and ______ are congruent.

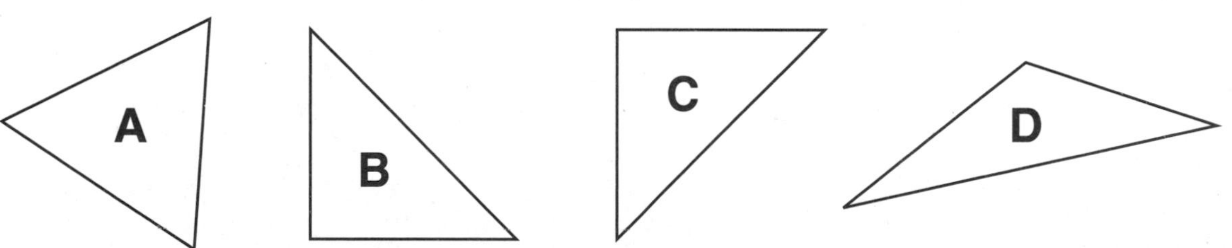

3. Figures ______ and ______ are congruent.

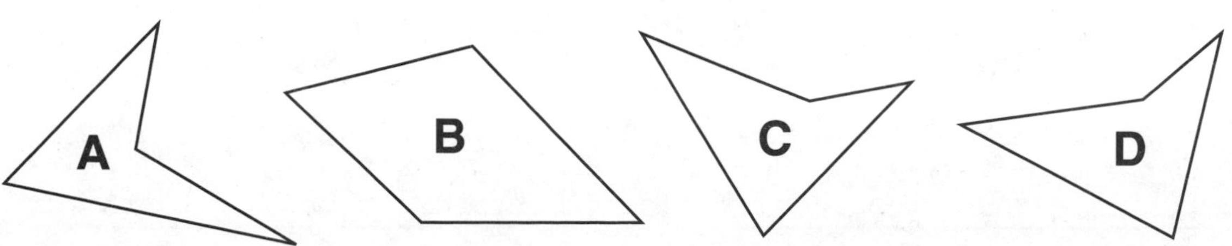

Name ____________________

Vocabulary
similar

▶ Similar Figures

Similar figures are the same shape. They may also be the same size, but they don't have to be.		
These figures are similar.	These figures are similar.	These figures are not similar.

Are the two figures similar? Write *similar* or *not similar*.

4. 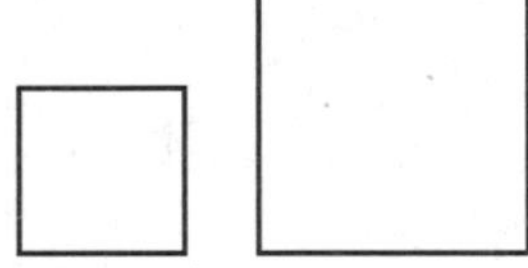

____

5. 

____

6. 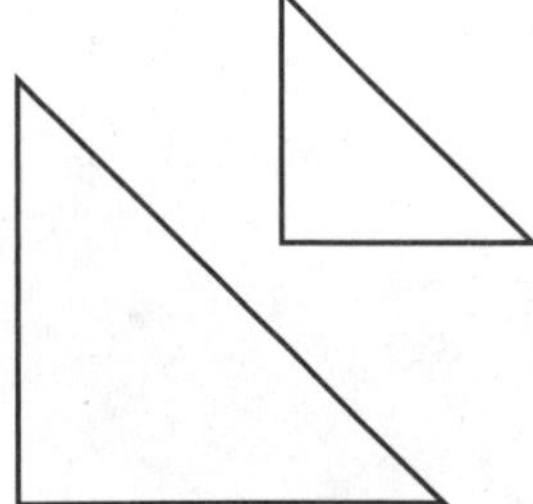

____

7. 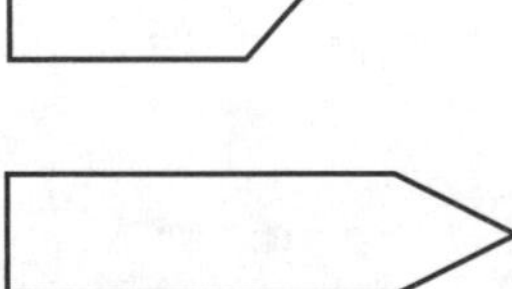

____

Name

► Sort Figures

A	B	C
D	E	F
G	H	J
K	L	M

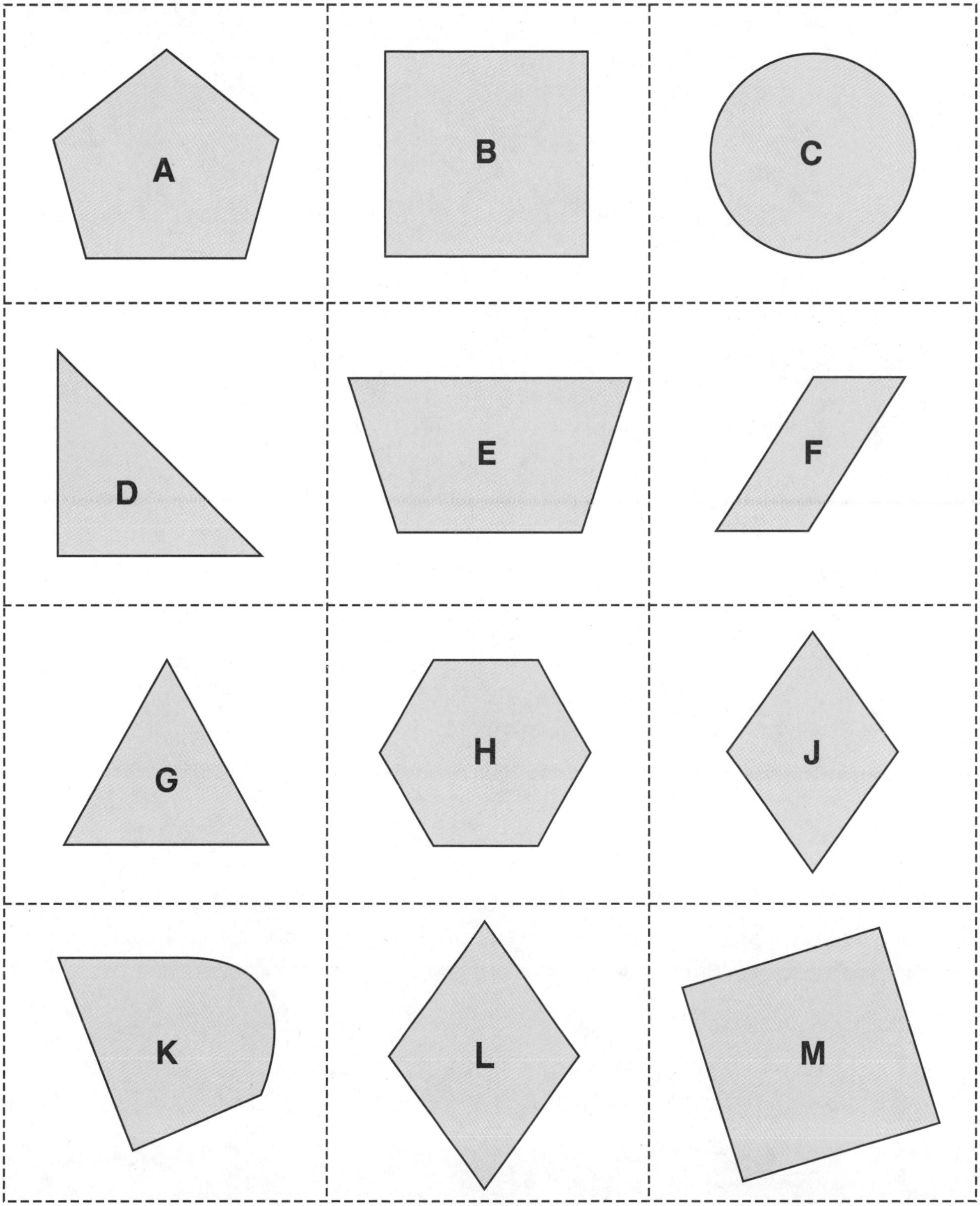

Dear Family,

Your child is working on a geometry unit about congruent figures: figures that are the same size and shape. The unit also covers similar figures: figures that are the same shape but not necessarily the same size.

Your child will be sliding figures up, down, left, and right; flipping figures over horizontal and vertical lines; and turning figures around a point.

He or she will also explore different types of patterns, including repeating patterns, growing patterns, and motion patterns (slides, flips, and turns).

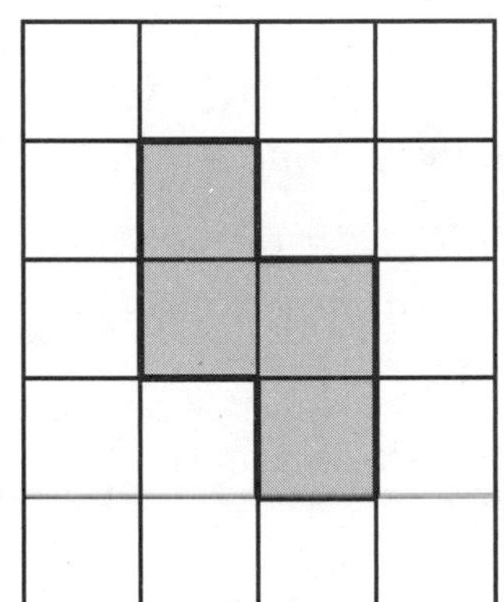

Area of shaded figure = 4 square centimeters

Your child will be asked to find the area of figures in square centimeters by counting the number of squares on centimeter-grid paper that a figure covers.

You can help reinforce your child's math learning at home.

- Encourage your child to work on jigsaw puzzles to practice sliding, flipping, and turning figures.
- Have your child find the area of tiled floors in square units by counting square tiles.
- Help your child identify patterns in fabrics, nature, music, and art.
- Create patterns using objects like buttons, paper clips, or coins. Ask your child to continue the pattern. Or you can remove one piece from the pattern and ask your child to identify the missing piece.

If you have any questions or comments, please call or write to me.

Sincerely,
Your child's teacher

Estimada familia:

Su niño está trabajando en una unidad de geometría sobre figuras congruentes: figuras que tienen el mismo tamaño y forma. La unidad también incluye figuras semejantes: figuras que tienen la misma forma pero no necesariamente el mismo tamaño.

Su niño trasladará figuras hacia arriba, hacia abajo, hacia la izquierda y hacia la derecha; invertirá figuras sobre rectas horizontales y verticales y hará girar figuras alrededor de un punto.

También explorará diferentes tipos de patrones, incluidos patrones que se repiten, patrones que aumentan y patrones de movimiento (traslaciones, inversiones y giros).

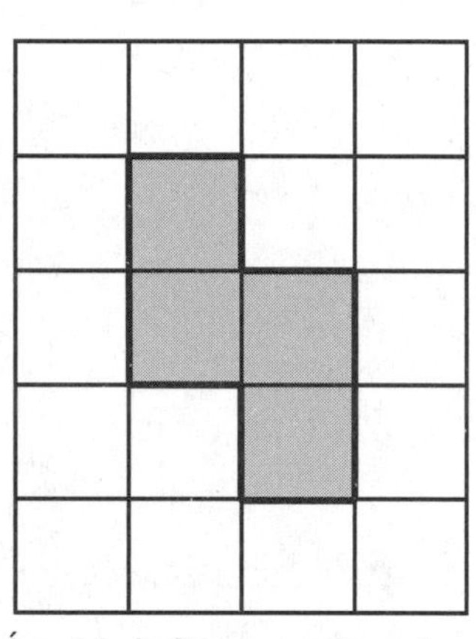

Área de la figura sombreada = 4 centímetros cuadrados

Se le pedirá a su niño que halle el área de figuras en centímetros cuadrados contando el número de cuadrados de un papel cuadriculado que están cubiertos por una figura.

Usted puede ayudar a que su niño refuerce el aprendizaje de matemáticas en casa.

- Anime a su niño a trabajar con rompecabezas para practicar la traslación, la inversión y el giro de figuras.
- Pídale a su niño que halle el área de pisos de baldosas en unidades cuadradas, contando baldosas cuadradas.
- Ayude a su niño a identificar patrones en las telas, la naturaleza, la música y el arte.
- Haga patrones utilizando objetos como botones, sujetapapeles o monedas. Pida a su niño que continúe el patrón. También, puede quitar una pieza del patrón y pedirle al niño que identifique la pieza que falta.

Si tiene alguna pregunta o comentario, por favor comuníquese conmigo.

Atentamente,
El maestro de su niño

Name ____________________

Vocabulary
slide

▶ Identify Slides

You can **slide** a figure right or left along a straight line.

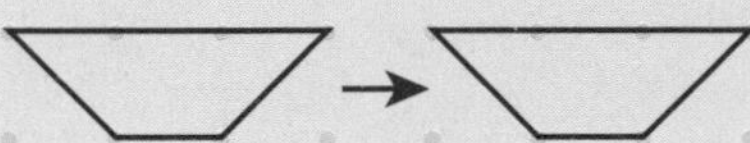

You can slide a figure up or down along a straight line.

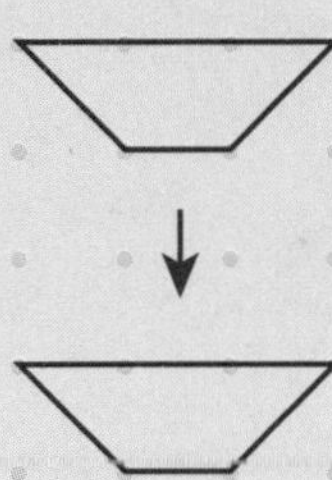

Does each picture show a slide? Write *yes* or *no.*

1. 

____

2. 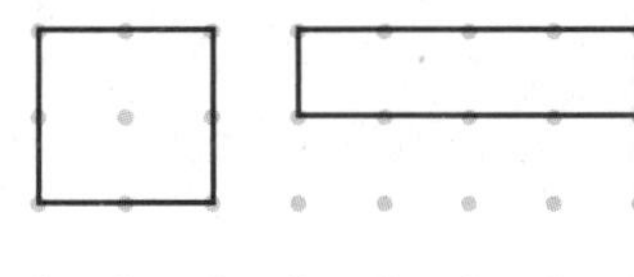

____

3. 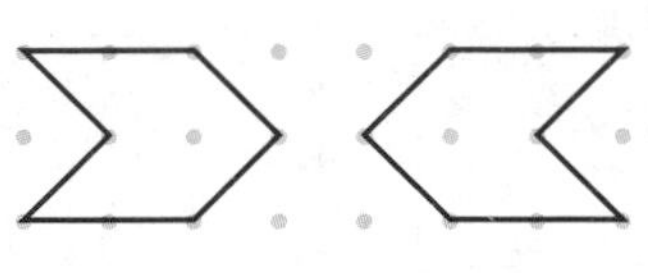

____

4. 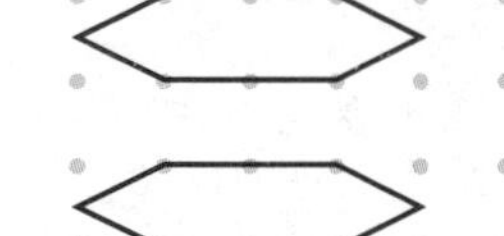

____

Class Activity

Name ____________________

Vocabulary
flip
horizontal line
vertical line

▶ Identify Flips

You can **flip** a figure over a **horizontal line**.

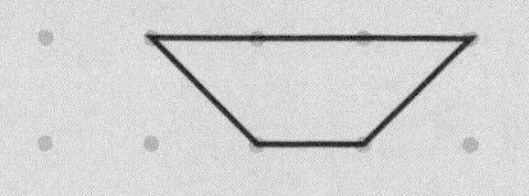

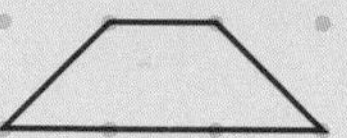

You can flip a figure over a **vertical line**.

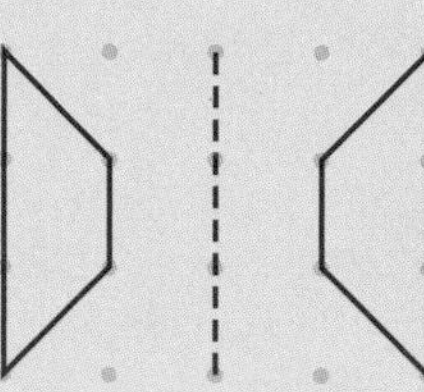

Does each picture show a flip over the line? Write *yes* or *no*.

5. 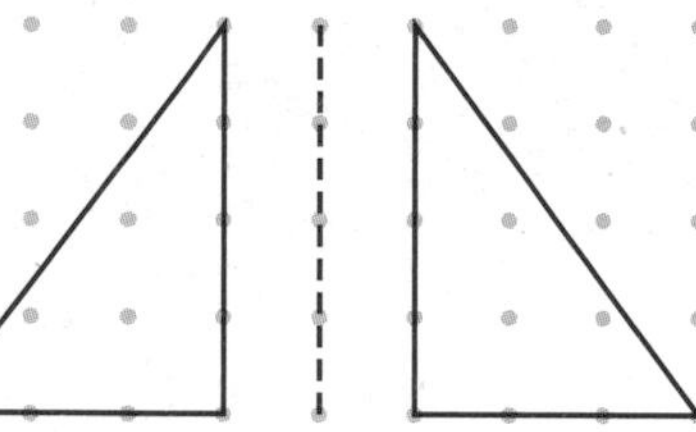

____

6. 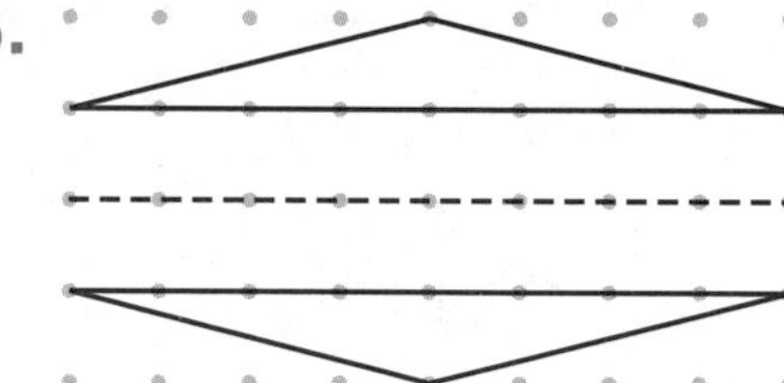

____

7. 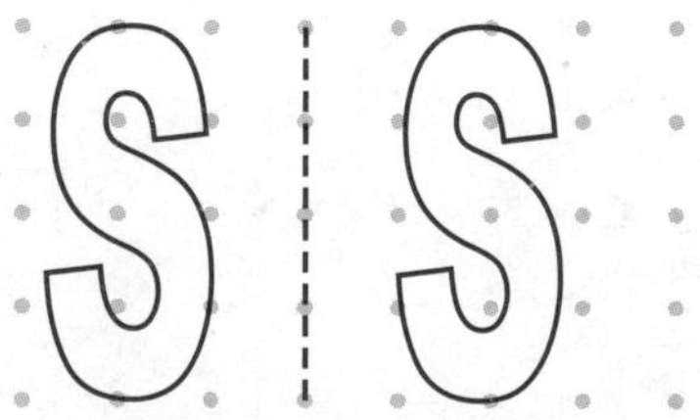

____

8. 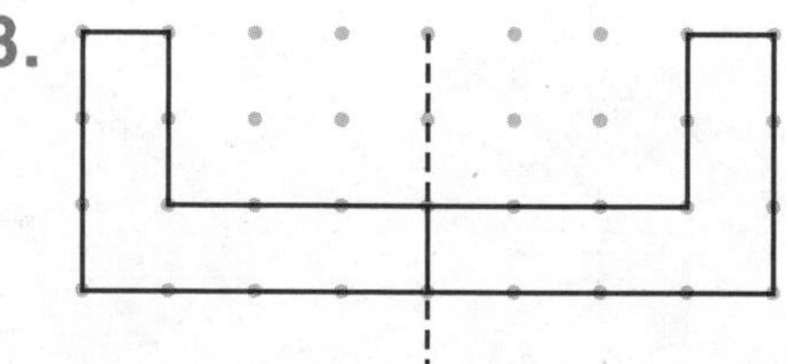

____

Name ______________________________

Vocabulary
turn
rotate

► Identify Turns

You can **turn** or **rotate** a figure around a point.

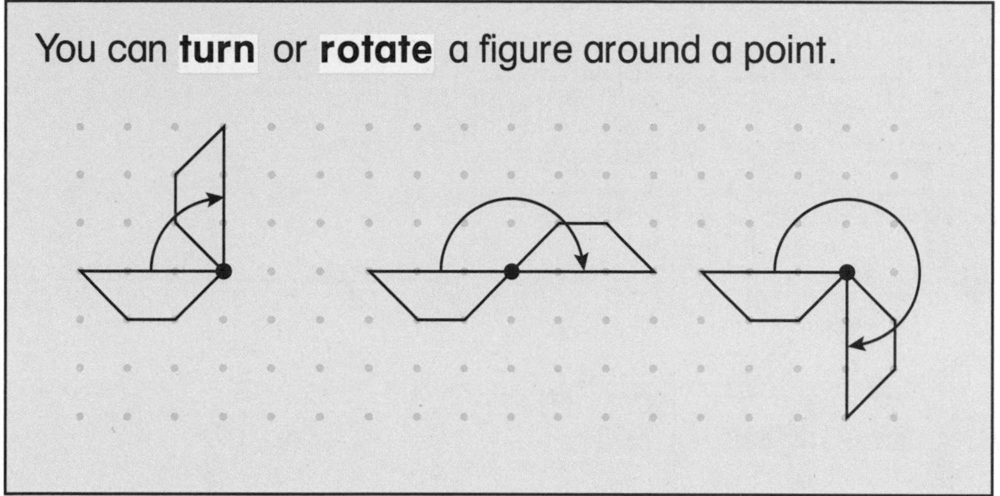

Does each picture show a turn around the point?
Write *yes* or *no*.

9.

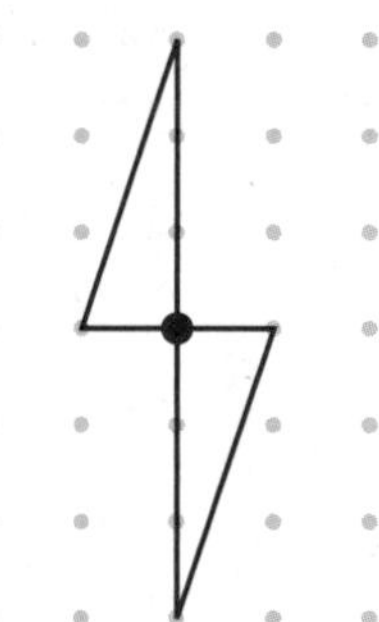

____

10.

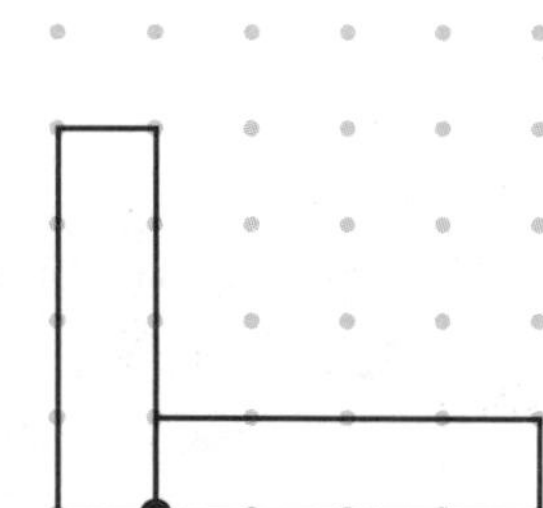

____

11.

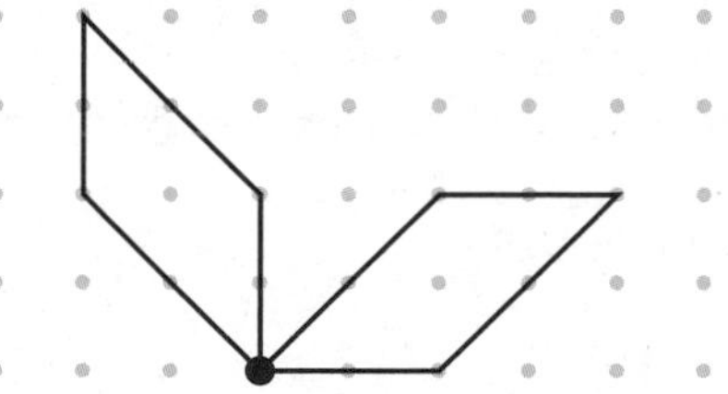

____

12.

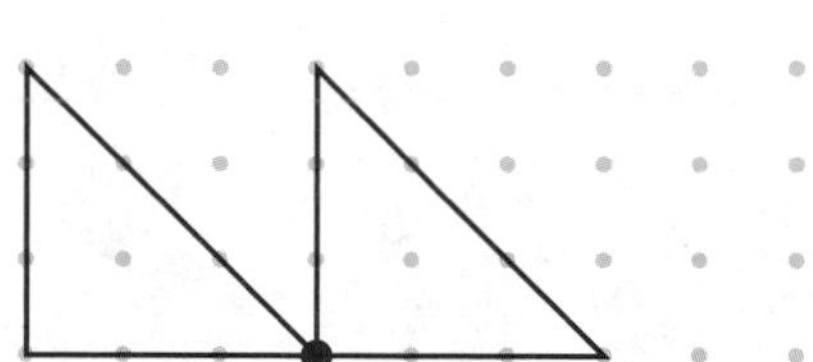

____

E-2 Class Activity

Name

Vocabulary
slide
flip
turn

▶ Identify Slides, Flips, and Turns

You can **slide, flip,** or **turn** a figure to make a pattern.

Write *slide, flip,* or *turn* to describe each pattern.

13.  ____________

14.  ____________

15. 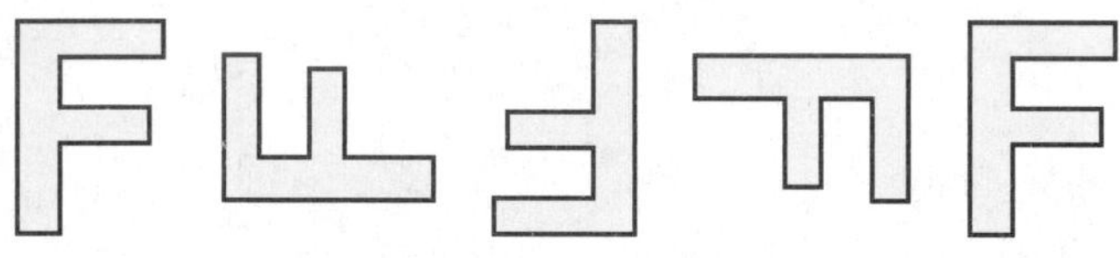 ____________

16. 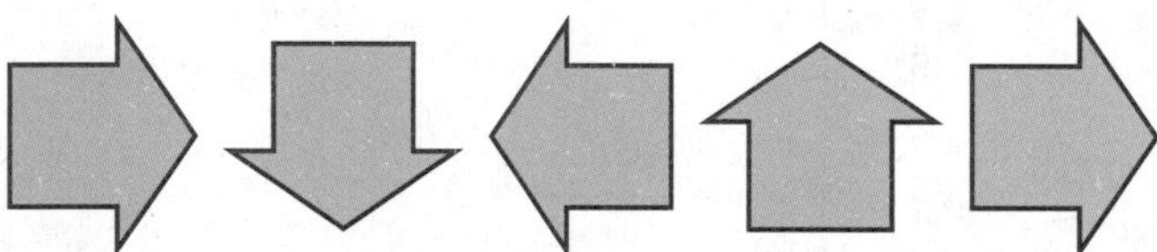 ____________

17.  ____________

18.  ____________

Name ______________________

▶ Extend Patterns

Draw the next figure in the pattern.

19. 

____

20. 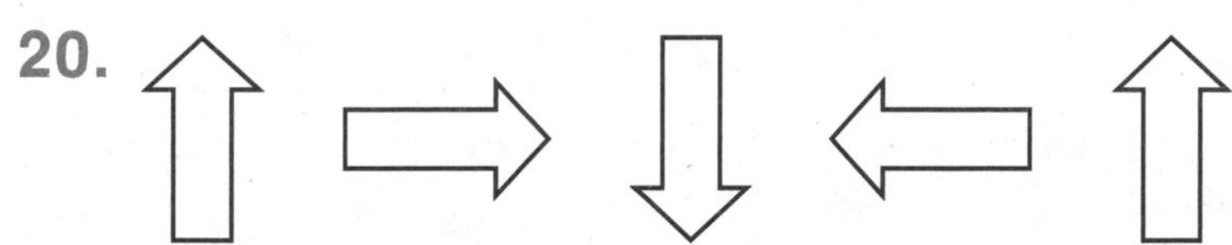

____

21. 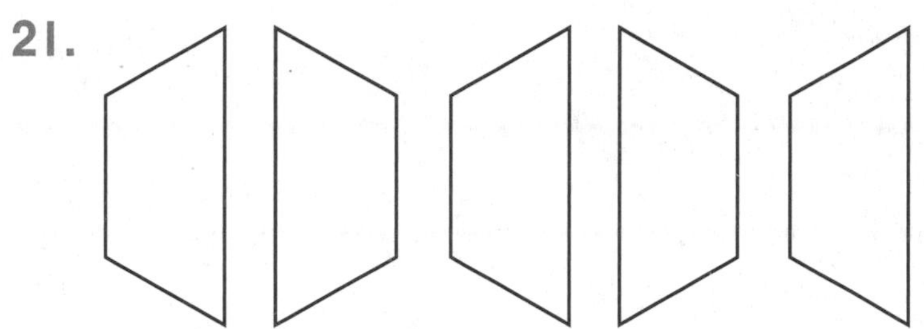

____

22. 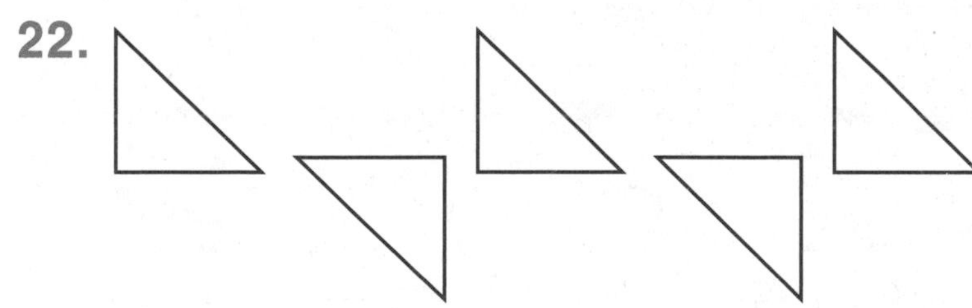

____

23. 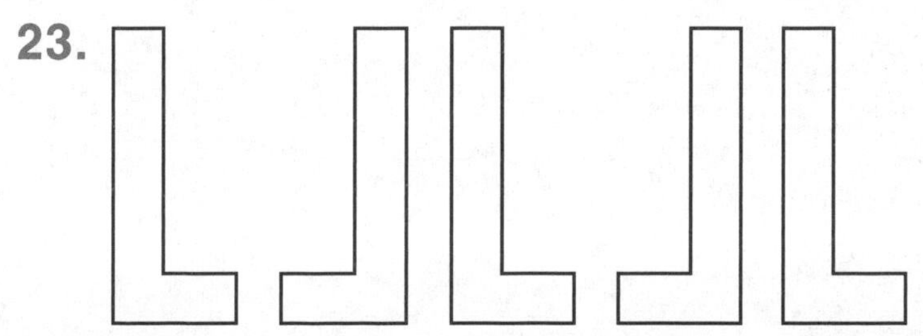

____

Name

Vocabulary
tessellation

▶ Explore Tessellations

A **tessellation** is a pattern made by congruent polygons that fit together exactly to cover a surface.

A tessellation is like a tiling pattern that covers a floor.

1. Use your ruler to continue the pattern to make a tessellation of triangles.

   Color the triangles to make a pattern.

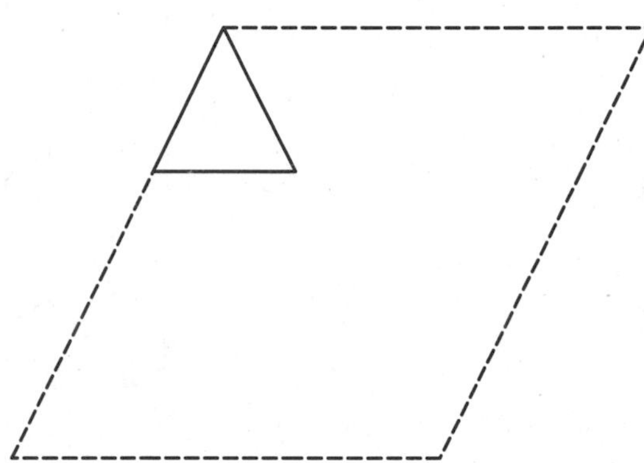

2. Use your ruler to draw more figures to extend this tessellation. Color the tessellation to make a pattern.

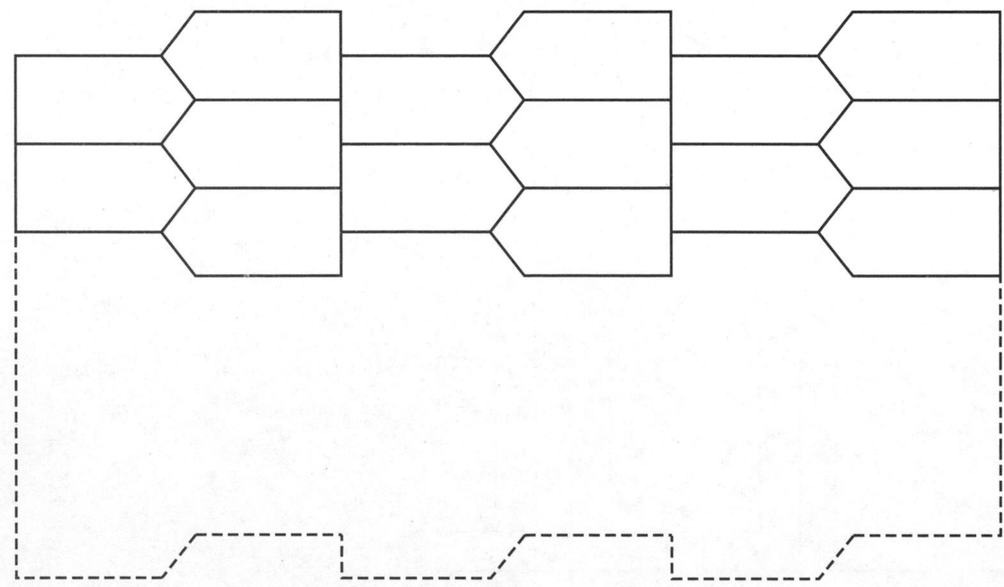

E-4 Class Activity

Name ______________________________

▶ Count Square Units

Vocabulary
area
square units

Cover each figure with **square units** and count them to find the **area**.

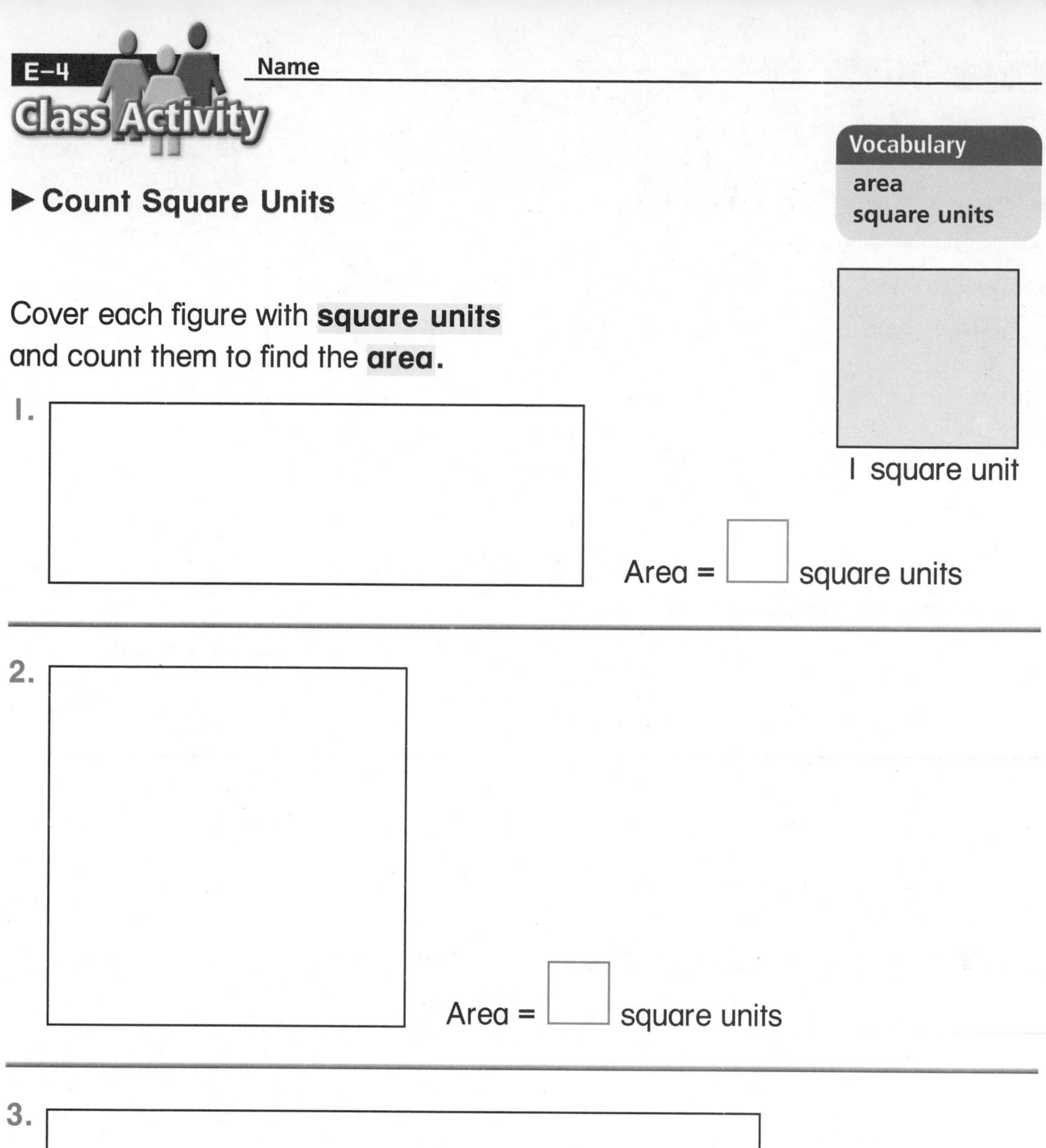

1 square unit

1. Area = ☐ square units

2. Area = ☐ square units

3. Area = ☐ square units

E–4 Class Activity

Name ____________________

Vocabulary
square centimeter

▶ Count Square Centimeters

You can measure area in **square centimeters**.
A square centimeter is a square with sides that measure 1 cm.

1 square centimeter

Count the number of squares in each shaded figure to find the area in square centimeters.

4.

Area = ☐ square centimeters

5.

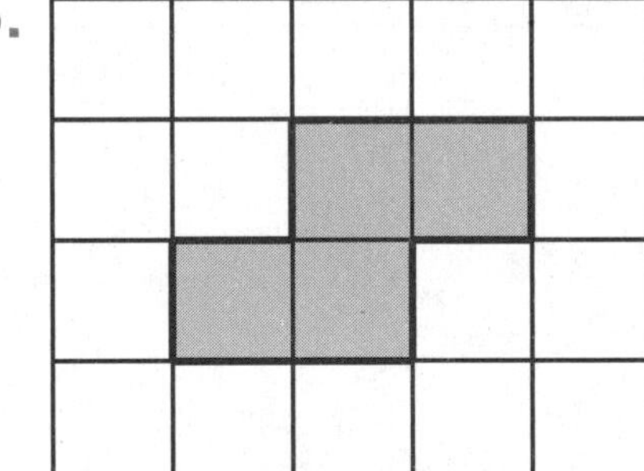

Area = ☐ square centimeters

6.

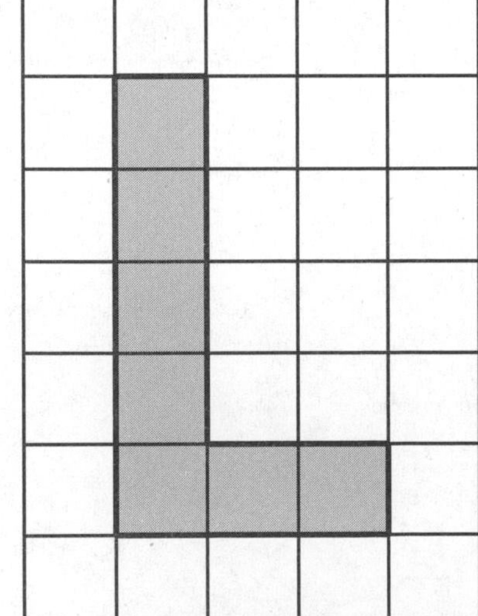

Area = ☐ square centimeters

7.

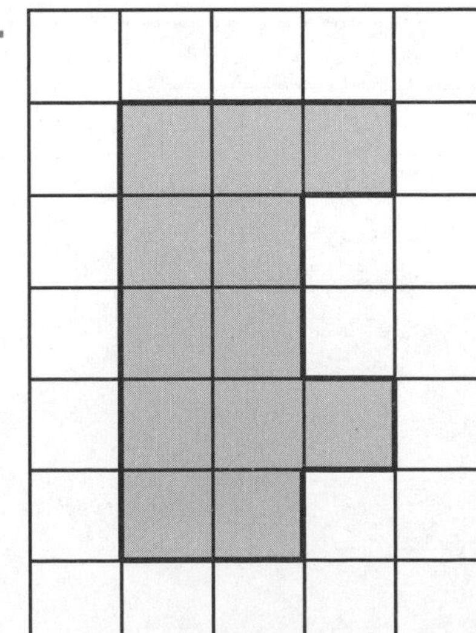

Area = ☐ square centimeters

Name ______________________________

1. Which two shapes are congruent?

Shapes ______ and ______ are congruent.

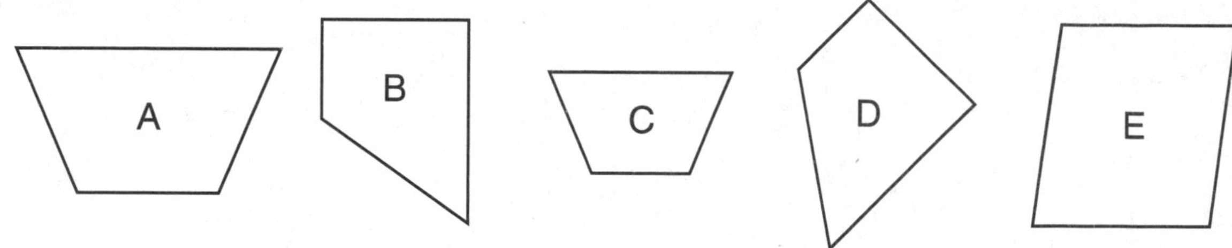

2. Are the two shapes similar? Write *similar* or *not similar.*

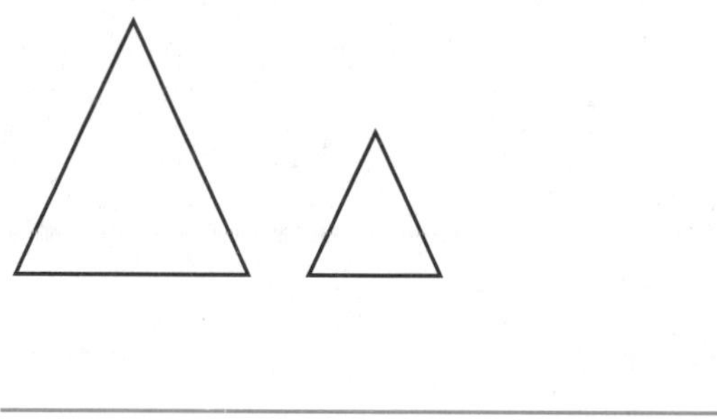

____

3. Sort these shapes using the rule: quadrilaterals and not quadrilaterals. Write the letters.

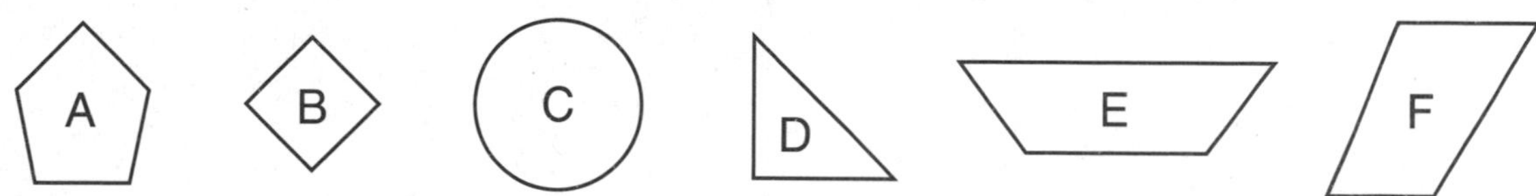

The shapes ____________ are quadrilaterals.

The shapes ____________ are not quadrilaterals.

Name ______________________________

4. Does the picture show a slide?
Write *yes* or *no.*

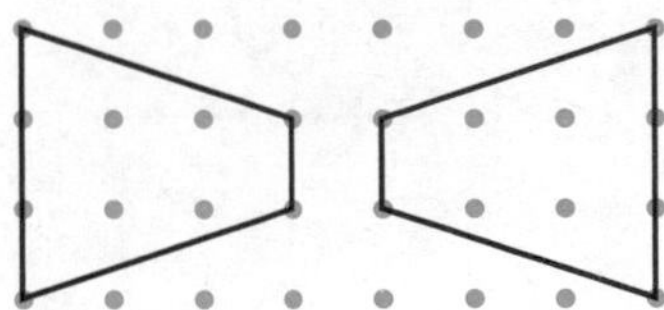

____

5. Does the picture show a flip over the line?
Write *yes* or *no.*

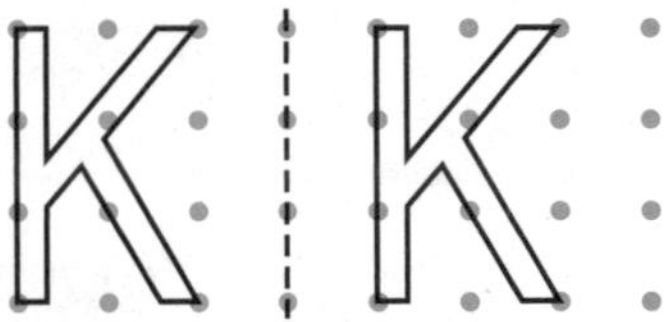

____

6. Does the picture show a turn around the point?
Write *yes* or *no.*

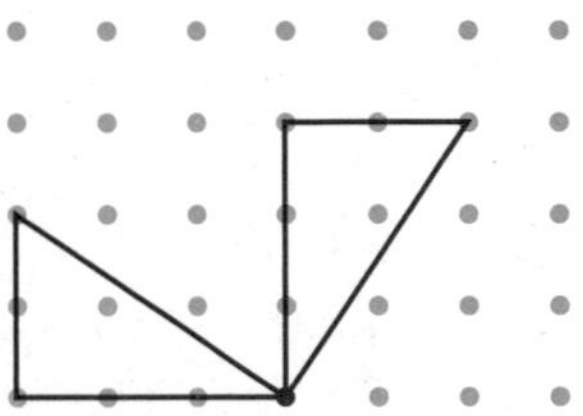

____

Name ______________________

7. Draw the next figure in the pattern.

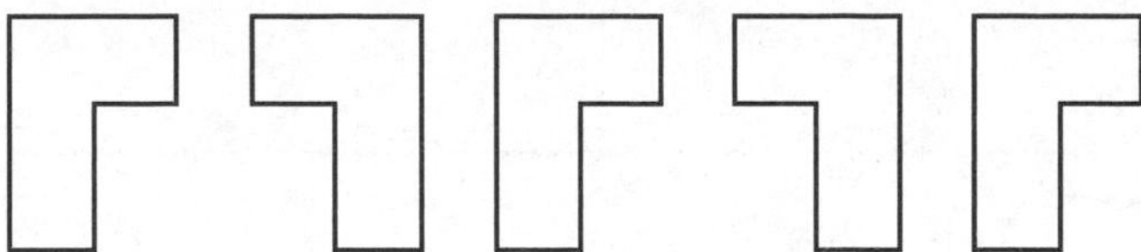

____

Find the area in square centimeters.

8.

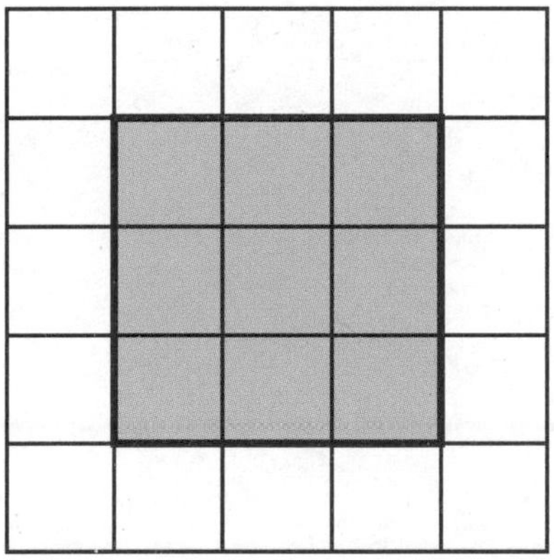

Area = ______ square centimeters

9.

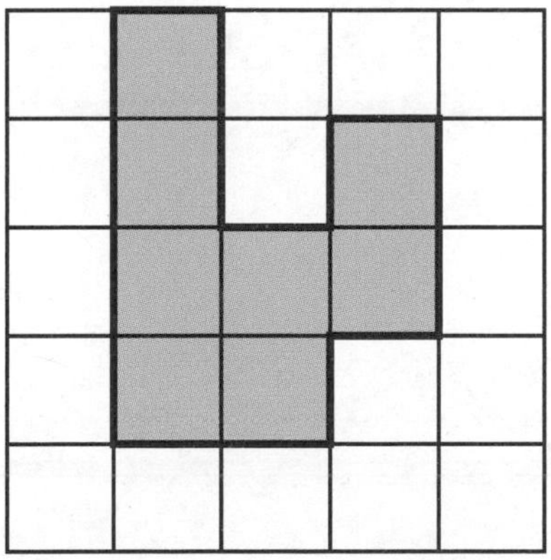

Area = ______ square centimeters

Name ______________________________

10. Extended Response Choose a sorting rule to sort the shapes into two groups.

My sorting rule is: ______________________________

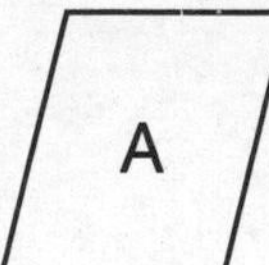

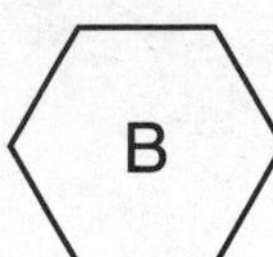

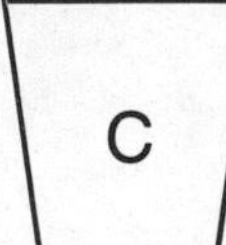

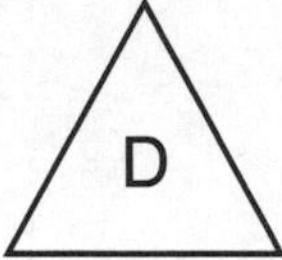

The shapes ____________ are ________________.

The shapes ____________ are ________________.

6–1 Class Activity

Name ___

▶ Count to 1,000 by Hundreds

Cut on dashed lines.

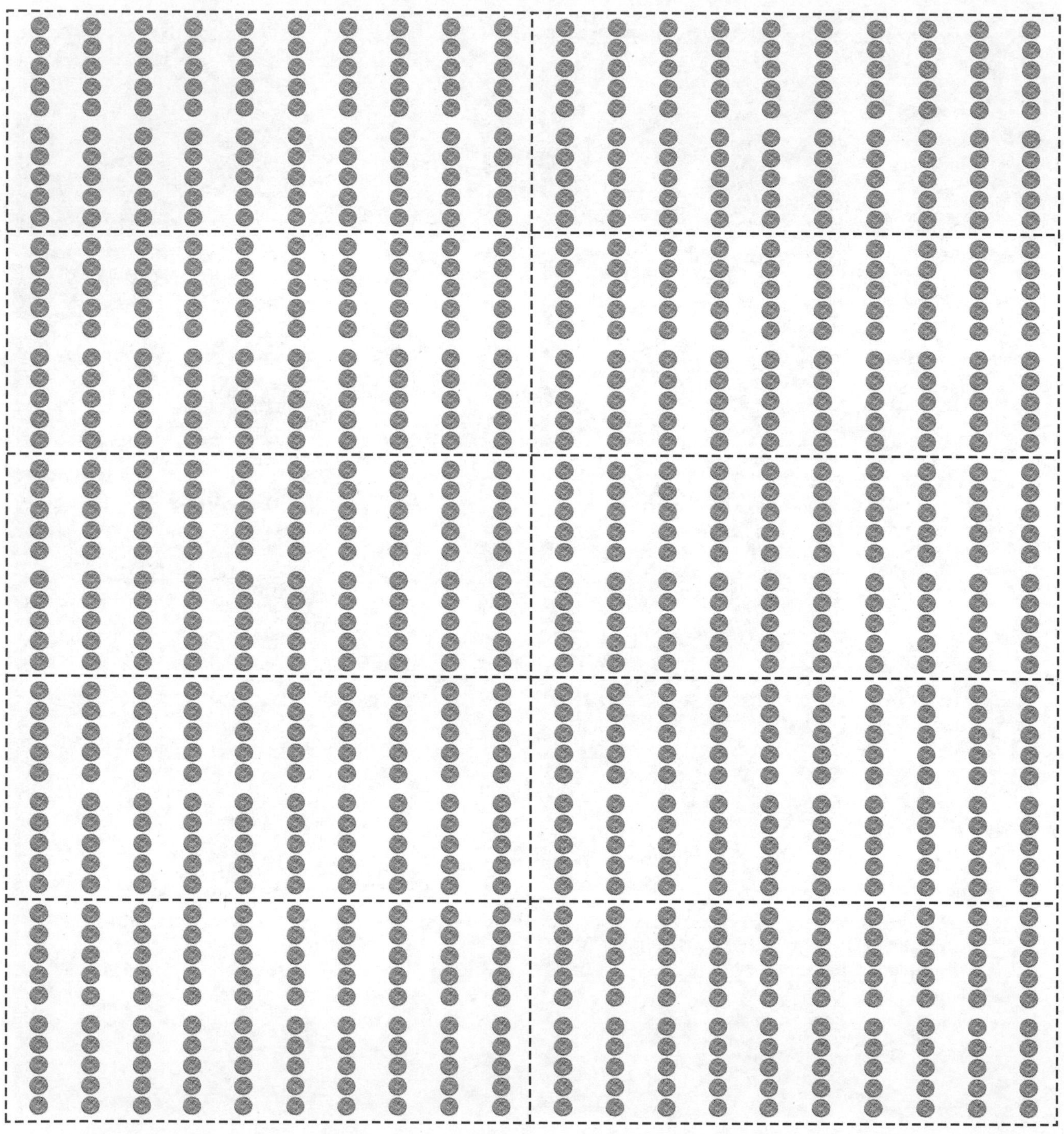

Dear Family,

In this unit, children will learn different ways to add 3-digit numbers that have totals less than 1,000, with and without regrouping. One way that children will add 3-digit numbers is by counting to 1,000 by tens and by hundreds.

Count to 1,000

Children count by ones from a number, over the hundred, and into the next hundred. For example, 498, 499, 500, 501, 502, 503.

Mistakes often occur when counting this way, so watch for errors that children may make.

Some children will write 5003 instead of 503 for five hundred three. Using Secret Code Cards will help children write the numbers correctly.

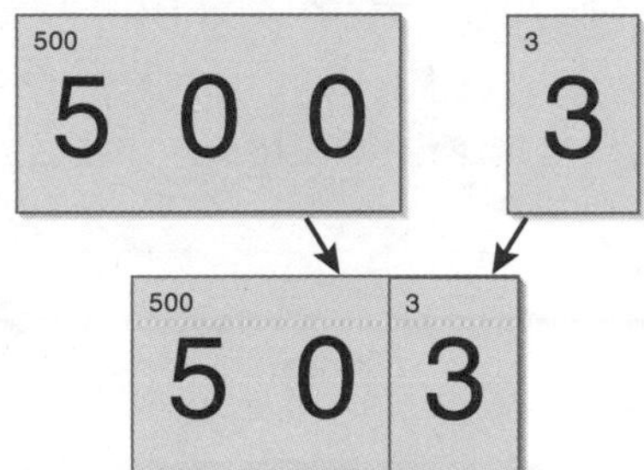

Counting aloud to 1,000 and grouping and labeling small objects provide written and oral practice, and are good ways to help children recognize the difference between 5,003 and 503.

Please call if you have any questions or concerns. Thank you for helping your child learn how to add 3-digit numbers by counting to 1,000.

Sincerely,
Your child's teacher

Estimada familia:

En esta unidad los niños están aprendiendo diferentes maneras de sumar números de 3 dígitos con totales de menos de 1,000, reagrupando y sin reagrupar. Una manera en que los niños sumarán números de 3 dígitos es contando hasta 1,000 de diez en diez y de cien en cien.

Contar hasta 1,000

Los niños cuentan de uno en uno a partir de un número, llegan a la centena y comienzan con la siguiente centena.

Por ejemplo, 498, 499, 500, 501, 502, 503.

Cuando se cuenta de esta manera los niños suelen cometer errores. Por lo tanto, preste atención a errores que los niños puedan cometer.

Algunos niños Podrian escribir 5003 en vez de 503 al intentar escribir quinientos tres. Usar las Tarjetas de código secreto ayudará a los niños a escribair correctamente los números.

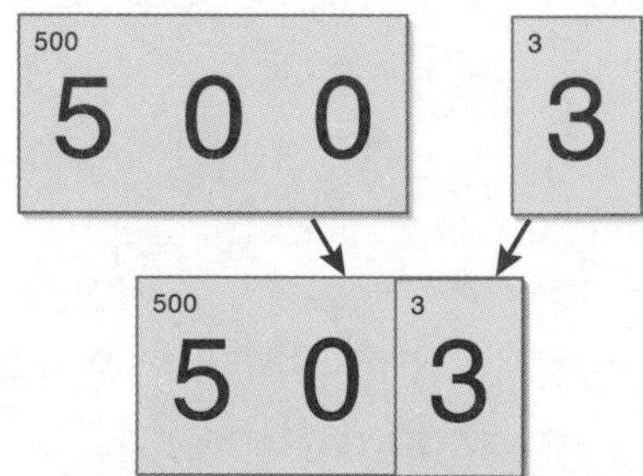

Contar hasta 1,000 en voz alta y poner objectos pequeños en grupos y rotularlos proporcionan práctica oral y escrita, y ayudan a los niños a reconocer la diferencia entre 5,003 y 503.

Si tiene alguna duda o pregunta, por favor comuníquese conmigo. Gracias por ayudar a su niño a aprender a sumar números de 3 dígitos contando hasta 1,000.

Atentamente,
El maestro de su niño

Name ______________________

Vocabulary
hundreds
tens
ones

▶ Expanded Numbers

Write the **hundreds**, **tens**, and **ones**.

1. 382 = 300 + 80 + 2
   H T O
2. 738 = _____ + _____ + _____
3. 526 = _____ + _____ + _____
4. 267 = _____ + _____ + _____

Write the number.

5. 400 + 50 + 9 = 459
   H T O
6. 800 + 10 + 3 = _____
7. 100 + 70 + 5 = _____
8. 600 + 40 + 1 = _____

Write the missing number.
Watch the hundreds, tens, and ones.
They are out of order.

9. _____ = 5 + 900 + 40
10. 30 + 7 + 200 = _____
11. _____ = 400 + 6 + 80
12. 9 + 800 + 40 = _____
13. _____ = 70 + 4 + 300
14. 60 + 500 + 3 = _____
15. _____ = 2 + 400 + 90
16. 9 + 90 + 200 = _____
17. 462 = 2 + 400 + _____
18. _____ + 90 + 700 = 798
19. 523 = 20 + 3 + _____
20. _____ + 4 + 200 = 224

21. **On the Back** Write or draw your own definition of hundreds, tens, and ones.

Name

6–3

Class Activity

Name ______________________

▶ Count Over a Hundred by Ones and by Tens

Count by ones. Write the numbers.

1. 396 397 398 399 400 401 402 403 404 405 406
2. 594 595 ____ ____ ____ ____ ____ ____ ____ ____ 604
3. 297 298 ____ ____ ____ ____ ____ ____ ____ ____ 307
4. 495 ____ ____ ____ ____ ____ ____ ____ ____ ____ 505
5. 598 ____ ____ ____ ____ ____ ____ ____ ____ ____ 608
6. 697 ____ ____ ____ ____ ____ ____ ____ ____ ____ 707

Count by tens. Write the numbers.

7. 830 840 850 860 870 880 890 900 910 920 930
8. 370 380 ____ ____ ____ ____ ____ ____ ____ ____ 470
9. 640 ____ ____ ____ ____ ____ ____ ____ ____ ____ 740
10. 580 ____ ____ ____ ____ ____ ____ ____ ____ ____ 680
11. 750 ____ ____ ____ ____ ____ ____ ____ ____ ____ 850
12. 460 ____ ____ ____ ____ ____ ____ ____ ____ ____ 560

6-3

Name ______________________

Going Further

▶ Read and Write Word Names for Numbers

You can read or write numbers with words or symbols.

1 one	11 eleven	10 ten	100 one hundred
2 two	12 twelve	20 twenty	200 two hundred
3 three	13 thirteen	30 thirty	300 three hundred
4 four	14 fourteen	40 forty	400 four hundred
5 five	15 fifteen	50 fifty	500 five hundred
6 six	16 sixteen	60 sixty	600 six hundred
7 seven	17 seventeen	70 seventy	700 seven hundred
8 eight	18 eighteen	80 eighty	800 eight hundred
9 nine	19 nineteen	90 ninety	900 nine hundred
			1,000 one thousand

Write each number.

1. one hundred twenty-five ________
2. four hundred fifty-eight ________
3. six hundred thirty-one ________
4. nine hundred sixty-two ________
5. eight hundred forty ________
6. seven hundred three ________

Write each word name.

7. 500 ______________________________
8. 592 ______________________________
9. 650 ______________________________
10. 605 ______________________________
11. 1,000 ______________________________

Name ____________________

Vocabulary
estimate
actual amount

▶ Estimate the Number of Objects in a Container

1. **Estimate** the number of objects.
Then count the **actual amount.**

Estimate			Actual (Real Amount)		
______ Groups of 100	______ Groups of 10	______ Extra Ones	______ Groups of 100	______ Groups of 10	______ Extra Ones

2. Draw boxes, sticks, and circles to show the number of objects the class has.

Groups of 100 (boxes)	Groups of 10 (sticks)	Extra Ones (circles)

3. **On the Back** Use the picture. Estimate to find the answer. Then explain how you found your estimate.

Lynn and Ramón picked some apples. About how many apples did they pick?

Name

Name ____________________

Class Activity

▶ Add Numbers with 1, 2, and 3 Digits

Solve.

1. 100 + 100 = ____ 100 + 10 = ____ 100 + 1 = ____

   200 + 200 = ____ 200 + 20 = ____ 200 + 2 = ____

   300 + 300 = ____ 300 + 30 = ____ 300 + 3 = ____

   400 + 400 = ____ 400 + 40 = ____ 400 + 4 = ____

   500 + 500 = ____ 500 + 50 = ____ 500 + 5 = ____

---

2. 600 + 200 = ____ 20 + 600 = ____ 2 + 600 = ____

   700 + 300 = ____ 30 + 700 = ____ 3 + 700 = ____

   800 + 100 = ____ 10 + 800 = ____ 1 + 800 = ____

   900 + 100 = ____ 10 + 900 = ____ 1 + 900 = ____

   100 + 900 = ____ 90 + 100 = ____ 9 + 100 = ____

---

3. 100 + 134 = ____ 100 + 34 = ____ 4 + 100 = ____

   200 + 245 = ____ 200 + 45 = ____ 200 + 5 = ____

   300 + 356 = ____ 56 + 300 = ____ 6 + 300 = ____

   400 + 467 = ____ 400 + 67 = ____ 400 + 7 = ____

   500 + 478 = ____ 78 + 500 = ____ 8 + 500 = ____

Name ______________________________

► Solve and Discuss

Solve each story problem. Use your Secret Code Cards or Proof Drawings if you wish.

4. A camping club bought some raisins. They bought 3 cartons that had 100 bags each. They had 24 bags left from their last trip. How many bags of raisins does the club have?

   [ ] ______________ label

5. Two friends want to make necklaces. They buy 1 package of a hundred red beads, 1 package of a hundred blue beads, and 1 package of a hundred green beads. They already have 12 loose beads. How many beads do they have altogether?

   [ ] ______________ label

6. Mia and Bo want to advertise their yard sale. They decide to make flyers. They buy 2 packs of paper. Each pack has 200 sheets in it. They have 32 sheets in their art box. How many sheets of paper do they have?

   [ ] ______________ label

7. All of the students at a school went out on the playground. They formed 8 groups of one hundred students and 6 groups of ten. There were 5 students left. How many students go to this school?

   [ ] ______________ label

6–5

Class Activity

Name ____________________

▶ More Story Problems

Solve each story problem.

8. The scout troop collected aluminum cans to recycle. They counted 2 groups of one hundred cans and 5 groups of ten. They had 7 more cans. How many cans did the troop collect?

   [ ] ____________ label

9. Angelica bought some toothpicks. She bought 8 packets of one hundred and 4 packets of ten. She already had 3 toothpicks. How many toothpicks does Angelica have in all?

   [ ] ____________ label

10. Dawn put up strings of lights in the yard. She used 4 strings that had one hundred lights on them. She also used 8 strings that had ten lights on them. How many lights did she use?

   [ ] ____________ label

11. Neil works at a newspaper stand. He counted 5 groups of one hundred newspapers and 3 groups of ten. He also counted 6 more loose newspapers. How many newspapers were at the stand?

   [ ] ____________ label

12. **On the Back** Write and solve another story problem like the ones above.

Name ______________________________

Name

Vocabulary
quarters

► Review Coins

Here are some coins and the amount of money they are worth.

The Quarter Machine turns **quarters** into other coins. What coins might the machine give you that equal 25¢? Draw some different ways. Use a circle with the number of cents inside for each coin.

1.

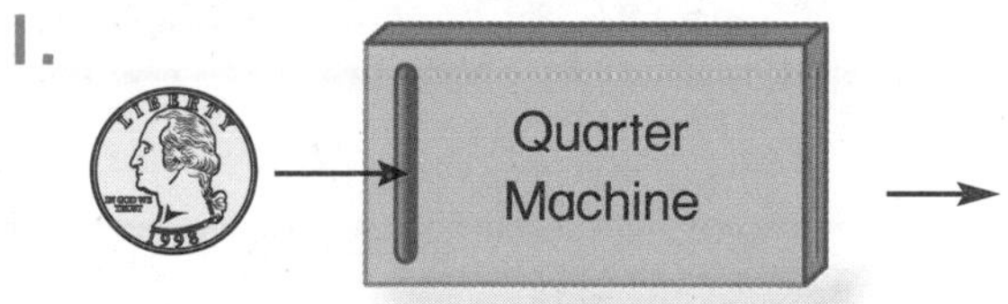

2.

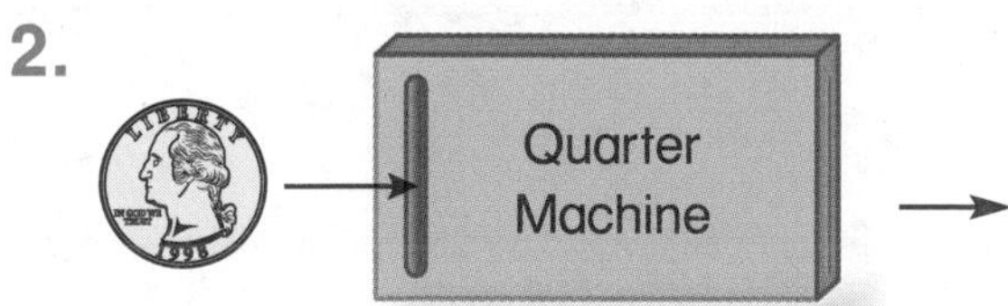

3.

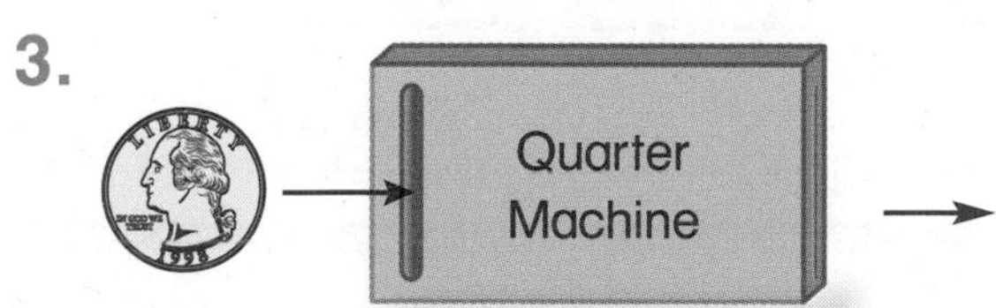

4.

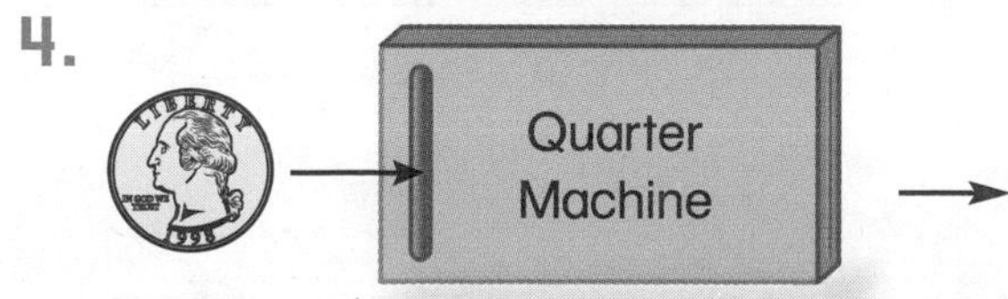

Going Further

Name

▶ Coin Combinations

For each Quarter Machine, draw a picture to show the coins it gives out.

1.

2.

3.

4.

5.

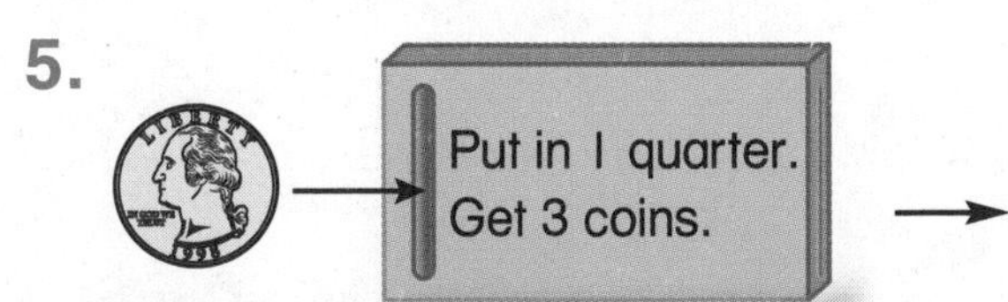

6.

Name ______________________

▶ Buy and Sell Items

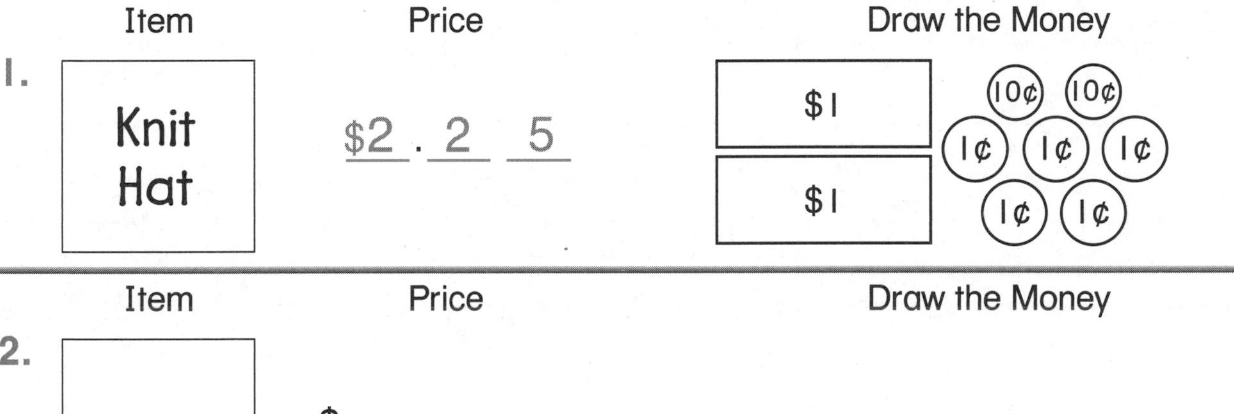

Item | Price | Draw the Money

2. [ ] $___.___ ___

Item | Price | Draw the Money

3. 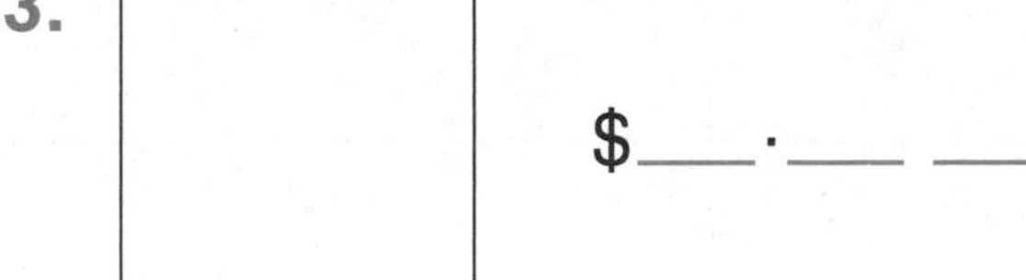 $___.___ ___

4. On the Back Make a list of the different ways you can make 80¢ using dimes and nickels.

Name

Name ____________________

▶ The Grocery Store

8 Bananas $1.29	12 Muffins $.99	1 Can of Tuna $2.38	1 Bushel of Apples $4.37
1 Dozen Eggs $1.68	6 Slices of Pizza $3.49	1 Sandwich $1.54	1 Box of Tacos $2.46
4 Yogurts $2.25	1 Jar of Pickles $.57	3 Bunches of Grapes $1.79	6 Oranges $2.07
3 Boxes of Pasta $3.72	2 Cans of Soup $1.45	1 Pound of Nuts $3.48	1 Dozen Peaches $1.10

On the Back Write about a time you spent money on something. How much did you start with? How much money did you spend? How much money did you have left?

Name

Name ________________________________

▶ Addition Sprint

5 + 7 =	9 + 6 =	7 + 6 =
4 + 8 =	7 + 8 =	4 + 6 =
3 + 9 =	9 + 7 =	0 + 7 =
7 + 5 =	9 + 2 =	4 + 9 =
4 + 5 =	5 + 2 =	6 + 8 =
8 + 4 =	6 + 4 =	8 + 5 =
8 + 6 =	8 + 7 =	6 + 1 =
6 + 9 =	5 + 5 =	5 + 4 =
9 + 9 =	1 + 9 =	7 + 4 =
6 + 3 =	7 + 9 =	3 + 6 =
9 + 0 =	4 + 7 =	9 + 4 =
7 + 7 =	8 + 8 =	5 + 8 =
9 + 1 =	6 + 6 =	3 + 4 =
8 + 9 =	3 + 5 =	6 + 7 =
2 + 5 =	9 + 3 =	1 + 6 =
3 + 9 =	2 + 9 =	5 + 6 =
2 + 7 =	2 + 6 =	5 + 5 =
9 + 4 =	5 + 9 =	6 + 8 =
2 + 8 =	8 + 2 =	4 + 4 =
0 + 8 =	9 + 8 =	1 + 8 =
8 + 3 =	6 + 5 =	6 + 7 =

Class Activity

Name ____________________

▶ Solve and Explain

Solve each story problem.
Be ready to explain what you did.

1. Milo made a display of plant and fish fossils for the library. He put in 478 plant fossils. He put in 67 fish fossils. How many fossils were in the display?

   ☐ ____________ label

2. The nature club planted some pine and birch trees. They planted 496 birch trees. Then they planted 283 pine trees. How many trees did the club plant in all?

   ☐ ____________ label

3. There were 504 yellow ducks entered in the Rubber Duck River Race. Then we added 38 white ones. How many ducks are in the race now?

   ☐ ____________ label

4. There are 189 children at Camp Sunshine. There are 375 children at Camp Bluebird. How many children are there at the two camps?

   ☐ ____________ label

Extra Practice

Name ____________________

▶ Solve and Discuss

Add using any method. Make a Proof Drawing if it helps.

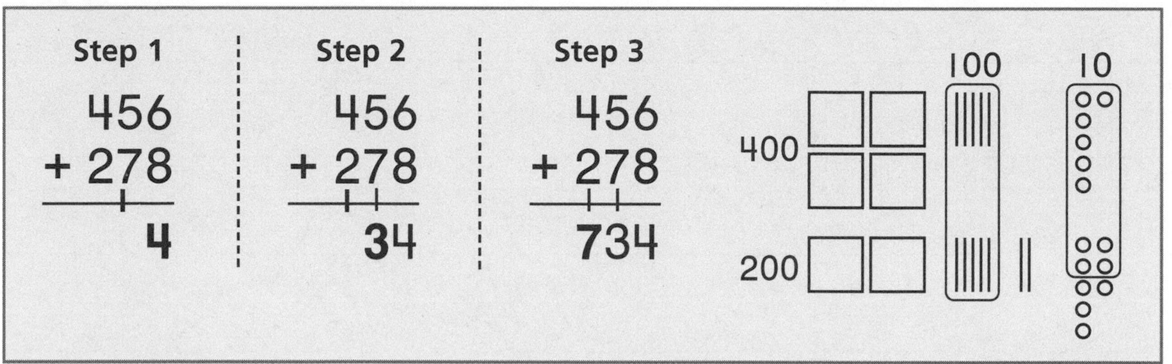

1. $\begin{array}{r} 375 \\ +\ 482 \\ \hline \end{array}$

2. $\begin{array}{r} 148 \\ +\ 236 \\ \hline \end{array}$

3. $\begin{array}{r} 584 \\ +\ 361 \\ \hline \end{array}$

4. $\begin{array}{r} 168 \\ +\ 674 \\ \hline \end{array}$

5. $\begin{array}{r} 289 \\ +\ 376 \\ \hline \end{array}$

6. $\begin{array}{r} 563 \\ +\ 157 \\ \hline \end{array}$

7. $\begin{array}{r} 497 \\ +\ 259 \\ \hline \end{array}$

8. $\begin{array}{r} 124 \\ +\ 563 \\ \hline \end{array}$

9. $\begin{array}{r} 348 \\ +\ 239 \\ \hline \end{array}$

10. **On the Back** Write two of your own story problems for a classmate to solve.

Name

Dear Family,

Your child is now learning how to add 3-digit numbers. First, children do this with methods they invent themselves or they extend the drawings they did for 2-digit addition.

Children solve the great "mystery" of addition: a hundred can be made from the extra tens, and a ten can be made from the extra ones. *Math Expressions* shows children these two simple methods for 3-digit addition.

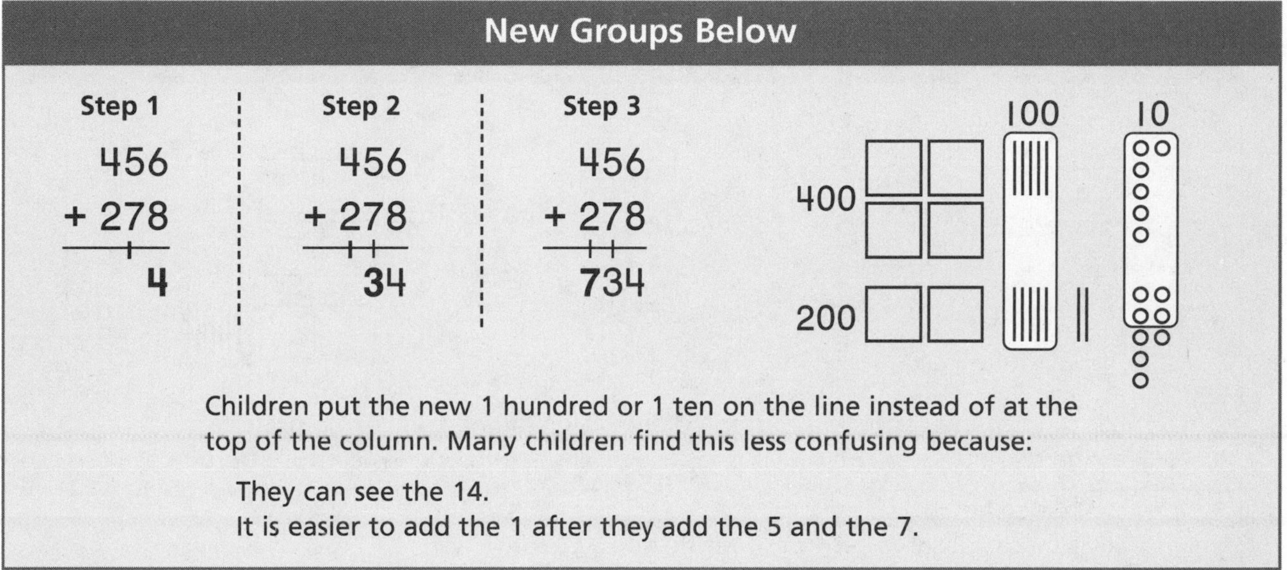

Children put the new 1 hundred or 1 ten on the line instead of at the top of the column. Many children find this less confusing because:

They can see the 14.
It is easier to add the 1 after they add the 5 and the 7.

Show All Totals

	456
	+ 278
hundreds →	600
tens →	120
ones →	14
	734

Children see the hundreds, tens, and ones they are adding. Children may also use the New Groups Above.

$$\begin{array}{r} {}^{1\,1} \\ 456 \\ +\,278 \\ \hline 734 \end{array}$$

These also can be seen when they make a math drawing like the one above.

Children may use any method that they understand, can explain, and can do fairly quickly. They should use hundreds, tens, and ones language to explain. This shows that they understand that they are adding 4 hundreds and 2 hundreds and not 4 and 2.

Please call if you have questions or comments.

Sincerely,
Your child's teacher

Estimada familia:

Su niño está aprendiendo a sumar números de 3 dígitos. Primero, lo hacen con métodos que ellos mismos inventan, o agregan objetos los dibujos que hicieron para la suma de números de dos dígitos.

Los niños resuelven el "misterio" de la suma: se puede formar una centena a partir de las decenas que sobran y se puede formar una decena a partir de las unidades que sobran. *Math Expressions* les muestra estos dos métodos simples de suma de números de tres dígitos.

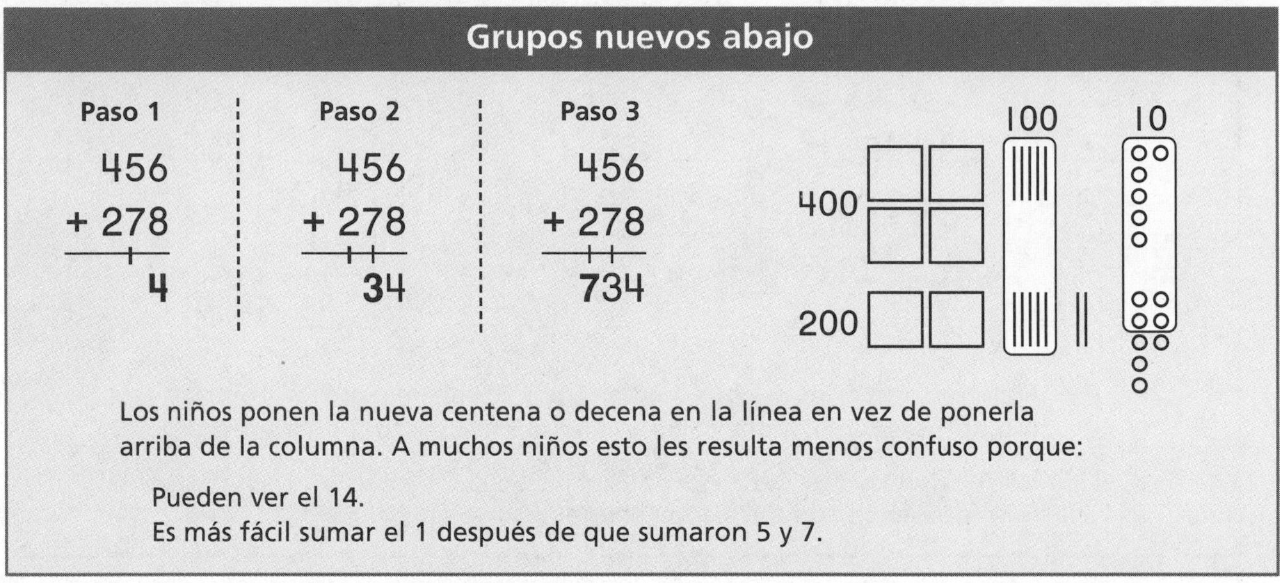

Mostrar todos los totales

	456
	+ 278
centenas →	600
decenas →	120
unidades →	14
	734

Los niños ven las centenas, las decenas y las unidades que están sumando. También pueden usar el método de Grupos nuevos arriba.

$$\begin{array}{r} {}^{1\,1} \\ 456 \\ +\ 278 \\ \hline 734 \end{array}$$

Esto también se puede observar cuando hacen un dibujo matemático como el de arriba.

Los niños pueden usar cualquier método que comprendan, puedan explicar y puedan hacer relativamente rápido. Para explicar deben usar un lenguaje relacionado con centenas, decenas y unidades. Esto mostrará que entienden que están sumando 4 centenas y 2 centenas, y no 4 y 2.

Si tiene alguna duda o pregunta, por favor comuníquese conmigo.

Atentamente,
El maestro de su niño

Name

▶ **Make a Table**

$1.86	$2.93	$4.67
Swan	Zebra	Leopard
$4.96	$2.68	$3.79
Bear	Raccoon	Elephant
$3.79	$1.55	$1.58
Kangaroo	Owl	Turtle
$4.94	$2.81	$3.57
Monkey	Penguin	Giraffe

6–11

Class Activity

Name ______________________________

▶ Add 3-Digit Money Amounts

1. Animals: ______________________

____

$.

+ $.

Make a new ten? ________

Make a new hundred? ________

2. Animals: ______________________

____

$.

+ $.

Make a new ten? ________

Make a new hundred? ________

3. Animals: ______________________

____

$.

+ $.

Make a new ten? ________

Make a new hundred? ________

4. Animals: ______________________

____

$.

+ $.

Make a new ten? ________

Make a new hundred? ________

5. Animals: ______________________

____

$.

+ $.

Make a new ten? ________

Make a new hundred? ________

6. Animals: ______________________

____

$.

+ $.

Make a new ten? ________

Make a new hundred? ________

6–12 Class Activity

Name ____________________

▶ Solve and Explain

Add. Use any method. Make a Proof Drawing if you wish.

1.
$$\begin{array}{r} 236 \\ +\,478 \\ \hline \end{array}$$

Make a new ten? ________

Make a new hundred? ________

2. 183 + 517 = ______

Make a new ten? ________

Make a new hundred? ________

3. 93 + 485 = ______

Make a new ten? ________

Make a new hundred? ________

4.
$$\begin{array}{r} 368 \\ +\,257 \\ \hline \end{array}$$

Make a new ten? ________

Make a new hundred? ________

5. 347 + 37 = ______

Make a new ten? ________

Make a new hundred? ________

6. 645 + 87 = ______

Make a new ten? ________

Make a new hundred? ________

7. **On the Back** Write and solve a story problem using 3-digit numbers. Explain how you made a new ten or hundred to add the numbers.

Name

Name ______________________________

Class Activity

▶ Find the Hidden Animal

Directions for the puzzle appearing on page 346.

1. Start by coloring in the six dotted squares. These are "free" squares. They are part of the puzzle solution.
2. Solve a problem below. Then look for the answer in the puzzle grid. Color it in.
3. Solve all 20 questions correctly. Color in all 20 correct answers.
4. Name the hidden picture. It is a(n) ______________.

$\begin{array}{r} 524 \\ +247 \\ \hline \end{array}$ $\begin{array}{r} 287 \\ +164 \\ \hline \end{array}$ $\begin{array}{r} 384 \\ +375 \\ \hline \end{array}$ $\begin{array}{r} 456 \\ +174 \\ \hline \end{array}$ $\begin{array}{r} 327 \\ +265 \\ \hline \end{array}$

$\begin{array}{r} 207 \\ +595 \\ \hline \end{array}$ $\begin{array}{r} 248 \\ +376 \\ \hline \end{array}$ $\begin{array}{r} 282 \\ +457 \\ \hline \end{array}$ $\begin{array}{r} 548 \\ +387 \\ \hline \end{array}$ $\begin{array}{r} 233 \\ +288 \\ \hline \end{array}$

$\begin{array}{r} 367 \\ +265 \\ \hline \end{array}$ $\begin{array}{r} 293 \\ +595 \\ \hline \end{array}$ $\begin{array}{r} 284 \\ +376 \\ \hline \end{array}$ $\begin{array}{r} 259 \\ +463 \\ \hline \end{array}$ $\begin{array}{r} 138 \\ +327 \\ \hline \end{array}$

$\begin{array}{r} 286 \\ +\ \ 78 \\ \hline \end{array}$ $\begin{array}{r} 407 \\ +266 \\ \hline \end{array}$ $\begin{array}{r} 503 \\ +148 \\ \hline \end{array}$ $\begin{array}{r} 78 \\ +65 \\ \hline \end{array}$ $\begin{array}{r} 192 \\ +339 \\ \hline \end{array}$

Name ______________________

See page 345 for directions on how to solve the puzzle.

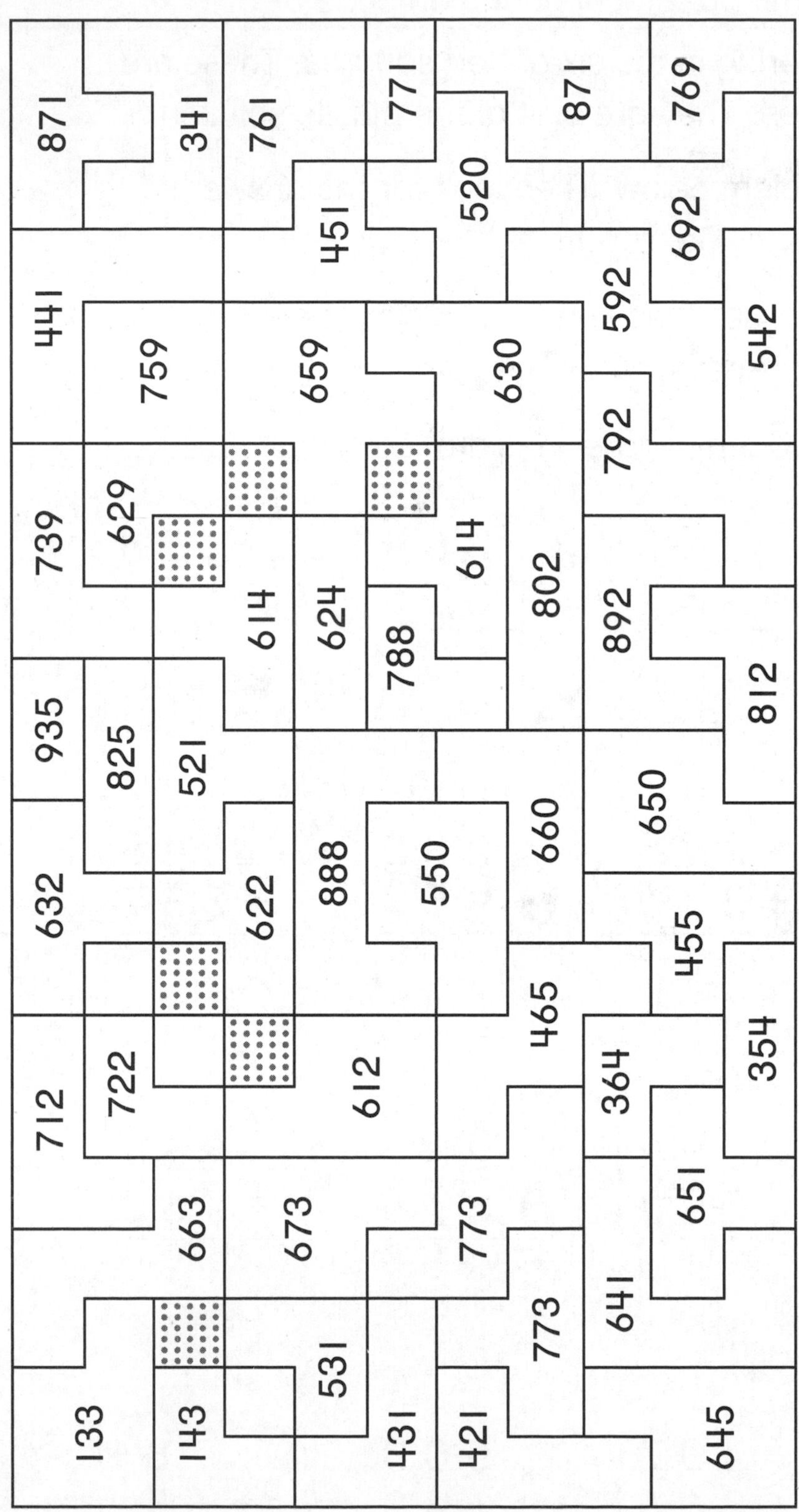

6–13

Class Activity

Name ____________________

► Adding Up to Solve Story Problems

Solve each story problem. | **Show your work.**

1. Mr. Cruz planted 750 yams to sell. After he sold some, he had 278 yams left. How many yams did he sell?

   [ ] ____________ label

2. Last year there were 692 houses in our town. This year some new houses were built. Now there are 976 houses. How many new houses were built this year?

   [ ] ____________ label

3. Delia had 524 rocks in her collection. She gave some to her sister. Then she had 462 rocks. How many rocks did she give away?

   [ ] ____________ label

4. On Saturday, 703 people went to a movie. 194 went in the afternoon. The rest went in the evening. How many people went in the evening?

   [ ] ____________ label

5. **On the Back** Write a story problem with the answer **235 seashells.**

Name

Name

▶ Subtraction Sprint

7 − 4 =	10 − 6 =	17 − 9 =
13 − 5 =	15 − 9 =	6 − 4 =
9 − 3 =	11 − 3 =	10 − 7 =
11 − 2 =	18 − 9 =	13 − 9 =
8 − 6 =	8 − 4 =	12 − 5 =
12 − 9 =	9 − 7 =	16 − 8 =
6 − 3 =	13 − 6 =	14 − 7 =
15 − 7 =	12 − 3 =	10 − 6 =
10 − 8 =	16 − 7 =	8 − 5 =
8 − 3 =	7 − 5 =	11 − 9 =
14 − 5 =	12 − 4 =	13 − 7 =
11 − 7 =	17 − 8 =	14 − 8 =
10 − 4 =	9 − 4 =	10 − 5 =
12 − 8 =	14 − 8 =	12 − 6 =
16 − 9 =	11 − 4 =	15 − 7 =
14 − 6 =	9 − 6 =	13 − 6 =
9 − 5 =	12 − 7 =	11 − 8 =
13 − 9 =	14 − 9 =	12 − 3 =
10 − 3 =	13 − 4 =	13 − 5 =
15 − 8 =	7 − 3 =	15 − 6 =
11 − 5 =	11 − 6 =	13 − 8 =

Class Activity

Name ______________________________

▶ Discuss Subtraction Problems

Solve each story problem. Use any method.
Make a Proof Drawing.

1. A teacher bought 200 erasers for his students. He gave 152 of them away. How many erasers does he have left over?

   ☐ ______________ label

2. The school cafeteria has 500 apples. Some of them were served with lunch. There are now 239 apples left. How many apples did the cafeteria serve?

   ☐ ______________ label

3. Teresa sells pianos. She must sell 600 of them. She has already sold 359. How many does she have left to sell?

   ☐ ______________ label

4. Jorge is on a basketball team. He scored 181 points last year. He scored some points this year too. He now has a total of 400 points. How many points did he score this year?

   ☐ ______________ label

Dear Family,

Your child is now learning how to subtract 3-digit numbers. The most important part is understanding and being able to explain a method. Children may use any method that they understand, can explain, and can perform fairly quickly.

Expanded Method

Step 1

$432 = 400 + 30 + 2$

$-273 = -200 + 70 + 3$

Step 2

$300 + 120 + 12$

$\cancel{400} + \cancel{30} + \cancel{2}$

$-200 + 70 + 3$

Step 3 $100 + 50 + 9 = 159$

Step 1 "Expand" each number to show that it is made up of hundreds, tens, and ones.

Step 2 Check to see if there are enough ones to subtract from. If not, ungroup a ten into 10 ones and add it to the existing ones. Check to see if there are enough tens to subtract from. If not, ungroup a hundred into 10 tens and add it to the existing tens. Children may also ungroup from the left.

Step 3 Subtract to find the answer. Children may subtract from left to right or right to left.

Ungroup First Method

−273

Ungroup from the right.

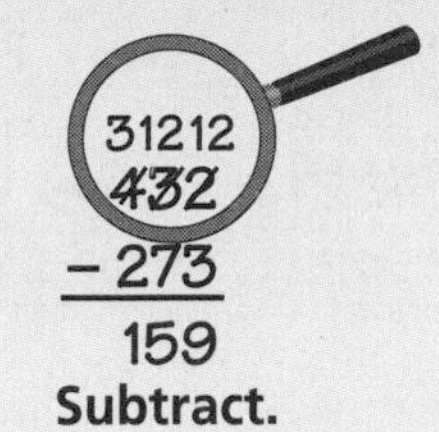

−273

159

Subtract.

Step 1 Check to see if there are enough ones and tens to subtract from. Ungroup where needed.

Look inside 432. Ungroup 432 and rename it as 3 hundreds, 12 tens, and 12 ones.

Ungroup from the left:

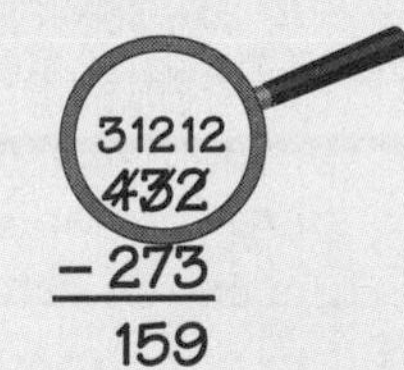

−273

159

Step 2 Subtract to find the answer. Children may subtract from the left or from the right.

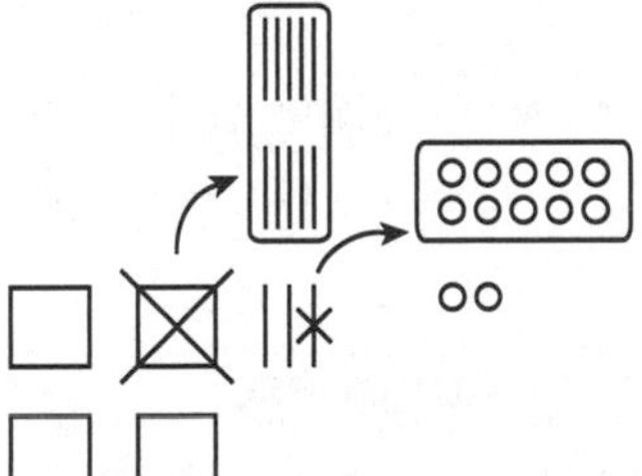

Ungroup

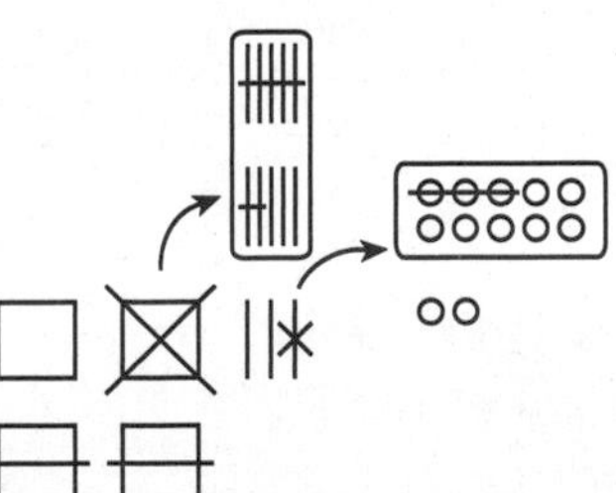

Subtract

In explaining any method they use, children are expected to use "hundreds, tens, and ones" language to show that they understand place value.

Please call if you have questions or comments.

Sincerely,
Your child's teacher

Carta a la familia

Estimada familia:

Su niño está aprendiendo a restar números de 3 dígitos. Lo más importante es comprender y saber explicar un método. Los niños pueden usar cualquier método que comprendan, puedan explicar y puedan hacer relativamente rápido.

Método extendido

Paso 1

$$\begin{aligned} 432 &= 400 + 30 + 2 \\ -\,273 &= -\,200 + 70 + 3 \end{aligned}$$

Paso 2

$$\begin{array}{r} 300 + 120 + 12 \\ \not{4}\not{0}\not{0} + \not{3}\not{0} + \not{2} \\ -\,200 + 70 + 3 \\ \hline \end{array}$$

Paso 3

$$\begin{cases} 100 + 50 + 9 \\ = 159 \end{cases}$$

Paso 1 "Extender" cada número para mostrar que consta de centenas, decenas y unidades.

Paso 2 Observar si hay suficientes unidades para restar. Si no, desagrupar una decena para formar 10 unidades y sumarlas a las unidades existentes. Observar si hay suficientes decenas para restar. Si no, desagrupar una centena para formar 10 decenas y sumarlas a las decenas existentes. Los niños también pueden desagrupar por la izquierda.

Paso 3 Restar para hallar la respuesta. Los niños pueden restar de izquierda a derecha o de derecha a izquierda.

Método de desagrupar primero

−273

Desagrupar por la derecha

31212
432
−273
159

Restar

Paso 1 Observar si hay suficientes unidades y decenas para restar. Desagrupar cuando haga falta.

Mirar dentro de 432. Desagrupar 432 y volver a nombrarlo como 3 centenas, 12 decenas y 12 unidades.

Desagrupar por la izquierda:

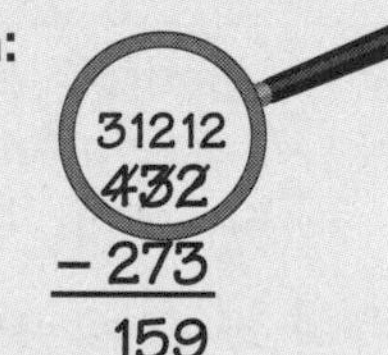

−273
159

Paso 2 Restar para hallar la respuesta. Los niños pueden restar empezando por la izquierda o por la derecha.

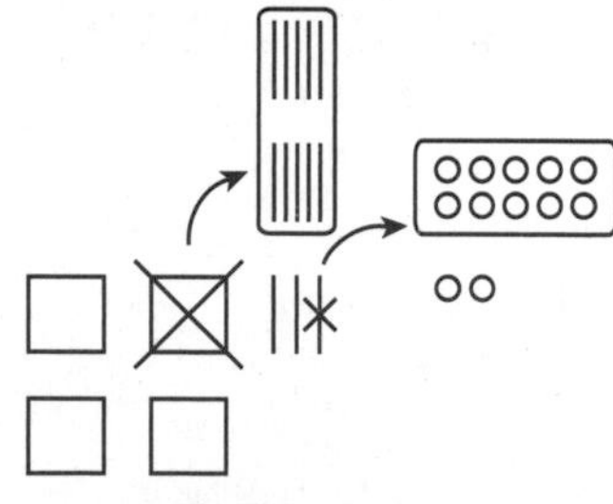

Desagrupar

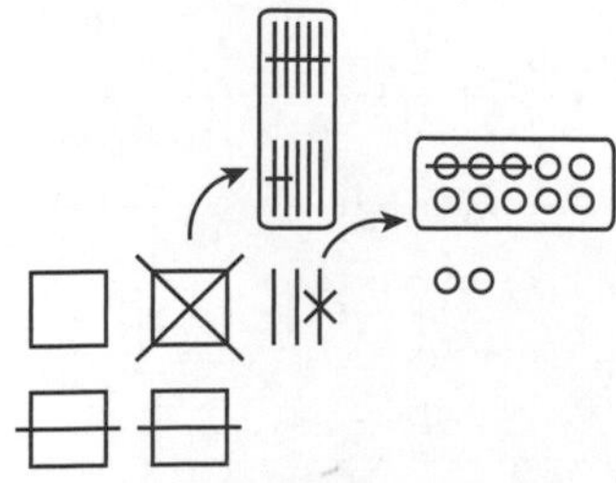

Restar

Para explicar cualquier método que usen, los niños deben usar un lenguaje relacionado con centenas, decenas y unidades para demostrar que comprenden el valor posicional.

Si tiene alguna duda o comentario, por favor comuníquese conmigo.

Atentamente,
El maestro de su niño

6–15 Class Activity

Name ______________________

Vocabulary
ungroup

▶ Represent a Subtraction Exercise

Decide if you need to **ungroup**. If you need to ungroup, draw a magnifying glass around the top number. Then find the answer.

1. $\begin{array}{r} 508 \\ -346 \\ \hline \end{array}$

   Ungroup to get 10 ones? ______

   Ungroup to get 10 tens? ______

2. $\begin{array}{r} 500 \\ -306 \\ \hline \end{array}$

   Ungroup to get 10 ones? ______

   Ungroup to get 10 tens? ______

3. $\begin{array}{r} 670 \\ -340 \\ \hline \end{array}$

   Ungroup to get 10 ones? ______

   Ungroup to get 10 tens? ______

4. $\begin{array}{r} 570 \\ -390 \\ \hline \end{array}$

   Ungroup to get 10 ones? ______

   Ungroup to get 10 tens? ______

5. **On the Back** Write and solve your own story problem. Use the number **505** in your problem.

Name

Name ________________________________

► Review Addition and Subtraction

Ring *add* or *subtract.* Check if you need to ungroup or make a new ten or hundred. Then find the answer.

1. $\begin{array}{r} 762 \\ -395 \\ \hline \end{array}$

Subtract

☐ Ungroup to get 10 ones

☐ Ungroup to get 10 tens

Add

☐ Make 1 new ten

☐ Make 1 new hundred

2. $\begin{array}{r} 395 \\ +367 \\ \hline \end{array}$

Subtract

☐ Ungroup to get 10 ones

☐ Ungroup to get 10 tens

Add

☐ Make 1 new ten

☐ Make 1 new hundred

3. $\begin{array}{r} 287 \\ -193 \\ \hline \end{array}$

Subtract

☐ Ungroup to get 10 ones

☐ Ungroup to get 10 tens

Add

☐ Make 1 new ten

☐ Make 1 new hundred

4. $\begin{array}{r} 437 \\ +324 \\ \hline \end{array}$

Subtract

☐ Ungroup to get 10 ones

☐ Ungroup to get 10 tens

Add

☐ Make 1 new ten

☐ Make 1 new hundred

5. **On the Back** Explain how you know when to ungroup in subtraction. Use the words *ones*, *tens*, and *hundreds.*

Name

Name ________________________________

▶ Subtraction Sprint

7 − 4 =	10 − 6 =	17 − 9 =
13 − 5 =	15 − 9 =	6 − 4 =
9 − 3 =	11 − 3 =	10 − 7 =
11 − 2 =	18 − 9 =	13 − 9 =
8 − 6 =	8 − 4 =	12 − 5 =
12 − 9 =	9 − 7 =	16 − 8 =
6 − 3 =	13 − 6 =	14 − 7 =
15 − 7 =	12 − 3 =	10 − 6 =
10 − 8 =	16 − 7 =	8 − 5 =
8 − 3 =	7 − 5 =	11 − 9 =
14 − 5 =	12 − 4 =	13 − 7 =
11 − 7 =	17 − 8 =	14 − 8 =
10 − 4 =	9 − 4 =	10 − 5 =
12 − 8 =	14 − 8 =	12 − 6 =
16 − 9 =	11 − 4 =	15 − 7 =
14 − 6 =	9 − 6 =	13 − 6 =
9 − 5 =	12 − 7 =	11 − 8 =
13 − 9 =	14 − 9 =	12 − 3 =
10 − 3 =	13 − 4 =	13 − 5 =
15 − 8 =	7 − 3 =	15 − 6 =
11 − 5 =	11 − 6 =	13 − 8 =

Class Activity

Name ________________________________

Vocabulary
unknown start problem
comparison problem

► Solve Complex Story Problems

Solve the **unknown start** and **comparison problems**.

1. Marian had a collection of miniature cars. Then she gave 465 cars to her brother Simon. Now Marian has 288 cars. How many cars did she have to begin with?

   ☐ ________________ label

2. In September the Shaws planted some bulbs. In October they planted 178 more bulbs. Altogether they planted 510 bulbs. How many bulbs did they plant in September?

   ☐ ________________ label

3. Lila has 288 mugs in her collection, which is 158 fewer than her friend Letty has. How many mugs does Letty have in her collection?

   ☐ ________________ label

4. One year the Ricos planted 640 flowers. This was 243 more than the Smiths planted. How many flowers did the Smiths plant?

   ☐ ________________ label

6-21 Class Activity

Name ______________________________

▶ Solve and Discuss

Solve each story problem.

1. Lucero spilled a bag of marbles. 219 fell on the floor. 316 were still in the bag. How many were in the bag before it spilled?

   ☐ ______________ label

2. Al counted bugs in the park. He counted 561 on Monday. He counted 273 fewer than that on Tuesday. How many bugs did he count on both days combined?

   ☐ ______________ label

3. Happy the Clown gives out balloons. She gave out 285 at the zoo and then she gave out some more at the amusement park. Altogether she gave out 503. How many balloons did she give out at the amusement park?

   ☐ ______________ label

4. Bobo the Clown gave out 842 balloons at the fun fair. He gave out 194 at the store. He gave out 367 at the playground. How many more balloons did he give out at the fun fair than at the playground?

   ☐ ______________ label

Extra Practice

Name ____________________

► Practice Story Problems

Solve. Show your work on a separate sheet of paper.

1. Damon collects stamps. He had 383 stamps. Then he bought 126 more at a yard sale. How many stamps does he have now?

   [ ] ____________ label

2. Mr. Lewis sold 438 melons yesterday. Now he has 294 melons left to sell. How many melons did he have to start?

   [ ] ____________ label

3. Ali is passing out ribbons for a race. She passed out 57 ribbons so far and she has 349 ribbons left. How many ribbons did she have at the start?

   [ ] ____________ label

4. Tanya is doing a puzzle. She has put together 643 pieces. There are 1,000 pieces in the puzzle. How many pieces are left to put together?

   [ ] ____________ label

5. Pawel passed out fliers to advertise a play. He passed out 194 fliers at the bakery. He passed out 358 at the grocery store. How many more fliers did he pass out at the grocery store than at the bakery?

   [ ] ____________ label

6. Cora collected 542 sports cards last year. She collected 247 fewer than that this year. How many cards did she collect in both years together?

   [ ] ____________ label

Name ______________________________

▶ The Yard Sale

Choose any two toys to buy. Pay for them with $10.00.

$4.87	$3.49	$2.59	$1.64
Baseball Glove	Globe	Perfume	Funny Glasses
$1.55	**$2.48**	**$4.86**	**$3.97**
Toy Binoculars	Toy Lamb	Ring	Toy Guitar

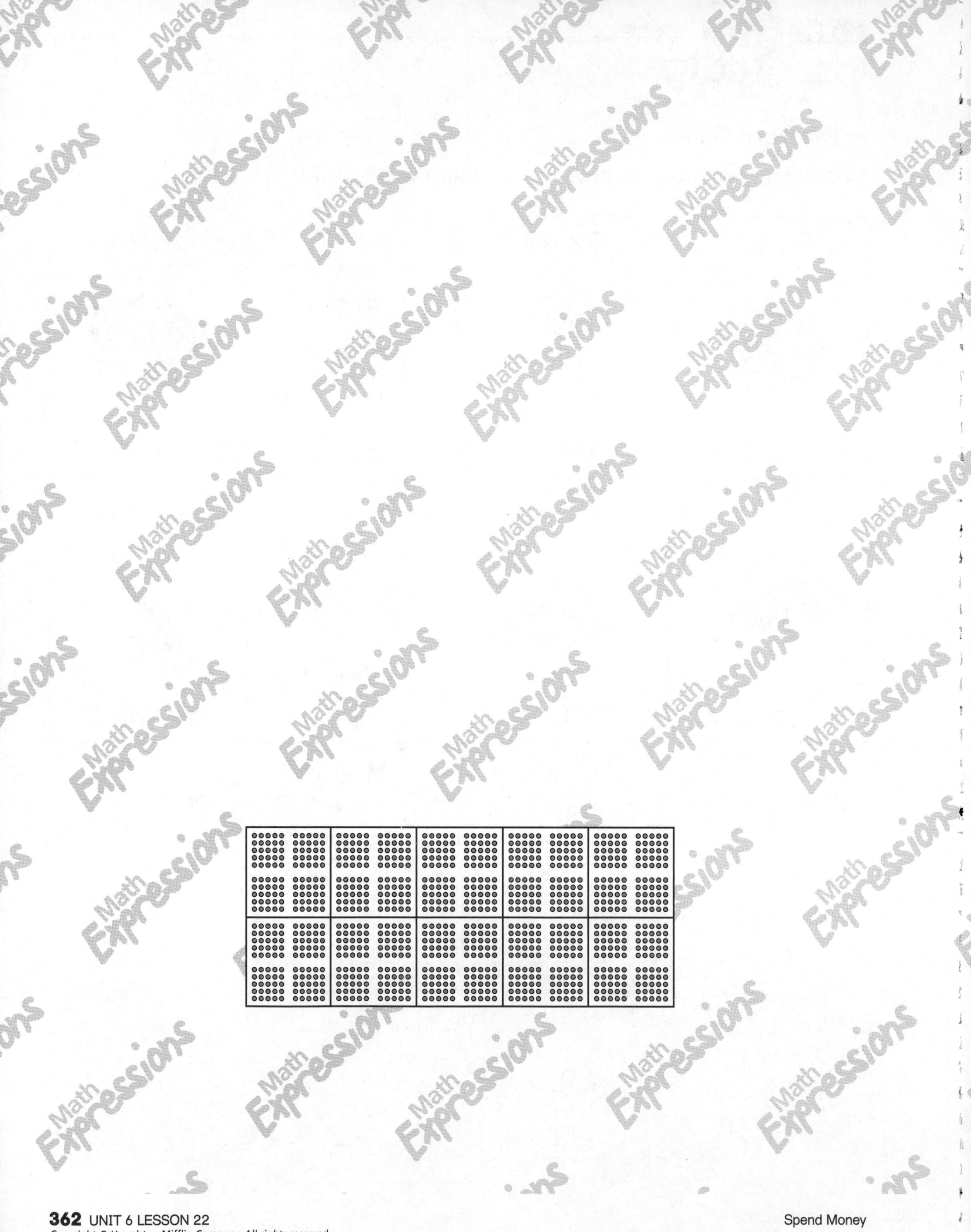

Name ______________________

Going Further

▶ Introduce Front-End Estimation

Follow these steps to use front-end estimation.

- Keep the front digit of each number.
- Use zeros for all the other digits.
- Add or subtract according to the sign.

1. 53 → 50
   + 27 → + 20

   The estimate is ________.

2. 53 → 50
   − 27 → − ____

   The estimate is ________.

3. 686 → 600
   + 259 → + ____

   The estimate is ________.

4. 686 → 600
   − 259 → − ____

   The estimate is ________.

▶ Practice Using Front-End Estimation

Estimate each sum or difference. Use front-end estimation.

5. 64 → ____
   + 53 → + ____

   The estimate is ________.

6. 842 → ____
   − 367 → − ____

   The estimate is ________.

7. **On the Back** Explain how you could use front-end estimation to choose the correct answer.

   34 − 15 = ☐ ○ 58 ○ 19 ○ 49 ○ 4

Name

Name ______________________

1. Write the total.

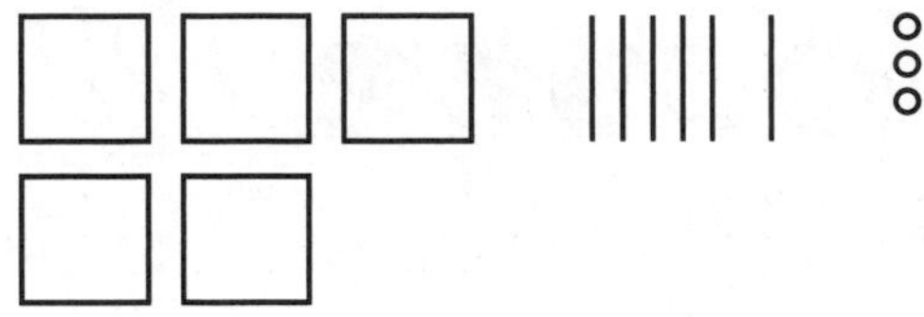

Total ______

2. Use boxes, sticks, and circles to show 478.

Total 478

Write the hundreds, tens, and ones.

Example: 456 = 400 + 50 + 6

3. 975 = ______ + ______ + ______

4. 283 = ______ + ______ + ______

---

5. Count by ones. Write the numbers.

294 295 ____ ____ ____ ____ ____ ____ ____ ____ 304

6. Count by tens. Write the numbers.

330 340 ____ ____ ____ ____ ____ ____ ____ ____ 430

Name ______________________

How much money is shown here? Use $ in your answer.

7.  ______

8.  ______

Add.

9. 745 + 138 = ______

10. 377 + 562 = ______

11. 488 + 354 = ______

12. 198 + 56 = ______

13. $3.98 + $2.81 = ______

14. $1.59 + $0.75 = ______

Subtract.

15. 618 − 473 = ______

16. 782 − 528 = ______

17. 447 − 178 = ______

Name ______________________

Subtract.

18. $\begin{array}{r} 505 \\ -\,371 \\ \hline \end{array}$

19. $\begin{array}{r} 300 \\ -\,239 \\ \hline \end{array}$

20. $\begin{array}{r} \$10.00 \\ -\,\$\ \ 4.81 \\ \hline \end{array}$

21. \$10.00 − \$2.72 = ______

Solve.

Show your work.

22. Dena picked 472 apples. She sold 187 at the Farmers Market. How many apples did she have left?

[ ] ______ label

23. This morning 256 books were returned to the library. 596 more were returned this afternoon. How many books were returned altogether?

[ ] ______ label

Name ____________________

Solve.	Show your work.
24. Ada read 124 pages in a book. The book has 300 pages. How many more pages does she still have to read to finish the book? ☐ ____________ label	

25. Extended Response Write and solve an addition or subtraction story problem using the numbers 458 and 279.

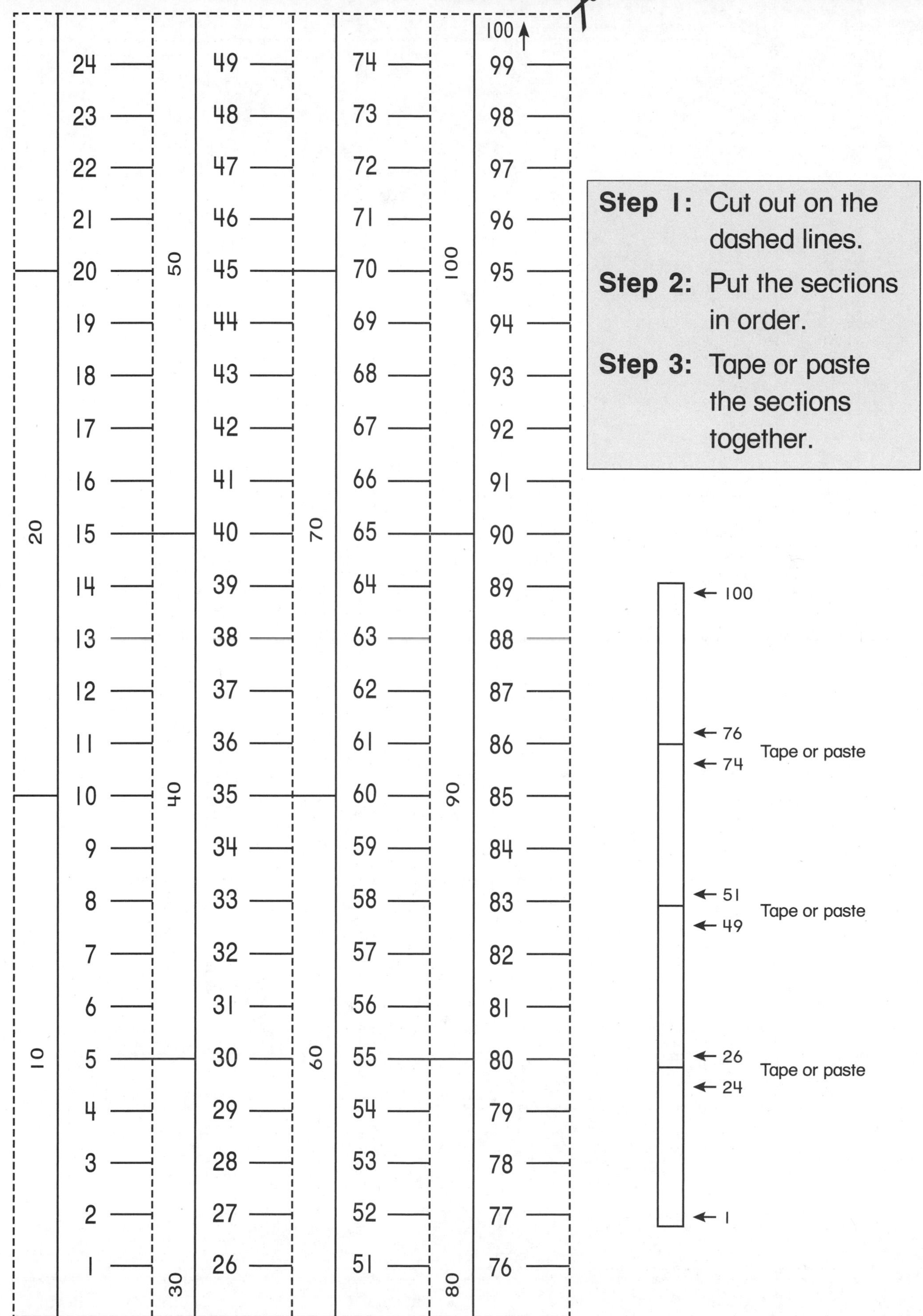

100
Step 1: Cut out on the dashed lines.
Step 2: Put the sections in order.
Step 3: Tape or paste the sections together.
100
76
74
Tape or paste
51
49
Tape or paste
26
24
Tape or paste
1

Name ____________________

▶ Estimate and Measure

Find a part of your hand that is about the length of each measure.

1. 1 cm ____________________

2. 1 dm ____________________

Find a part of your body that is about 1 meter long.

3. 1 m ____________________

Find the real object. Estimate and measure its length. Round if necessary.

4. 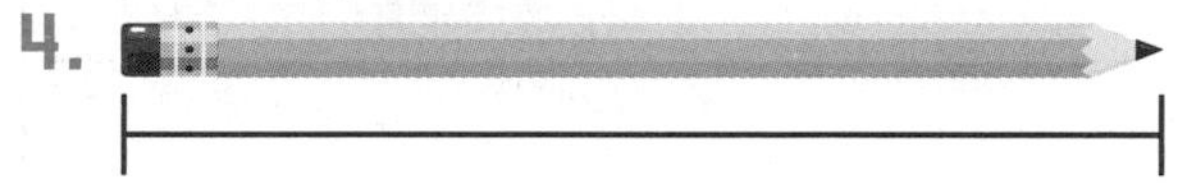

Estimate: about ________ cm

Measure: ________ cm

5. 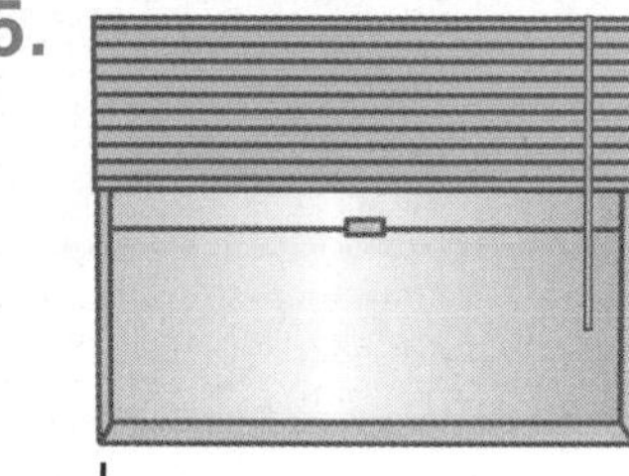

Estimate: about ________ cm

Measure: ________ cm

6. 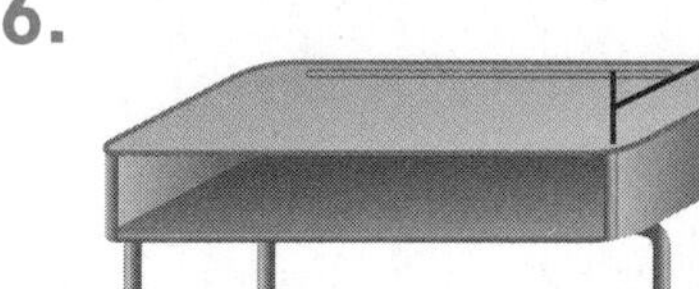

Estimate: about ________ dm

Measure: ________ dm

7. 

Estimate: about ________ m

Measure: ________ m

Draw a line segment to show each length.

8. 1 cm

9. 1 dm

F-1

Name ______________________________

Class Activity

▶ Measure Heights

When you measure a height greater than 1 m, you can place two meter sticks end-to-end. The first meter stick is 100 cm, so you can add 100 to the number of centimeters you read from the second meter stick. The height of the child shown here is 100 cm + 18 cm or 118 cm.

10. Complete the table for each person in your group.

Person's name	Estimated height in cm	Actual height in cm	Difference between estimated and actual height in cm

Use the data you collected to answer these questions.

11. Who is the tallest person in your group?

____

12. How much taller is the tallest person than the shortest person? _______________

13. Whose estimated height was closest to his or her actual height? _______________

14. On a separate sheet of paper, write four more questions you could ask about this data. Trade your questions with another group and answer each other's questions.

Dear Family,

In this geometry unit, your child will measure in centimeters, meters, and decimeters. Children develop a sense of the size of each metric unit by finding personal or body referents, drawing line segments, and measuring objects and distances with a meter stick.

Children compare the metric units for length to the U.S. monetary system, both of which use the base ten number system.

1 decimeter = 10 centimeters	1 dime = 10 cents
1 meter = 10 decimeters	1 dollar = 10 dimes
1 meter = 100 centimeters	1 dollar = 100 cents

Children convert units of linear measurement and units of the monetary system. They solve story problems to strengthen their understanding of the base ten system, while reinforcing their skills in the addition of 3-digit numbers.

The last two lessons of this unit introduce children to three-dimensional shapes. They use unit cubes to build rectangular prisms, and they draw these prisms from the top, side, and front view. They also learn how to find the volume of a three-dimensional shape by counting unit cubes.

In the last lesson, children look at attributes of three-dimensional shapes, like vertices, faces, and edges.

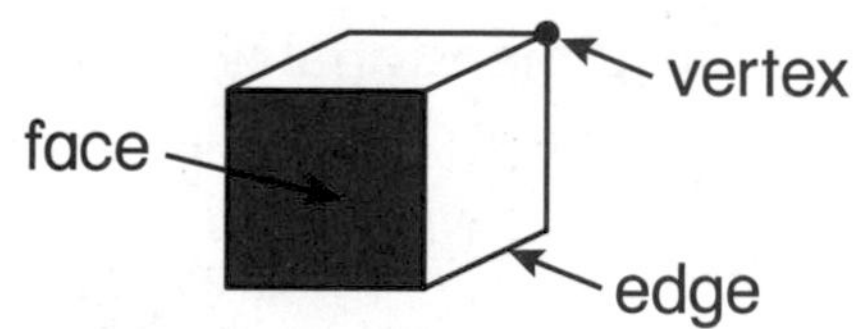

Children also investigate how different three-dimensional shapes stack and if they roll or slide across a surface. They then sort three-dimensional shapes by attributes.

If you have any questions or comments, please call or write to me.

Sincerely,
Your child's teacher

Estimada familia:

En esta unidad sobre geometría, su niño medirá con centímetros, metros y decímetros. Los niños van a comprender el tamaño de cada unidad métrica usando el cuerpo como punto de referencia, dibujando segmentos de recta y midiendo objetos y distancias con una regla de un metro.

Los niños van a comparar las unidades métricas de longitud con el sistema monetario de los EE. UU., ya que ambos utilizan el sistema de base diez.

1 decímetro = 10 centímetros	1 moneda de 10¢ = 10 centavos
1 metro = 10 decímetros	1 dólar = 10 monedas de 10¢
1 metro = 100 centímetros	1 dólar = 100 centavos

Los niños van a convertir unidades de longitud y unidades del sistema monetario. También resolverán problemas para reforzar su comprensión del sistema de base diez, a la vez que refuerzan su habilidad de sumar números de 3 dígitos.

Las dos últimas lecciones de esta unidad presentan las figuras tridimensionales. Los niños usarán cubos de unidad para construir prismas rectangulares y dibujarán los prismas desde arriba, desde el lado y desde adelante. También aprenderán cómo se calcula el volumen de una figura tridimensional contando cubos de unidad.

En la última lección, los niños estudiar los atributos de figuras tridimensionales tales como vértices, caras y aristas.

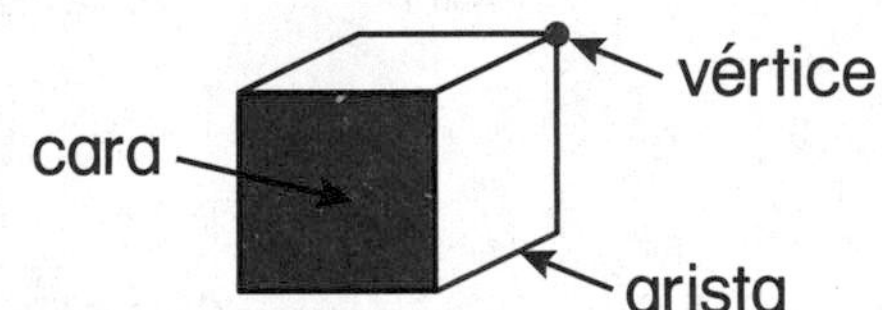

También verán cómo se pueden apilar las figuras tridimensionales y si ruedan o se deslizan sobre una superficie. Luego clasificarán las figuras tridimensionales según sus atributos.

Si tiene alguna duda o comentario, por favor comuníquese conmigo.

Atentamente,
El maestro de su niño

Name ______________________________

Vocabulary
centimeter (cm)
decimeter (dm)
meter (m)

▶ Equivalent Metric Lengths

1. Draw a line segment 10 **cm** long.

2. Draw a line segment 1 **dm** long.

3. What do you notice about the measurements 10 cm and 1 dm?

   ____

4. Fill in the correct number: 1 dm = ______ cm

5. Work in partners. One partner shows 1 m on a meter stick and the other partner shows 10 dm on a meter stick. What do you notice about the measurements 1 **m** and 10 dm?

   ____

6. Fill in the correct number: 1 m = ______ dm

7. Work in partners. Find 1 m and then 100 cm on a meter stick. What do you notice about the measurements 1 m and 100 cm?

   ____

Fill in the correct unit of measurement.

8. 1 ______ = 10 cm

9. 1 ______ = 10 dm

10. 1 ______ = 100 cm

F–2

Class Activity

Name ______________________________

▶ Jumping Game

In this game, you will stand at a start line and jump as far as possible.

Step 1: One person at a time, stand with toes at the start line.

Step 2: Jump as far as you can.

Step 3: Have another member in your group mark where your toes landed and measure the distance from the start line, in centimeters.

Step 4: Record the results in the table below.

Step 5: After everyone has jumped once, take a second turn.

Jumping Game		
Name	**First turn**	**Second turn**

11. Who jumped the farthest? ______________

12. How many people jumped farther than 50 cm? ______________

13. On a separate sheet of paper, write three more comparison questions about the data you collected. Share your questions with the group and answer them together.

Name ____________________

▶ Guessing Game

In this game, you and a partner will write clues that describe rectangular objects in the classroom. You will trade clues with another pair and try to find their objects.

Step 1: Measure the length and width of 3 objects. Record your measurements in the table below.

Object Dimensions		
Object	**Length (cm)**	**Width (cm)**

Step 2: Write 2 clues that describe each object.
Clue 1: Write the object's length and width.
Clue 2: Describe the object by color, location, shape, or use.

Step 3: Write the name of the object on the back of the index card.

What Am I?
Clue 1: I am 67 cm long and 44 cm wide.
Clue 2: I usually hang on the wall at the front of the classroom.

Answer
bulletin board

Step 4: Read your clues to another pair. Ask them to guess each of your objects by first estimating and then measuring to check.

F-2

Class Activity

Name ______________________________

▶ Penny Toss Game

In this game, you will stand at the start line and toss a penny as close as possible to the goal line.

Step 1: Take turns tossing a penny as close as possible to the goal line.

Step 2: Measure the distance of your toss in centimeters from the goal line.

Step 3: Complete the table below.

Penny Toss Game	
Name	**Distance from the goal line (cm)**

14. Whose penny landed closest to the goal line?

____

15. How many children's pennies landed less than 10 cm from the goal line? _______________

16. On a separate sheet of paper, write three more comparison questions about the data you collected. Share your questions with the group and answer them together.

F–4

Class Activity

Name ______________________

▶ Money and Length Equivalencies

Answer each question. Draw a picture if you need to.

1. How many ones in 1 ten? ______
2. How many dimes in 1 dollar? ______
3. How many pennies in 1 dime? ______
4. How many tens in 1 hundred? ______
5. How many centimeters in 1 dm? ______
6. How many cents in 1 dime? ______
7. How many pennies in 1 dollar? ______
8. How many ones in 1 hundred? ______
9. Write the numbers.

5 m 8 dm 4 cm = ______ dm 4 cm = ______ cm	_____ m _____ dm _____ cm = 41 dm 2 cm = ______ cm
$3.18 = _____ dimes _____ pennies = ______ pennies	$ ________ = _____ dimes _____ pennies = 412 pennies

10. **On the Back** Draw a picture to show the relationship between metric lengths (meters, decimeters, centimeters) and money (dollars, dimes, pennies).

Name

Name

▶ Rectangular Prisms

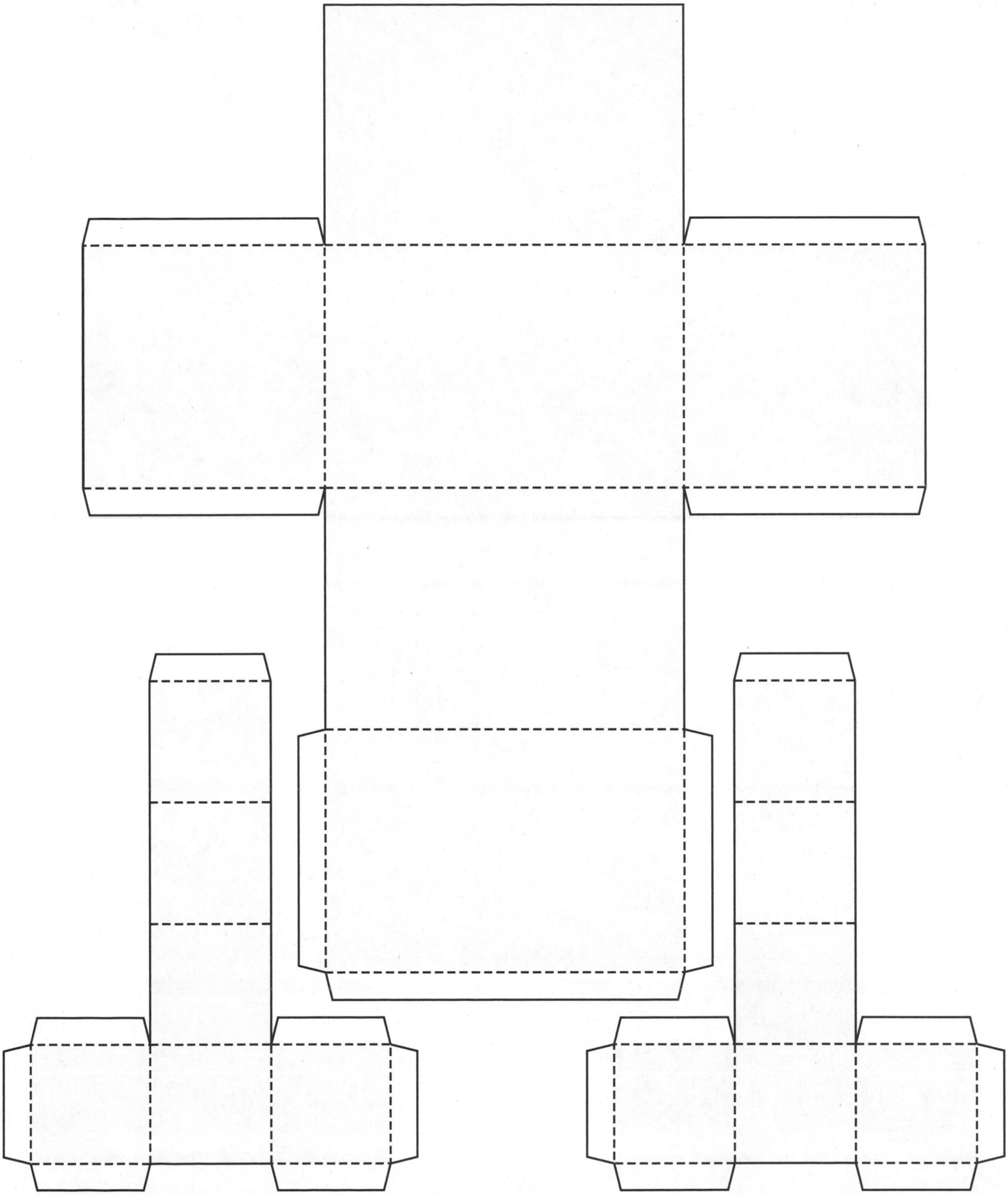

Cut on solid lines.
Fold on dashed lines.

Name ______________________

Vocabulary
rectangular prism
views

▶ Build and Draw Rectangular Prisms

Using unit cubes, build a **rectangular prism** to match each description. Draw the rectangular prism from the top, front, and side **views**.

1. two rows of three unit cubes

top view **front view** **side view**

2. one row of two unit cubes stacked on top of another row of two unit cubes

top view **front view** **side view**

▶ Build Rectangular Prisms from Drawings

Build a rectangular prism to match each set of views.

3.

top view **front view** **side view**

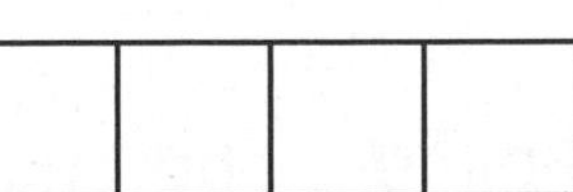

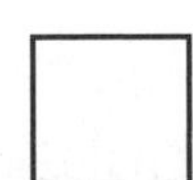

4.

top view **front view** **side view**

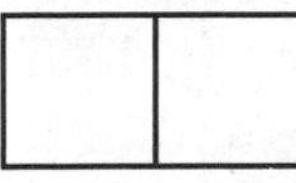

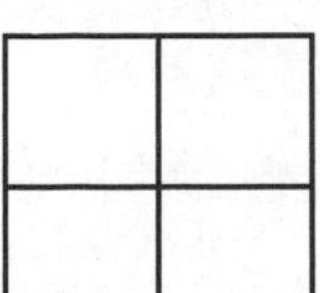

F–5 Class Activity

Name ____________________

Vocabulary
volume
cubic units

▶ Volume of 3-Dimensional Shapes

The **volume** of a 3-dimensional shape is the amount of space it occupies.

1 cubic unit

To measure volume, you can find the number of **cubic units** that make up the 3-dimensional shape.

Find the volume of each shape in cubic units.

5. 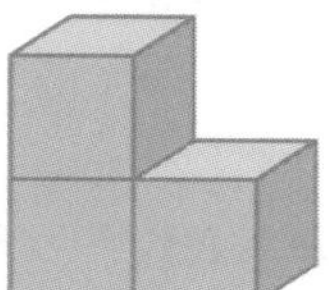
_______ cubic units

6. 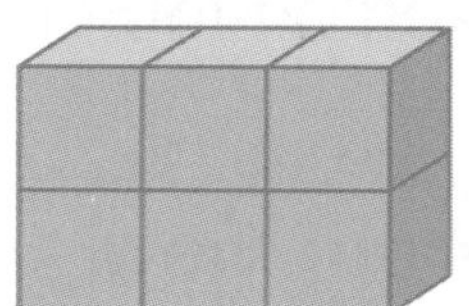
_______ cubic units

7. 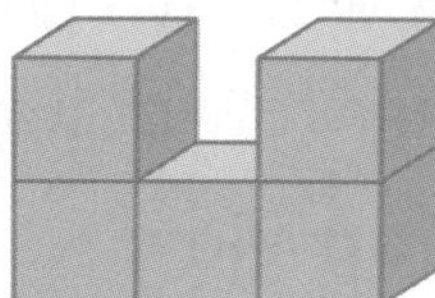
_______ cubic units

8. 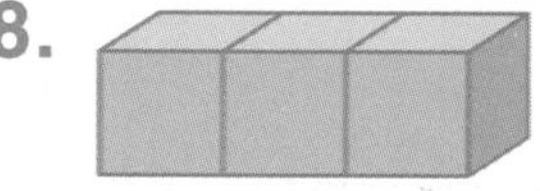
_______ cubic units

9. 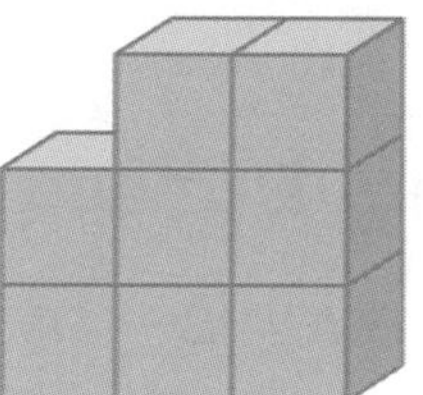
_______ cubic units

10. 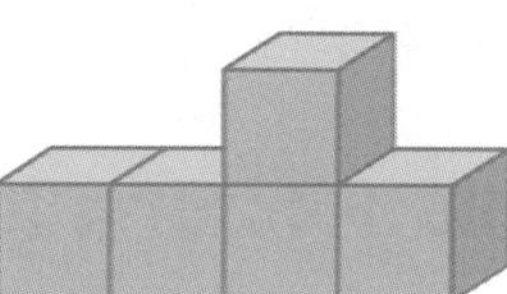
_______ cubic units

Use unit cubes to build each 3-dimensional shape. Find the volume by counting cubic units.

11. 
_______ cubic units

12. 
_______ cubic units

13. 
_______ cubic units

Name ____________________

Class Activity

Vocabulary
three-dimensional (3-D)

► Identify Solid Shapes

Name each **three-dimensional (3-D)** shape.

1. 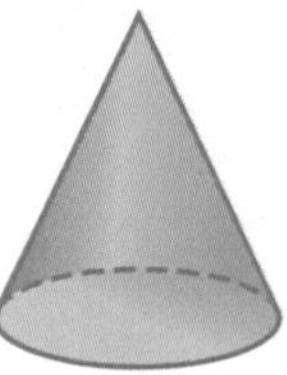
____

2. 
____

3. 
____

4. 
____

5. 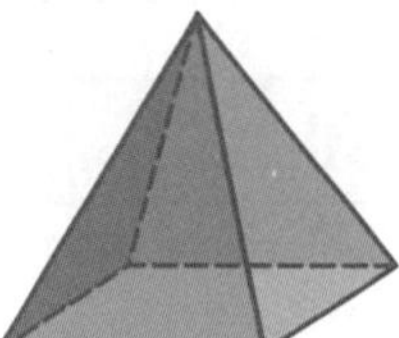
____

6. 
____

7. Hunt for shapes in your classroom. Find examples of each shape and list them in the table below.

Shape	Examples
cone	
cube	
rectangular prism	
sphere	
square pyramid	
cylinder	

F-6 Class Activity

Name ______________________________

Vocabulary
stack
slide
roll

► Stack, Slide, and Roll

You can **stack** some shapes.

You can **slide** some shapes.

You can **roll** some shapes.

8. Experiment with three-dimensional shapes to find out if you can stack, slide, or roll them. Place a checkmark in the column that applies to each shape.

Shape	Stack	Slide	Roll
cube			
square pyramid			
cone			
cylinder			
rectangular prism			
sphere			

Name

▶ Alike and Different

Describe how each pair of shapes is alike and different.

Shapes	How these shapes are alike	How these shapes are different
9.		
10.		
11.		
12.		

Name ______________________________

Class Activity

▶ Sort Three-Dimensional Shapes

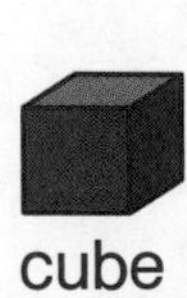
cube

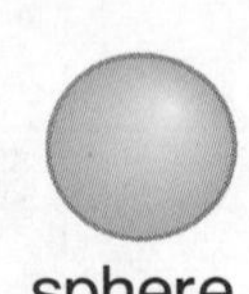
sphere

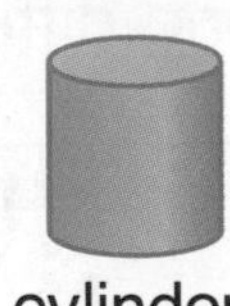
cylinder

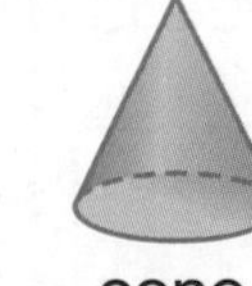
cone

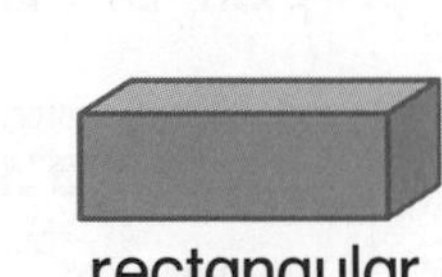
rectangular prism

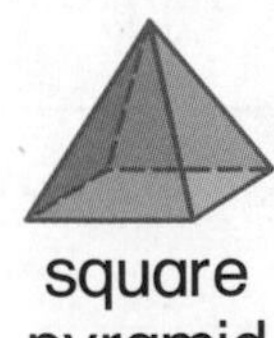
square pyramid

13. Choose your own sorting rule to sort these three-dimensional shapes into two groups.

My sorting rule is ______________________________

The shapes ______________________________

____

The shapes ______________________________

____

▶ Venn Diagram

14. Sort the shapes above into two groups: shapes that roll and shapes that slide. Write the names of the shapes in the Venn diagram. If a shape rolls and slides, place it in the overlap between the two circles.

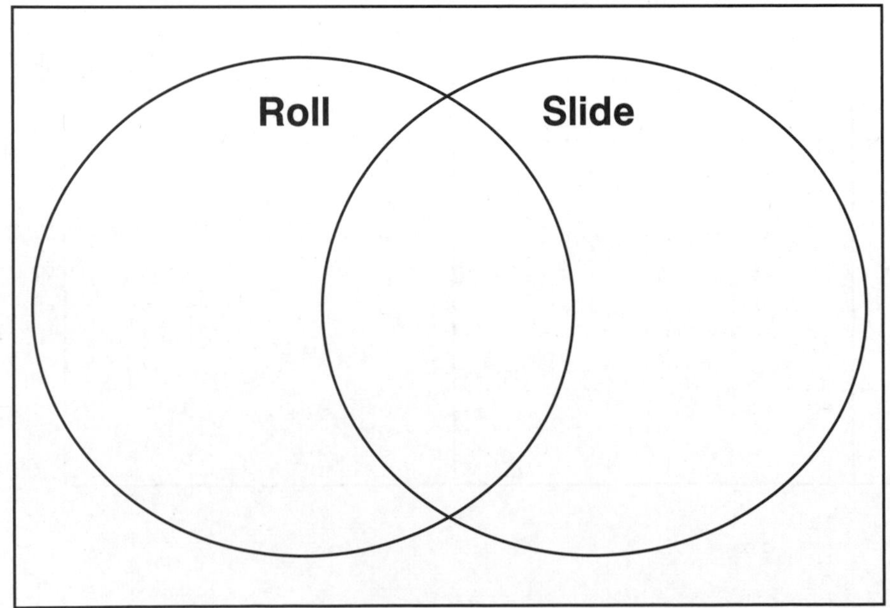

Name ______________________________

Write the numbers.

1. 170 cm = ______ m ______ dm

2. 654 cm = ______ m ______ dm ______ cm

3. 575 cm = ______ m ______ dm ______ cm

Is each shape 2-D (two-dimensional) or 3-D (three-dimensional)?

4. 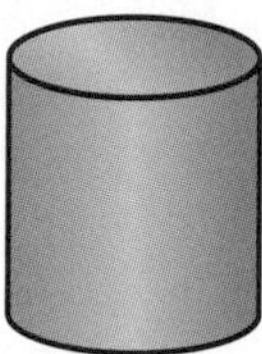 ______________

5. 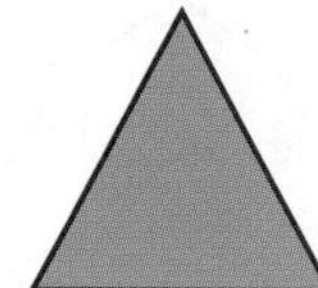 ______________

6. Draw the top, front, and side views. 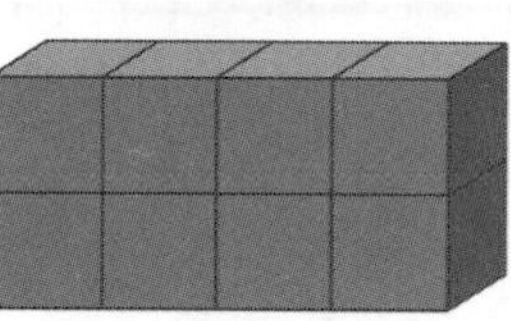

Top View **Front View** **Side View**

Find the volume of each shape in cubic units.

7. 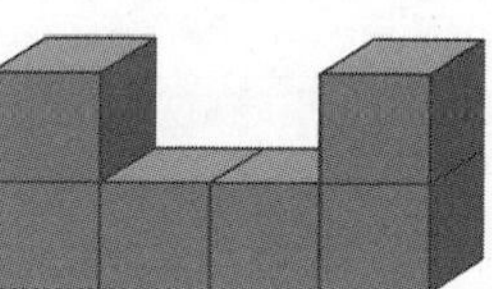

______________ cubic units

8. 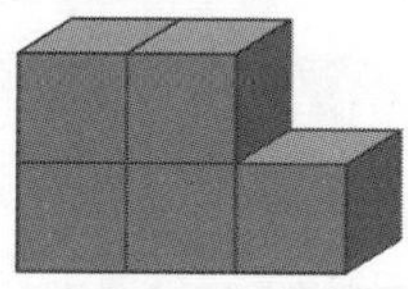

______________ cubic units

Name ______________________________

9. Sort the shapes. Write the names of the shapes in the Venn diagram.

cube

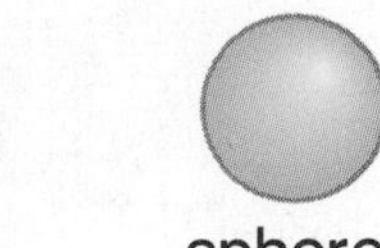
sphere

cylinder

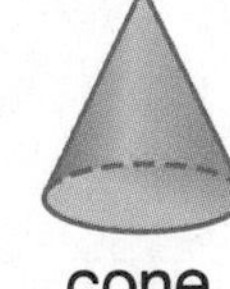
cone

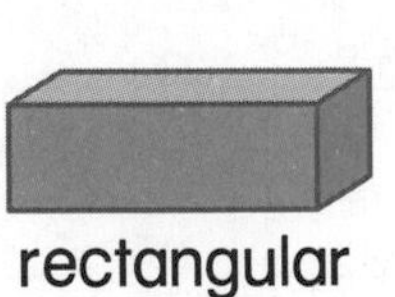
rectangular prism

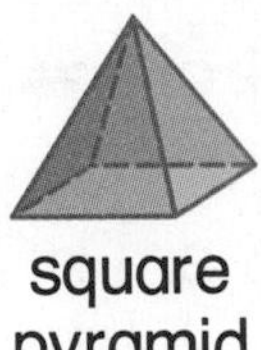
square pyramid

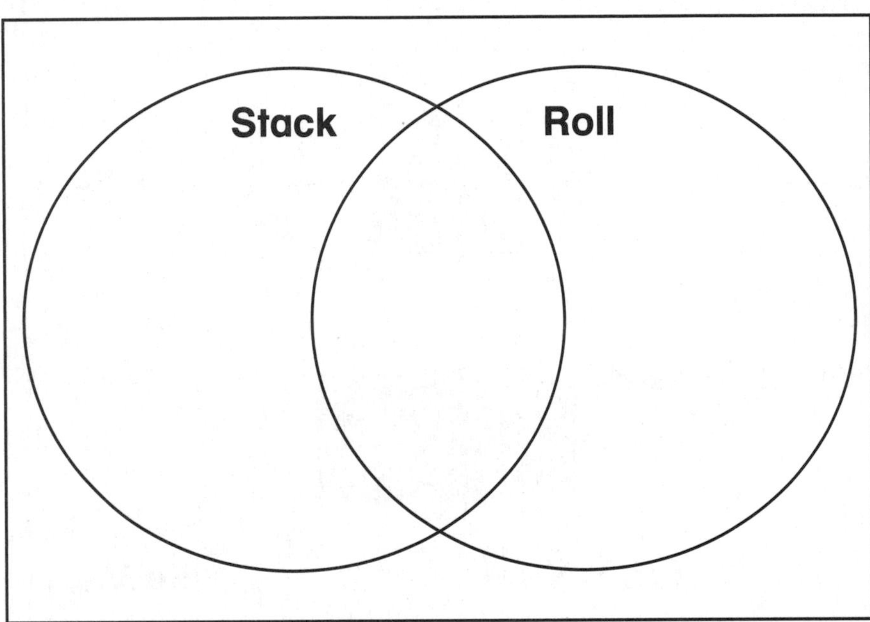

10. **Extended Response** Explain how knowing about ones, tens, and hundreds can help you write 138 centimeters as meters, decimeters, and centimeters.

____

____

____

____

____

Name ______________________________

Vocabulary
multiplication

▶ Practice Multiplication

I have 5 vases. There are 2 flowers in each vase.

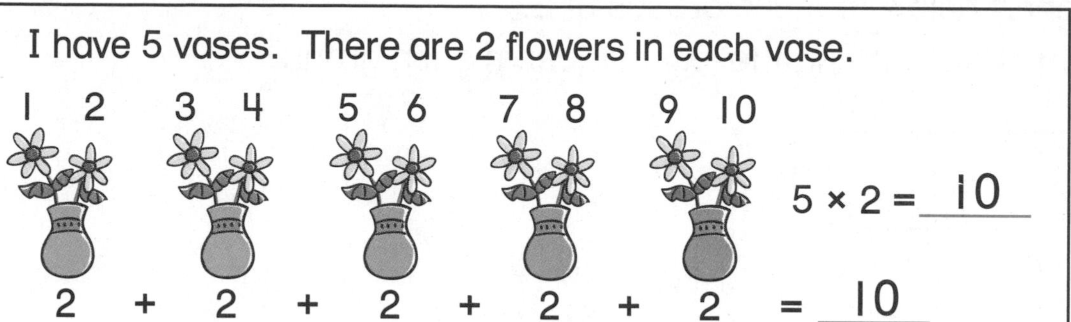

5 × 2 = 10

2 + 2 + 2 + 2 + 2 = 10

Write the addition and **multiplication** equation for each story. Make a math drawing to help you solve the problem.

1. I have 4 cats. Each cat has 3 toy mice. How many mice are there?

   3 + 3 + 3 + 3 = ______

   4 × 3 = ______ ☐ ______ label

2. I eat 4 pieces of fruit every day. How many pieces of fruit do I eat in 5 days?

   ___ + ___ + ___ + ___ + ___ = ______

   5 × 4 = ______ ☐ ______ label

3. I have 3 packs of pencils. There are 5 pencils in each pack. How many pencils do I have?

   5 + 5 + 5 = ______

   ______ × ______ = ______

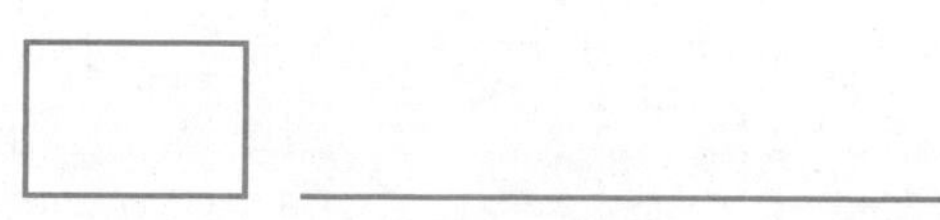
☐ ______ label

Name ______________________________

Vocabulary
count by
count-bys

▶ 2s Count-Bys

4. Fill in the chart below to make groups of 2.
Then **count by** 2s by saying the last number in each group.

1	2
3	4
	10
	16

5. Write out the 2s **count-bys** below.

2 ___ 4 ___ ___ ___ 10 ___ ___ ___ 16 ___ ___ ___

Name ______________________________

▶ Count by 2s to Multiply

Count by 2s. Then multiply.

6. Beach balls on a seal's nose

______ ______ ______ ______

4 × 2 = 8

7. Humps on a camel

______ ______ ______

3 × 2 = ______

8. Ice cubes in a pitcher

______ ______ ______ ______ ______ ______

6 × 2 = ______

9. Funny shoes on a clown

______ ______ ______ ______ ______

5 × 2 = ______

7-1

Name

Going Further

▶ Draw Pictures and Write Equations

Draw a picture. Write the multiplication equation.

1. 1 bag of 2 marbles

$1 \times 2 =$ _____

2. 2 bags of 1 marble

$2 \times 1 =$ _____

3. 1 bag of 3 marbles

____

4. 3 bags of 1 marble

____

5. 1 bag of 5 marbles

____

6. 5 bags of 1 marble

____

7. What pattern do you see? Draw or write to explain.

Dear Family,

In this unit, children are introduced to multiplication in three ways.

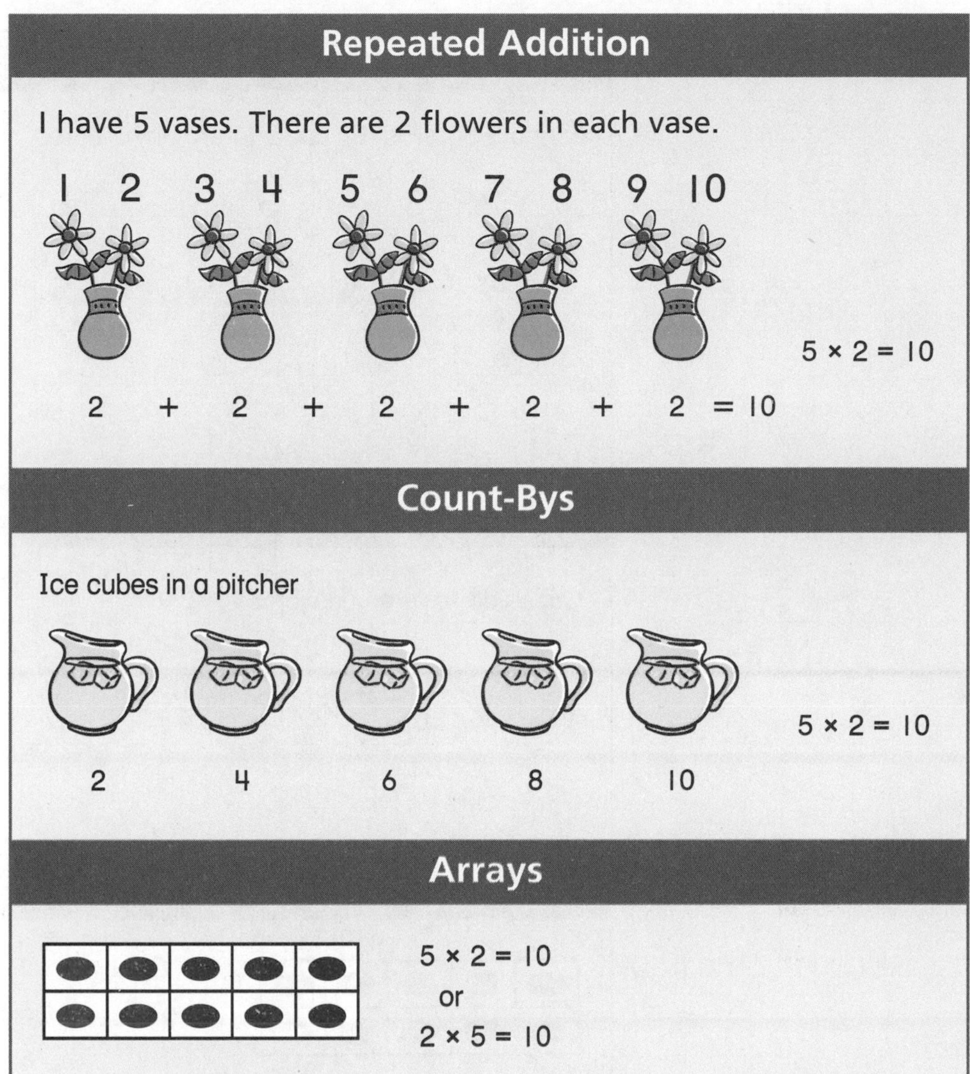

Please call if you have any questions or comments. Thank you for helping your child learn about multiplication.

Sincerely,
Your child's teacher

Estimada familia:

En esta unidad se la multiplicación de tres maneras.

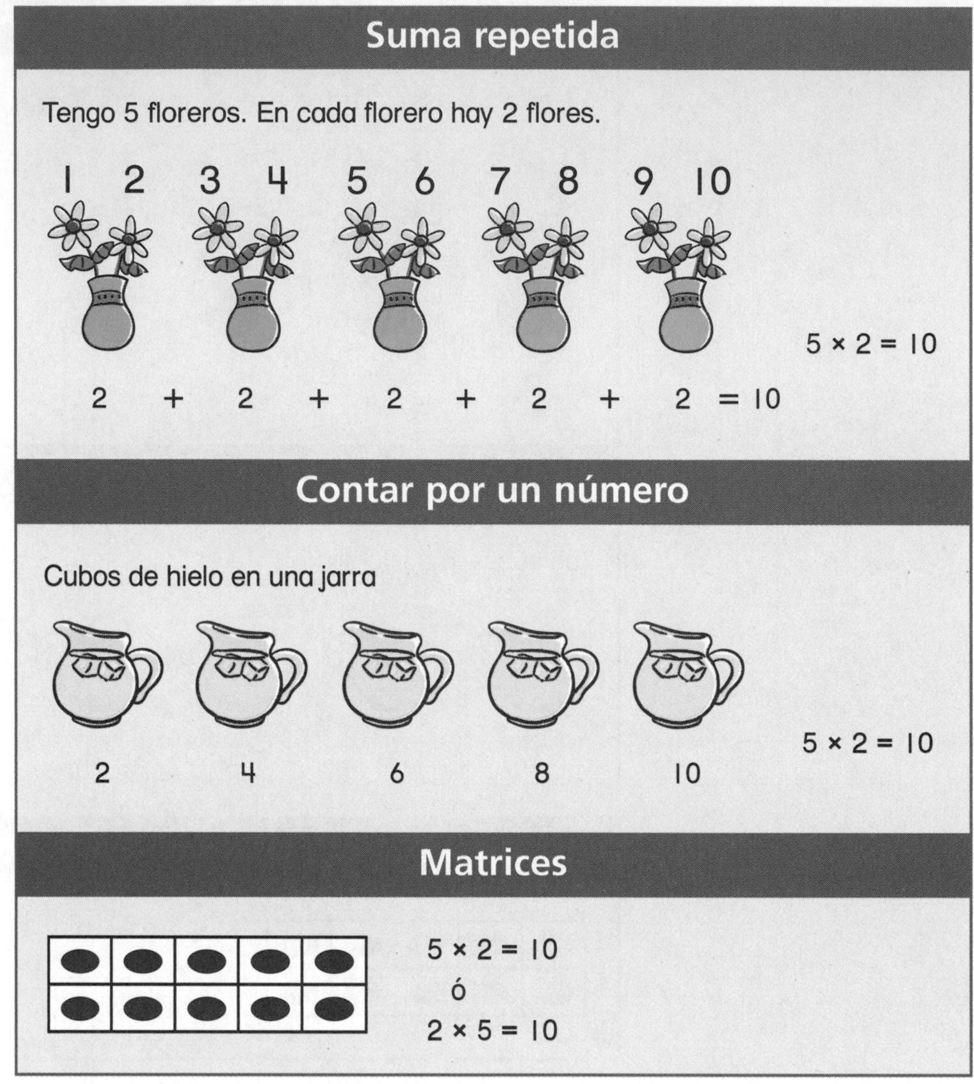

Si tiene alguna duda o comentario, por favor comuníquese conmigo. Gracias por ayudar a su niño a aprender sobre la multiplicación.

Atentamente,
El maestro de su niño

7–2 Name ____________________

Class Activity

Vocabulary
count by
count-bys

▶ 3s Count-Bys

1. Fill in the chart below to make groups of 3. Then **count by** 3s by saying the last number in each group.

1	2	3
4	5	6
		15
	20	
		27

2. Write out the 3s **count-bys** below.

3 ___ 6 ___ ___ ___ 15 ___ ___ ___ 27 ___

7-2 Class Activity

Name ____________________

Vocabulary
multiply

▶ Count by 3s to Multiply

Count by 3s. Then **multiply**.

3. Sides on a triangle

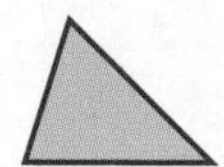 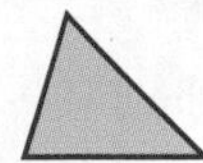 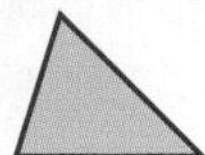 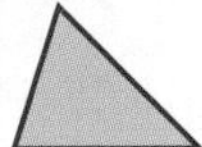

____ ____ ____ ____

$4 \times 3 =$ 12

4. Fried eggs on a plate

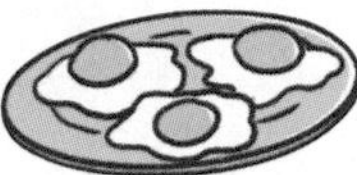 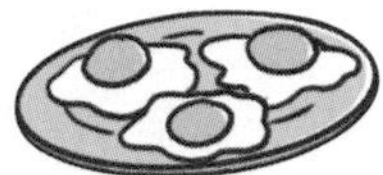

____ ____

$2 \times 3 =$ ____

5. Leaves on a branch

____ ____ ____ ____ ____ ____ ____ ____

$8 \times 3 =$ ____

6. Leaves on a shamrock

____ ____ ____ ____ ____ ____ ____ ____ ____

$9 \times 3 =$ ____

7. Holes in a bowling ball

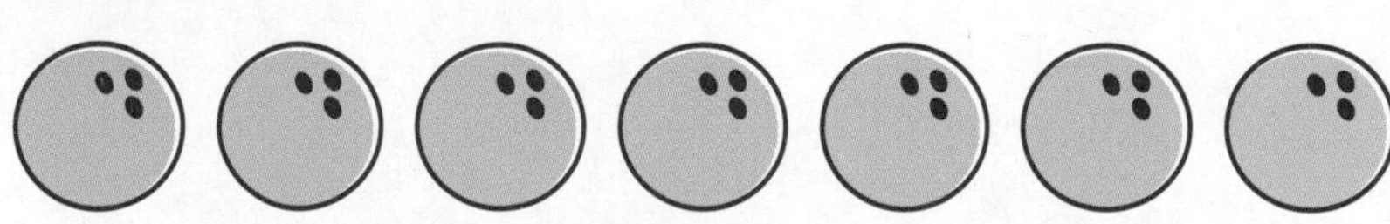

____ ____ ____ ____ ____ ____ ____

$7 \times 3 =$ ____

7–2

Name

Going Further

▶ Hats for Sale

Use the pictograph to answer the questions.

Hats for Sale

Color	Hats
Green	🎩 🎩 🎩
Red	🎩 🎩
Blue	🎩
Yellow	🎩 🎩

Key: Each 🎩 = 3 hats

1. How many hats does each 🎩 stand for?

   ☐ ____________ label

2. How many red hats are for sale?

   ☐ ____________ label

3. How many blue hats are for sale?

   ☐ ____________ label

4. The store has 6 purple hats. How many symbols are needed to show the purple hats on the pictograph?

   ☐ ____________ label

5. **On the Back** Write the answer and show your work for the following problem.

   If each 🎩 stands for only 2 hats, how many symbols do you need to show the red hats?

Name

Class Activity

Name ______

Vocabulary
count by
count-bys

▶ 4s Count-Bys

1. Fill in the chart below to make groups of 4. Then **count by** 4s by saying the last number in each group.

1	2	3	4
5	6	7	8
	18		
			32

2. Write out the 4s **count-bys** below.

4 8 ___ ___ 20 ___ ___ 32 ___ ___

Name ______________________

► Count by 4s to Multiply

Count by 4s. Then multiply.

3. Sides of a square

   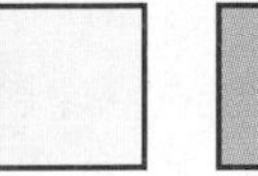 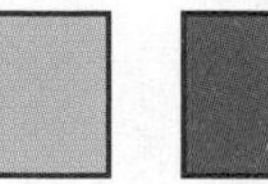 

____ ____ ____ ____ ____

5 × 4 = ______

4. Legs on a lion

____ ____ ____ ____ ____ ____ ____

7 × 4 = ______

5. Strings on a violin

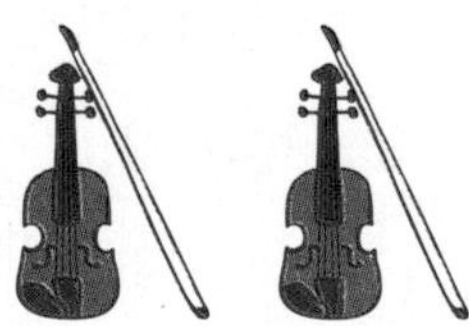

____ ____

2 × 4 = ______

6. Holes in a button

  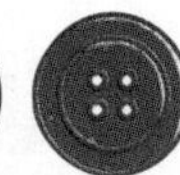       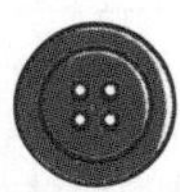

____ ____ ____ ____ ____ ____ ____ ____ ____

9 × 4 = ______

7. Cherries on a plate

____ ____ ____

3 × 4 = ______

Name ____________________

▶ Using Pictographs

Use the pictograph to answer the questions.

Playground Toys

Soccer balls	☆ ☆ ☆
Jump ropes	☆ ☆ ☆ ☆
Bats	☆ ☆

Key: Each ☆ = 4 toys

1. How many jump ropes are there in all? ☐ ____________ label

2. How many more soccer balls are there than bats?

☐ ____________ label

3. A school has 8 tennis rackets. How many ☆s are needed to show the tennis rackets in this pictograph?

☐ ____________ label

4. **On the Back** How many ☆s are needed to show the soccer balls if each ☆ represents 2 toys? Write the answer and show your work on the back.

Name

Name ______________________________

Vocabulary
count by
count-bys

▶ 5s Count-Bys

1. Fill in the chart below to make groups of 5. Then **count by** 5s by saying the last number in each group.

1	2	3	4	5
6	7	8	9	10
	17			
				25
		33		

2. Write out the 5s **count-bys** below.

5 ___ ___ ___ ___ 25 ___ ___ ___ ___ ___

7–4 Class Activity

Name ______________________

▶ Solve Array Problems.

Write the numbers.

3. 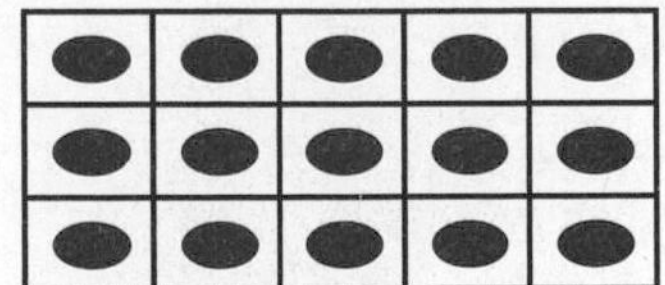

_______ × _______ or

_______ × _______

4. 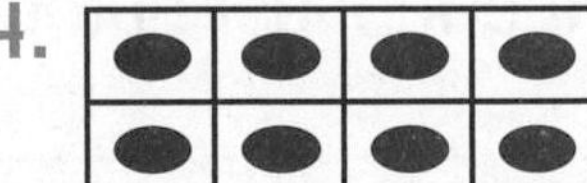

_______ × _______ or

_______ × _______

5. 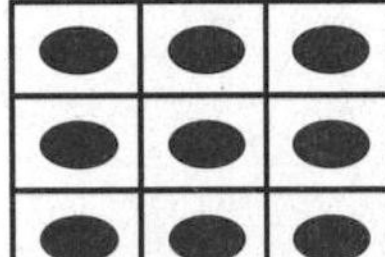

_______ × _______

6. 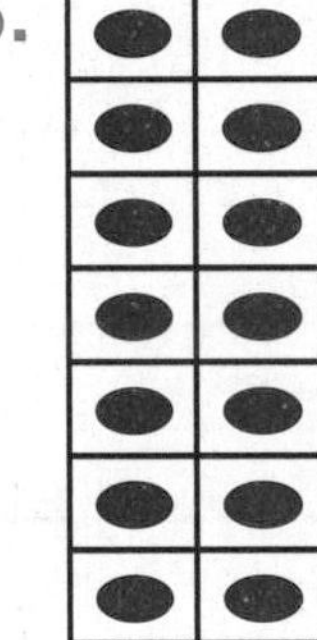

_______ × _______ or

_______ × _______

Plant some beans in your garden.
Your teacher will tell you how.

7.

Name ____________________

Vocabulary
count-bys
multiplication

► Use Arrays to Solve Problems

Here is Mr. and Mrs. Green's orchard.

1. How many apple trees are in the orchard?
   Write the **count-bys** and the **multiplication.**
   Count by 5s.

   5 ___ 10 ___ ___ ___ ___ ___ ___ ___

   8 × ___ = ___

2. Count by 8s.

   8 ___ 16 ___ ___ ___ ___

   5 × ___ = ___

Name ______________________

Going Further

Vocabulary
array

▶ Introduce Mystery Multiplication

You can use an **array** to find the unknown number in a multiplication sentence.

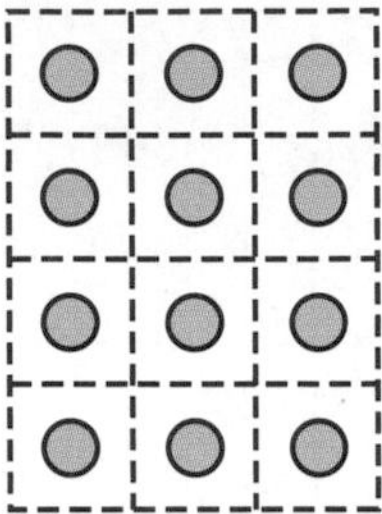

1. How many rows are there in the array? ☐ ______ label

2. How many columns are there in the array? ☐ ______ label

3. How many circles are there in all? ☐ ______ label

4. Complete the multiplication sentence.

☐ × 3 = 12

Find the unknown number in each multiplication sentence. Place beans on the grid to make an array to help you.

5. 5 × ☐ = 20

6. 4 × ☐ = 8

7. ☐ × 2 = 10

8. ☐ × 3 = 9

7–6 Class Activity

Name ______________________

Vocabulary
half
equal shares
twice
double

▶ Solve and Discuss

Draw in your answers. Write the numbers.

1. Kathy has **half** as many marbles as Yao.

   Kathy has ________.

   Yao has ________.

   Kathy

   Yao

2. Paulo and Leah have **equal shares** of blocks.

   Paulo has ________.

   Leah has ________.

   Leah

3. Nicole has **twice** as many stickers as Reggie.

   Nicole has ________.

   Reggie has ________.

   Nicole

4. Dean has **double** the number of stamps that Yolanda has.

   Yolanda has ________.

   Dean has ________.

   Yolanda

   Dean

5. **On the Back** Draw a picture to show equal shares of 14. Explain how you know your picture shows equal shares.

Name

Name ______________________

Vocabulary
symmetrical

► Find Lines of Symmetry

Cut out the shapes. Try to fold them in half so that the two parts match exactly. Sort the shapes into two groups: **symmetrical** and not symmetrical.

A

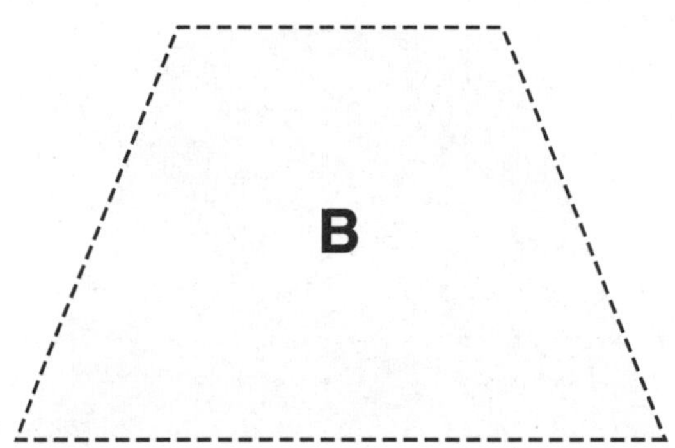

C

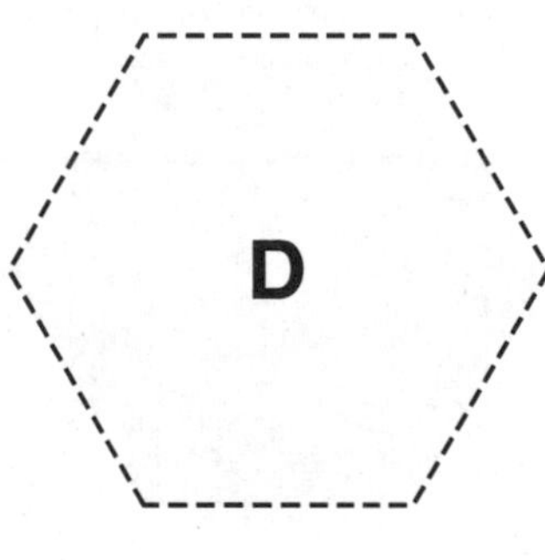

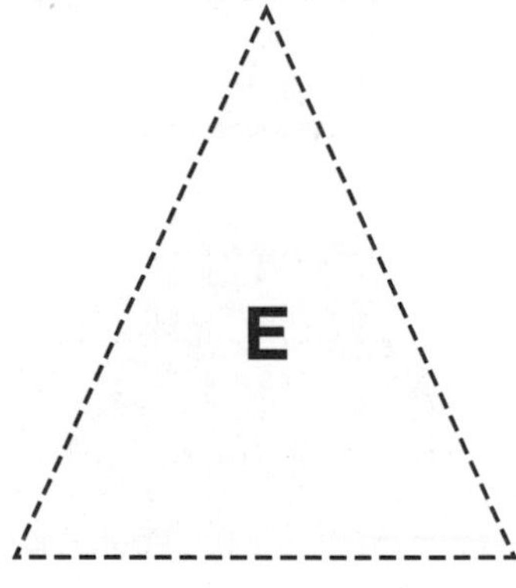

F

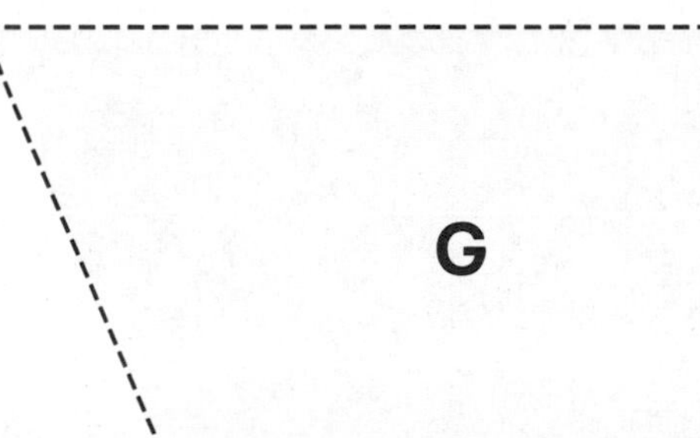

Name

Vocabulary
line of symmetry

► Complete Drawings of Symmetrical Shapes

Finish drawing the shapes.

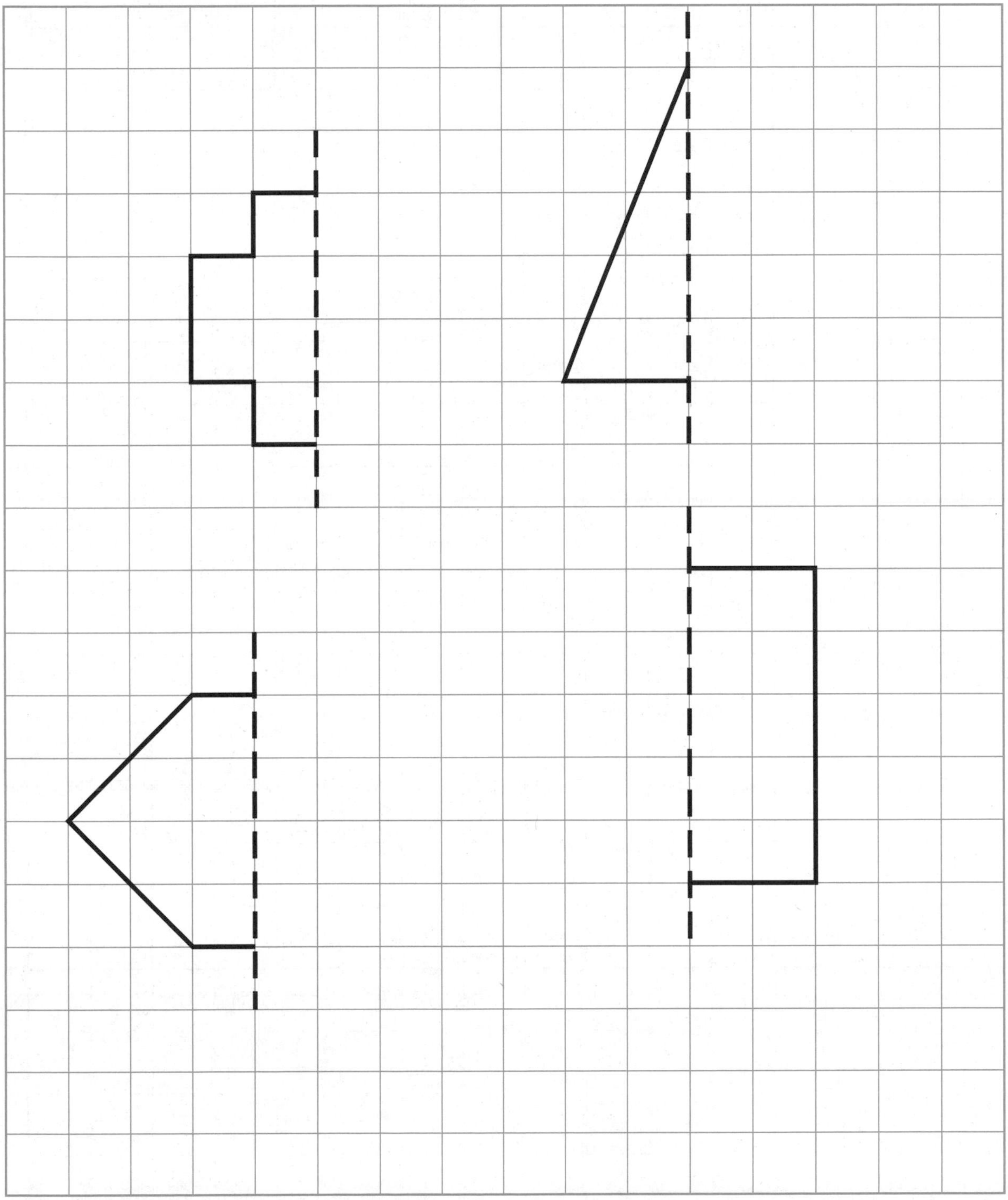

On the Back Draw some symmetrical shapes of your own. Draw a **line of symmetry** for each shape.

Name

Name ____________________

▶ Shade Unit Fractions

1. Shade in the fractions for the shapes.

$\frac{1}{2}$

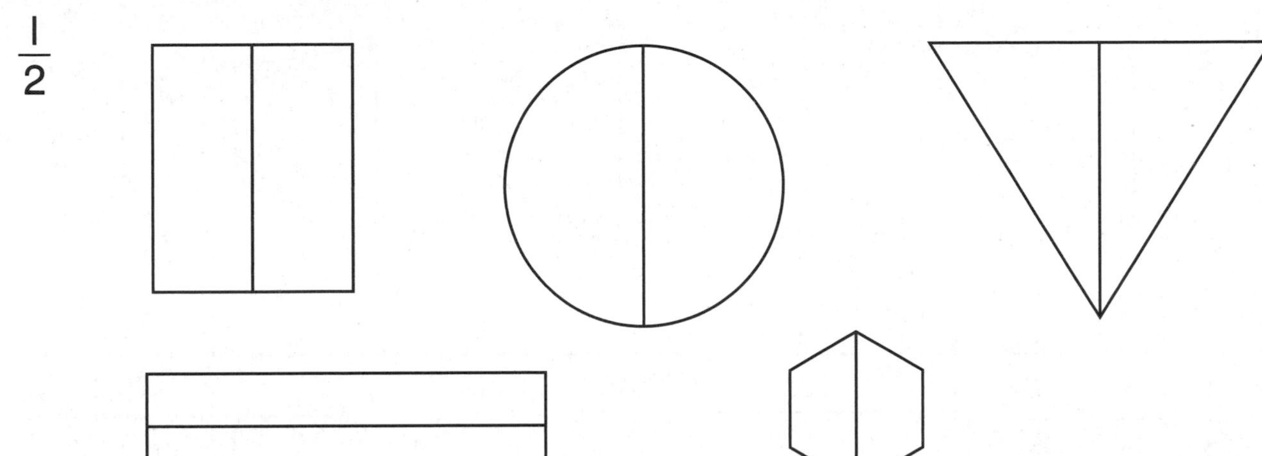

$\frac{1}{3}$

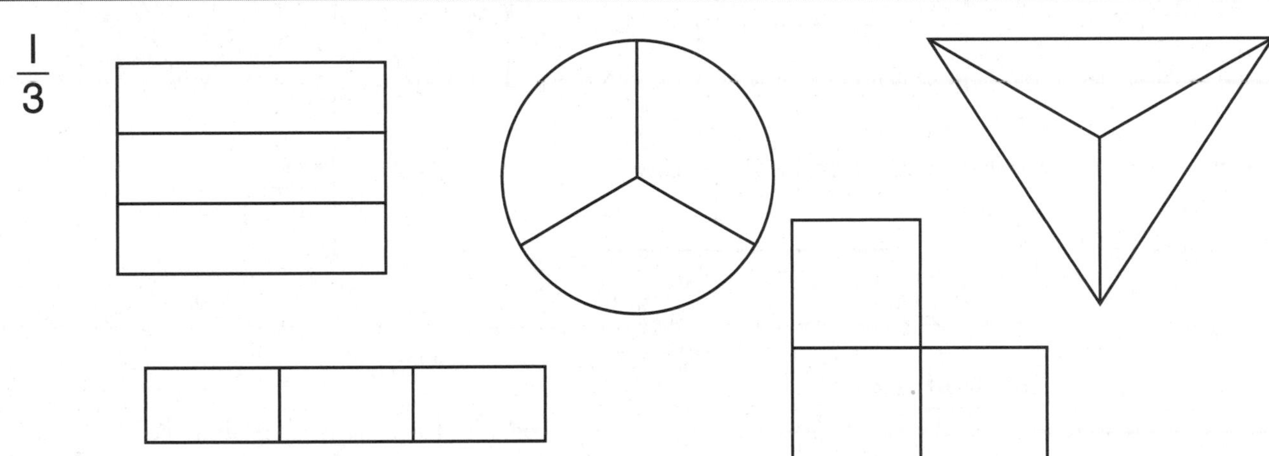

$\frac{1}{4}$

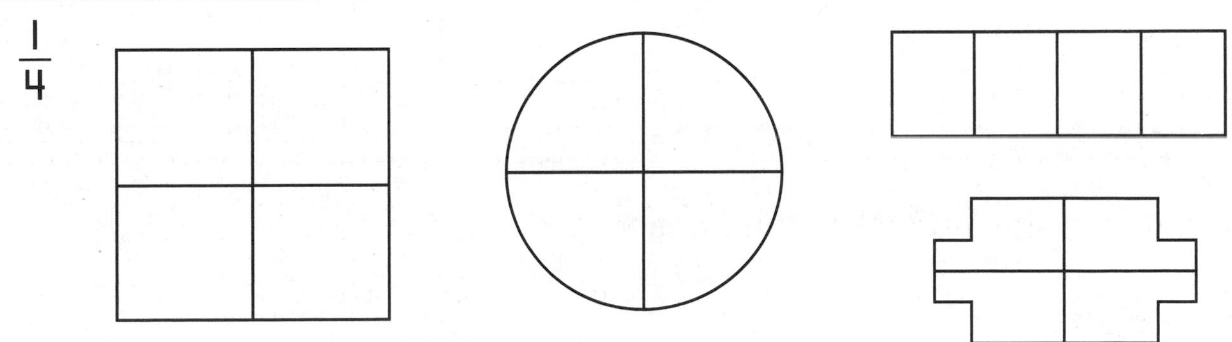

Name ______________________________

► Shade and Write Fractions

2. Shade in the fractions for the shapes.

$\frac{1}{2}$

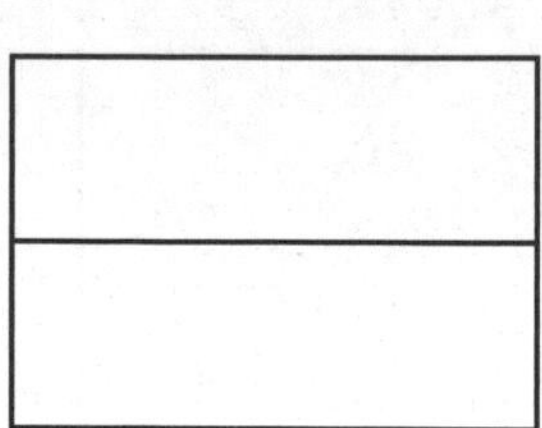
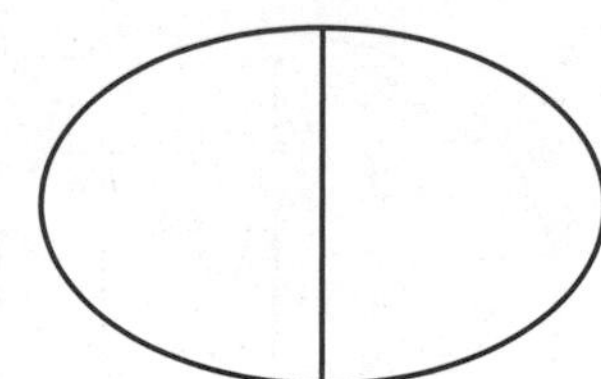
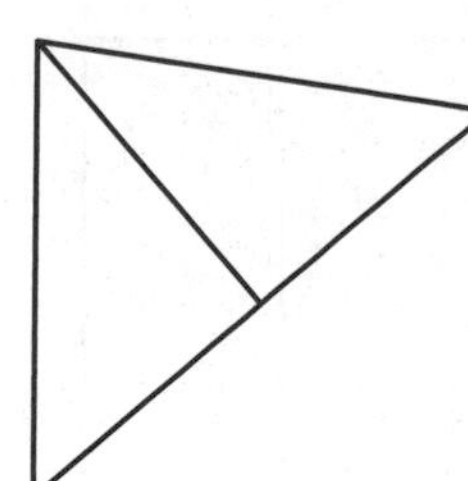

$\frac{2}{3} = \frac{1}{3} + \frac{1}{3}$

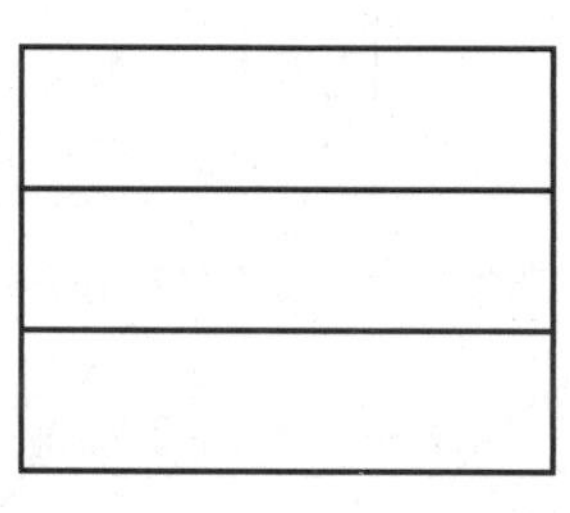
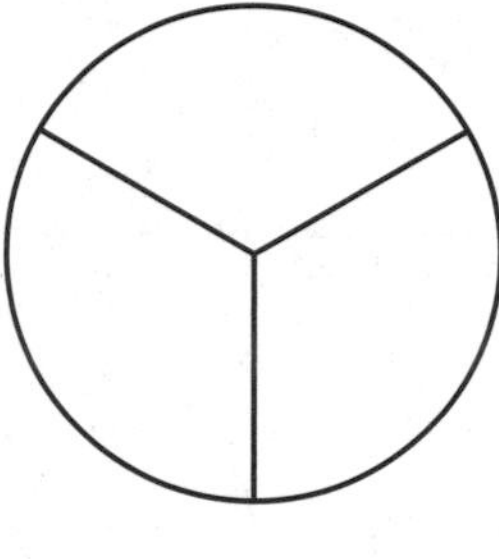
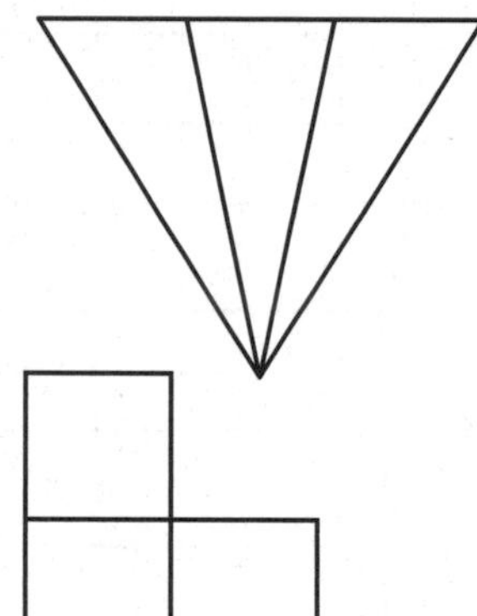

$\frac{3}{4} = \frac{1}{4} + \frac{1}{4} + \frac{1}{4}$

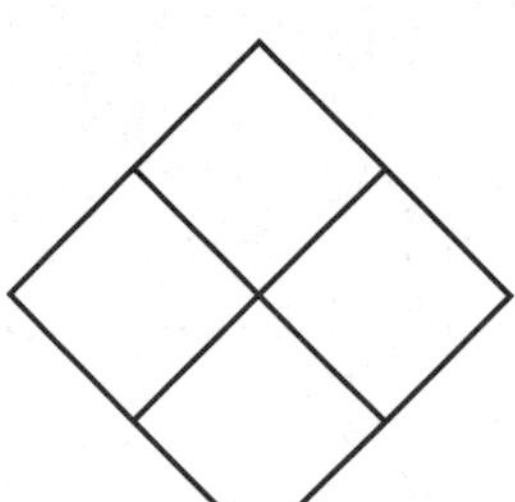
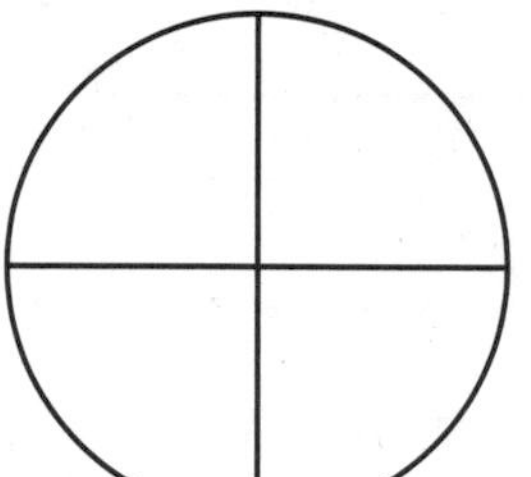
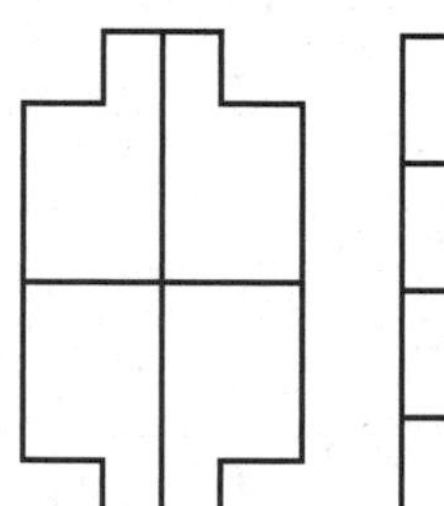

How much is shaded? Write the fraction.

3. 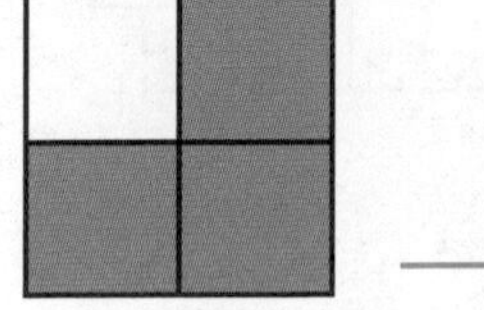 ______

4. 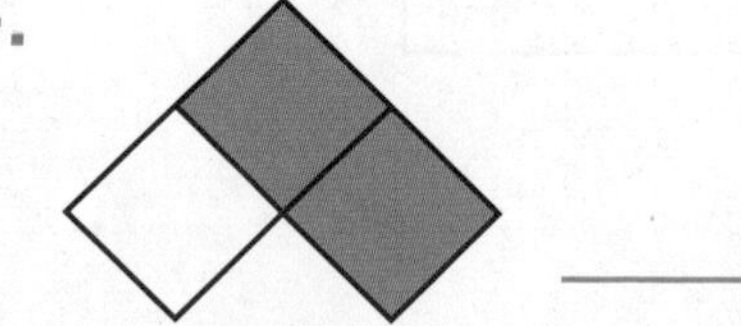 ______

Name

▶ Divide Shapes Into Equal Parts

Shade in the fractions of the shapes.

5. $\frac{1}{2}$

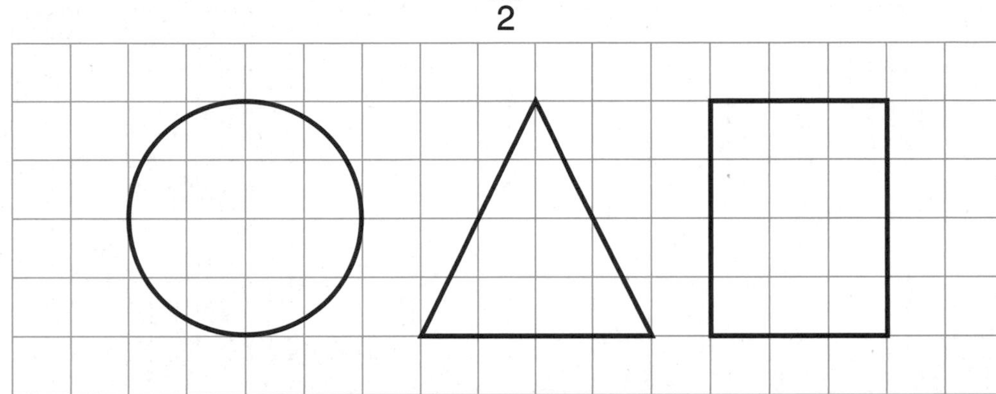

6. $\frac{2}{3} = \frac{1}{3} + \frac{1}{3}$

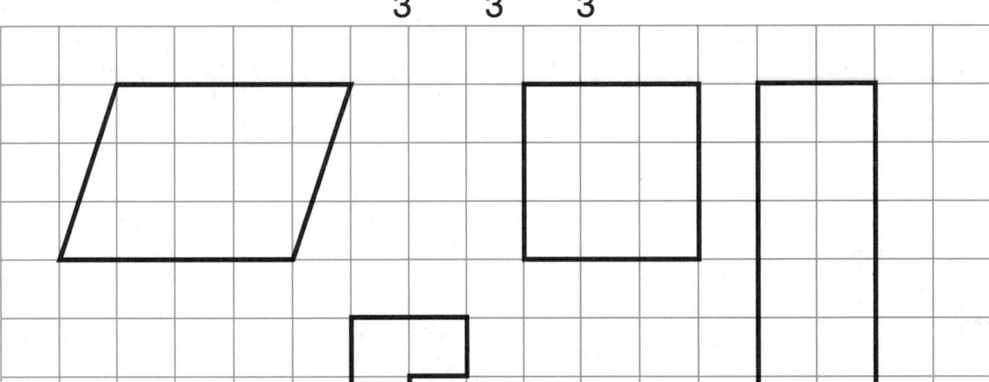

7. $\frac{3}{4} = \frac{1}{4} + \frac{1}{4} + \frac{1}{4}$

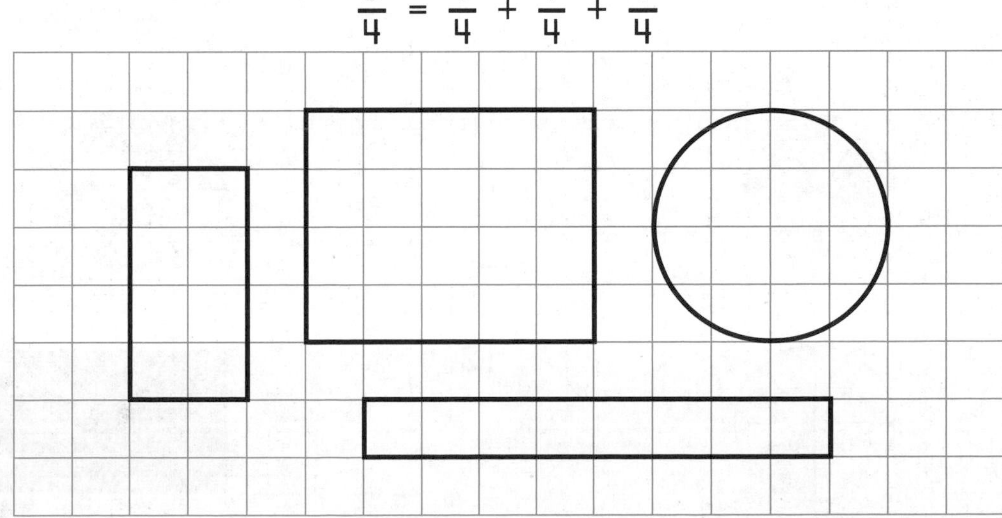

Name

▶ Solve and Discuss

Color to show each fraction.

1. $\frac{1}{5}$

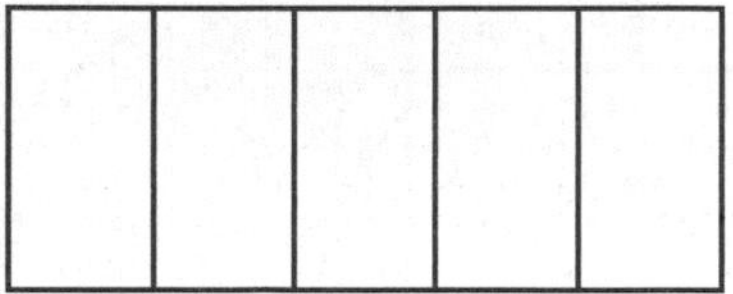

2. $\frac{4}{6} = \frac{1}{6} + \frac{1}{6} + \frac{1}{6} + \frac{1}{6}$

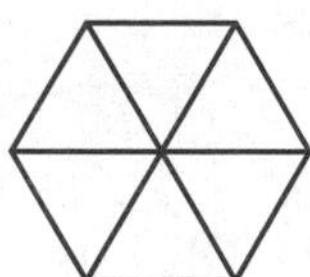

3. $\frac{3}{7} = \frac{1}{7} + \frac{1}{7} + \frac{1}{7}$

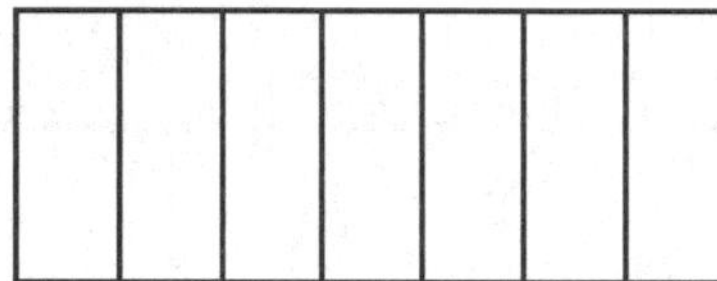

4. $\frac{2}{8} = \frac{1}{8} + \frac{1}{8}$

5. $\frac{3}{10} = \frac{1}{10} + \frac{1}{10} + \frac{1}{10}$

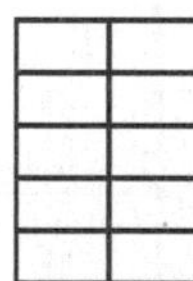

6. $\frac{2}{9} = \frac{1}{9} + \frac{1}{9}$

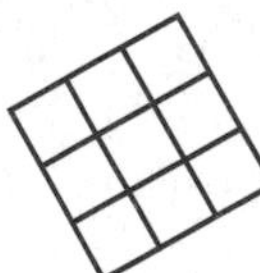

Write the fraction for the shaded part.

7. ______

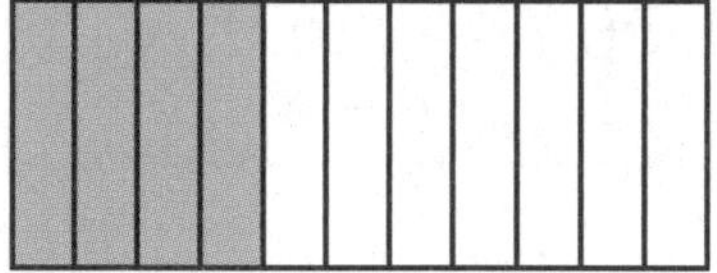

8. ______

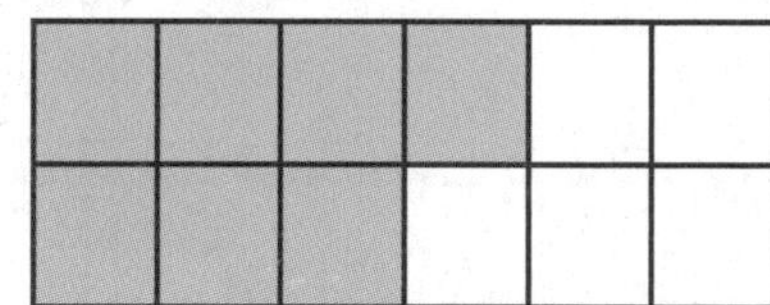

9. ______

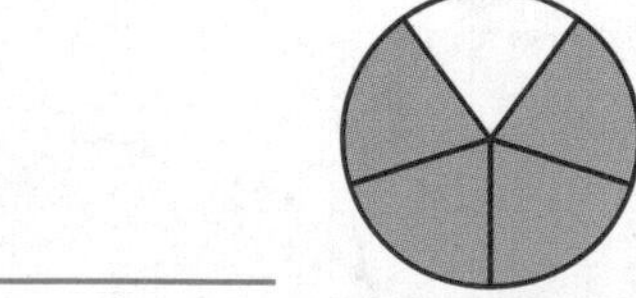

10. ______

11. ______

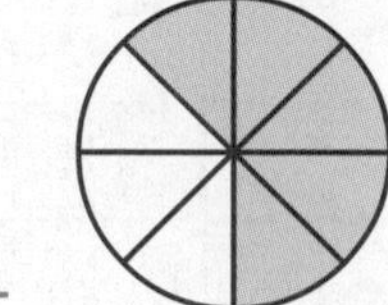

12. ______

Name

▶ Make Fraction Strips

Color the fraction strips. Cut on the dashed lines.

1. Color 1 whole.	
2. Color $\frac{1}{2}$.	
3. Color $\frac{1}{3}$.	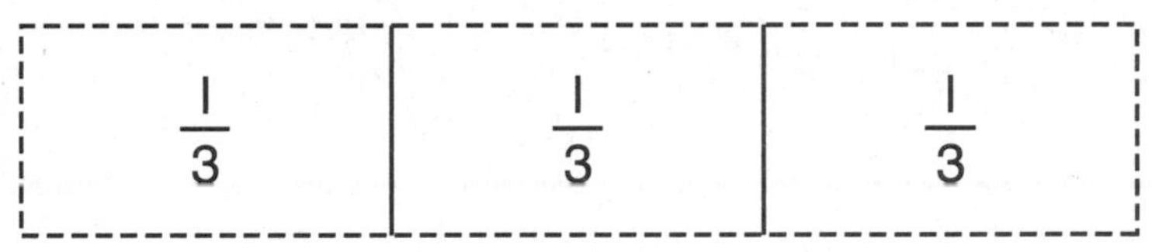
4. Color $\frac{2}{3} = \frac{1}{3} + \frac{1}{3}$.	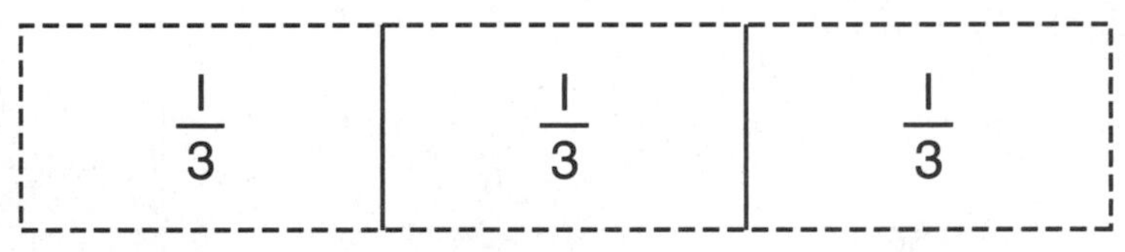
5. Color $\frac{1}{4}$.	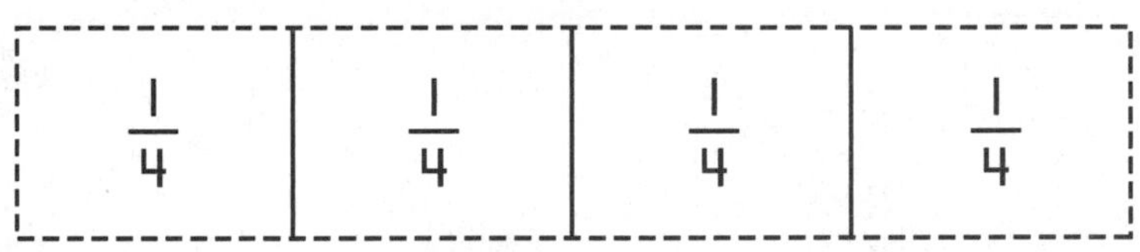
6. Color $\frac{2}{4} = \frac{1}{4} + \frac{1}{4}$.	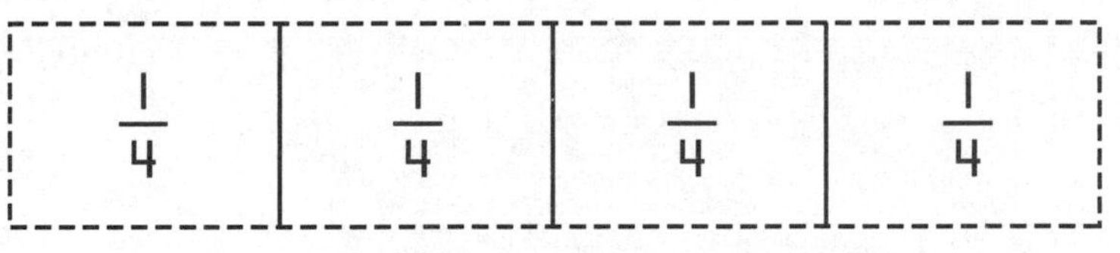
7. Color $\frac{3}{4} = \frac{1}{4} + \frac{1}{4} + \frac{1}{4}$.	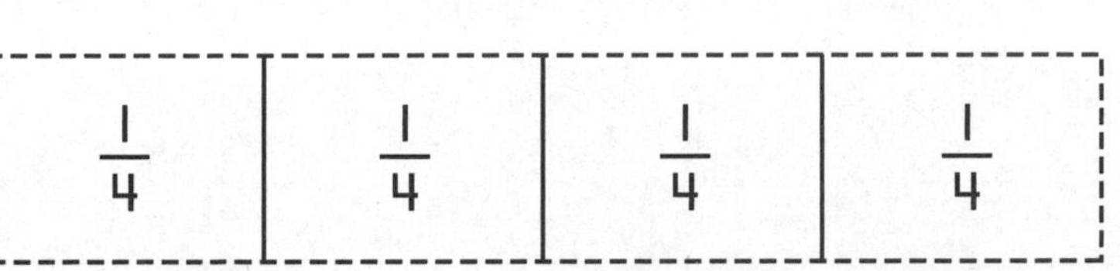

Name ____________________

Class Activity

▶ Compare Fractions

Use your fraction strips to compare the fractions. Then write <, >, or =.

Remember
$>$ means **is greater than**
$<$ means **is less than**
$=$ means **is equal to**

8. Compare $\frac{1}{3}$ and $\frac{1}{2}$. $\frac{1}{3}$  $\frac{1}{2}$	9. Compare $\frac{2}{4}$ and $\frac{3}{4}$. $\frac{2}{4}$ ◯ $\frac{3}{4}$
10. Compare $\frac{2}{3}$ and $\frac{1}{3}$. $\frac{2}{3}$ ◯ $\frac{1}{3}$	11. Compare $\frac{1}{4}$ and $\frac{1}{2}$. $\frac{1}{4}$ ◯ $\frac{1}{2}$
12. Compare $\frac{3}{4}$ and $\frac{2}{3}$. $\frac{3}{4}$ ◯ $\frac{2}{3}$	13. Compare $\frac{2}{3}$ and $\frac{1}{2}$. $\frac{2}{3}$ ◯ $\frac{1}{2}$
14. Compare $\frac{2}{4}$ and $\frac{1}{2}$. $\frac{2}{4}$ ◯ $\frac{1}{2}$	15. Compare $\frac{2}{3}$ and $\frac{2}{4}$. $\frac{2}{3}$ ◯ $\frac{2}{4}$

▶ Visual Thinking

Ring the picture that shows the correct amount.

16. less than $\frac{1}{2}$

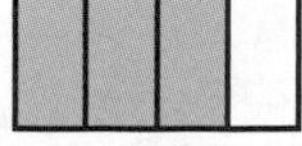 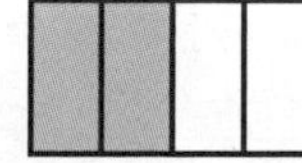 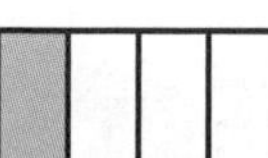

17. more than $\frac{1}{2}$

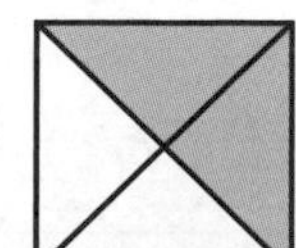 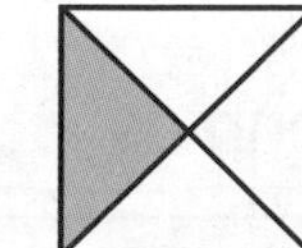 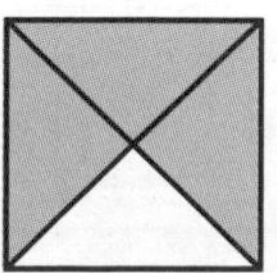

Name ______________________________

▶ Write Money in Different Ways

Complete the chart.

	Money Amount	Number of Cents	Dollars and Cents	Fraction of a Dollar
18.	1 dime	10¢	$0.10	$\frac{1}{10}$
19.	2 dimes	20¢	$0. ______	$\frac{\_\_}{10}$
20.	3 dimes	______ ¢	$0. ______	$\frac{\_\_}{10}$
21.	6 dimes	60¢	$ ______	$\frac{\_\_}{\_\_}$
22.	8 dimes	80¢	$ ______	$\frac{\_\_}{\_\_}$
23.	10 dimes	______ ¢	$1.00	$\frac{\_\_}{\_\_}$ or 1
24.	1 penny	1¢	$0.01	$\frac{1}{100}$
25.	2 pennies	2¢	$______	$\frac{\_\_}{100}$
26.	8 pennies	______¢	$______	$\frac{\_\_}{100}$
27.	35 pennies	35¢	$______	$\frac{\_\_}{100}$
28.	80 pennies	______ ¢	$0.80	$\frac{\_\_}{\_\_}$
29.	100 pennies	100¢	$______	$\frac{\_\_}{\_\_}$ or 1

Name

▶ Estimate Fractions

Cut on the dashed lines.

0	$\frac{1}{2}$	1

$\frac{1}{5}$	$\frac{1}{5}$	$\frac{1}{5}$	$\frac{1}{5}$	$\frac{1}{5}$
$\frac{1}{5}$	$\frac{1}{5}$	$\frac{1}{5}$	$\frac{1}{5}$	$\frac{1}{5}$
$\frac{1}{5}$	$\frac{1}{5}$	$\frac{1}{5}$	$\frac{1}{5}$	$\frac{1}{5}$

$\frac{1}{8}$	$\frac{1}{8}$	$\frac{1}{8}$	$\frac{1}{8}$	$\frac{1}{8}$	$\frac{1}{8}$	$\frac{1}{8}$	$\frac{1}{8}$
$\frac{1}{8}$	$\frac{1}{8}$	$\frac{1}{8}$	$\frac{1}{8}$	$\frac{1}{8}$	$\frac{1}{8}$	$\frac{1}{8}$	$\frac{1}{8}$
$\frac{1}{8}$	$\frac{1}{8}$	$\frac{1}{8}$	$\frac{1}{8}$	$\frac{1}{8}$	$\frac{1}{8}$	$\frac{1}{8}$	$\frac{1}{8}$

Name ______________________________

▶ The Spinner Game

Color the larger part of the spinner blue.

Color the smaller part of the spinner red.

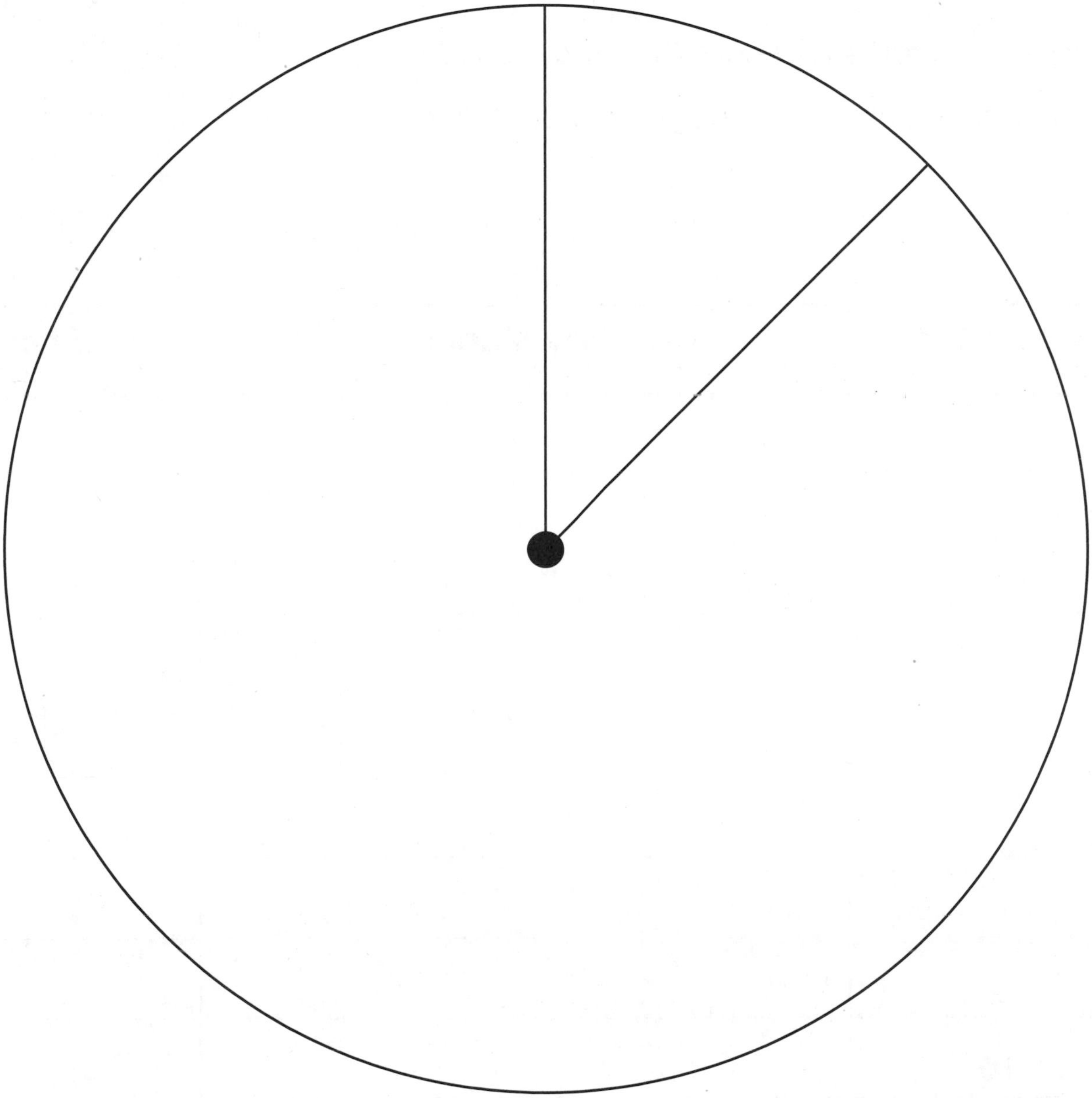

7-10 Name ____________________

Class Activity

Vocabulary
prediction
more likely

▶ Probability Experiment

1. Make a **prediction**. Is it **more likely** that you will roll a total of 2 or a total of 7? __________

2. Do the experiment.
   - Toss the number cubes 30 times.
   - Use tally marks to record the totals you roll.
   - Find the number of times you got each total.

Remember

| means 1

卌 means 5

Possible Totals	Tally Marks	Number
2		
3		
4		
5		
6		
7		
8		
9		
10		
11		
12		

Name ______________________________

Vocabulary
organized list
combinations

▶ Find All Possible Combinations

Make an **organized list** to solve the problems.

1. Nadia has a red coat and a blue coat. She also has a yellow hat and a green hat. How many different combinations of a coat and a hat can she wear?

☐ different **combinations**

Coat Color		Hat Color
red	→	
red	→	
blue	→	
blue	→	

2. Tia has white, wheat, and rye bread. She also has ham and tuna. How many different kinds of sandwiches can she make?

☐ different sandwiches

Bread		Filling
white	→	
white	→	
rye	→	

3. Michael has blue pants and black pants. He also has a red shirt and a green shirt. How many different combinations of pants and shirts can he wear?

☐ different combinations

Pants Color		Shirt Color
blue	→	
blue	→	

4. **On the Back** Kara is buying frozen yogurt. She can buy a cone or a cup. She can get vanilla, chocolate, or mint. Make a list of all the different combinations she can buy.

Name

Name ______________________

1. Count by 2s. Then multiply.
Shoes

$7 \times 2 =$ ______

______ ______ ______ ______ ______ ______ ______

2. Count by 3s. Then multiply.
Wheels on a tricycle

$5 \times 3 =$ ______

______ ______ ______ ______ ______

3. Count by 4s. Then multiply.
Legs on a dog

$6 \times 4 =$ ______

______ ______ ______ ______ ______ ______

4. Count by 5s. Then multiply.
Fingers on a hand

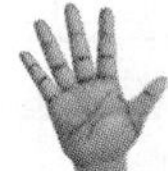 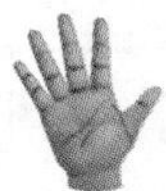  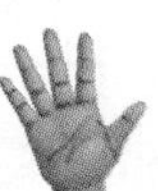    

$8 \times 5 =$ ______

______ ______ ______ ______ ______ ______ ______ ______

Name ____________________

Write the numbers.

5. 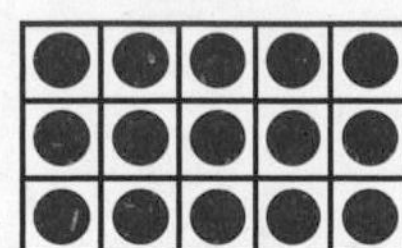

____ × ____ or

____ × ____

6. 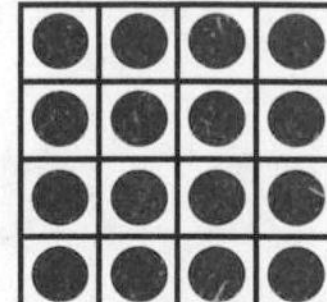

____ × ____

7. 

____ × ____ or

____ × ____

8. 

____ × ____ or

____ × ____

Draw in your answers. Write the numbers, too.

9. Walt has **twice** as many crayons as Carla.

Carla has ____.

Walt has ____.

Carla	Walt
○ ○ ○ ○ ○ ○ ○	

10. Tony has **half** as many toy cars as Harvey.

Tony has ____.

Harvey has ____.

Tony	Harvey
	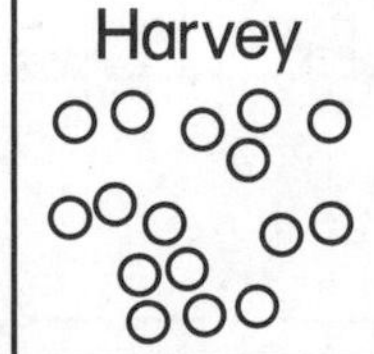

Name ____________________

Draw in your answers. Write the numbers, too.

11. Maria and Rachel have **equal shares** of toys.

Maria has ______.

Rachel has ______.

Maria	Rachel
○ ○ ○ ○ ○ ○	

12. Judy has **double** the number of pens that Aaron has.

Judy has ______.

Aaron has ______.

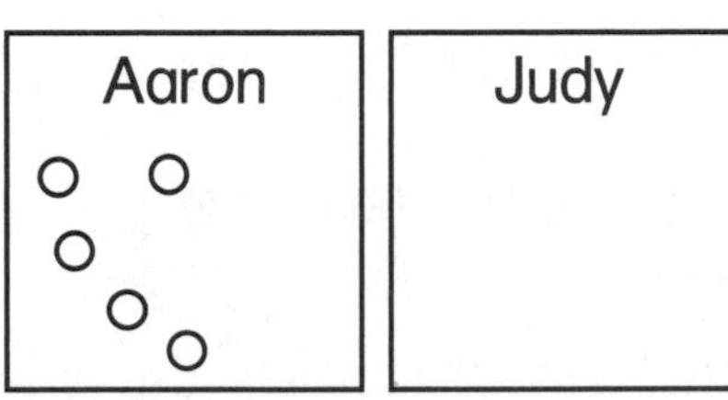

Is the figure symmetrical? Write *yes* or *no*.
If yes, draw one line of symmetry.

13. 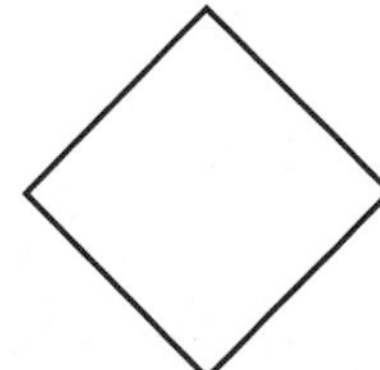

______

14. 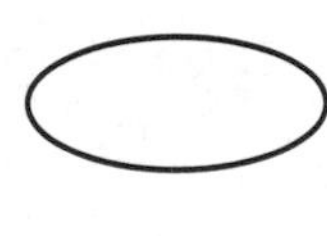

______

15. 

______

16. 

______

Write the fraction for the shaded part.

17. 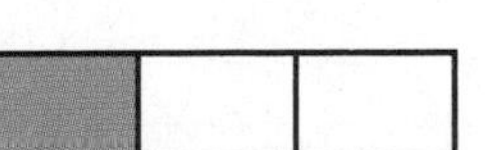

______

18. 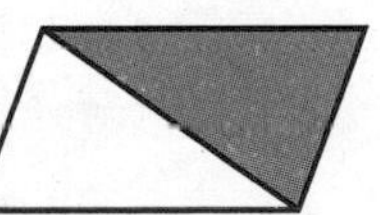

______

19. 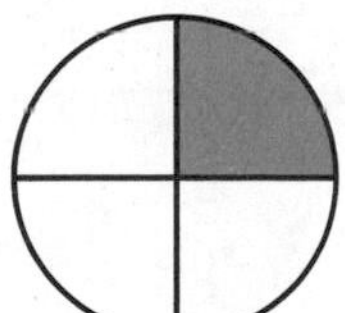

______

20. 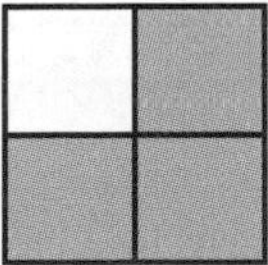

______

Name ________________________________

Look at the bag of cubes. Circle the correct event.

21. Which event is certain?

22. Which event is impossible?

21.
I will pick a black cube.

I will pick a white cube.

22.
I will pick a black cube.

I will pick a white cube.

Look at the bag of cubes. How likely are you to pick a black cube than a white cube?

23.

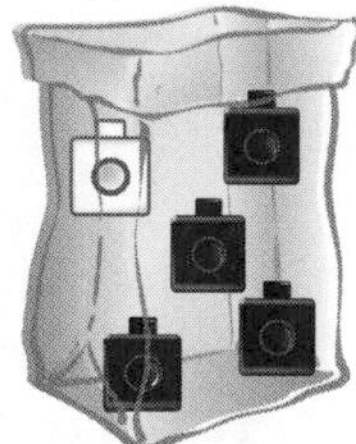

more likely

less likely

24.

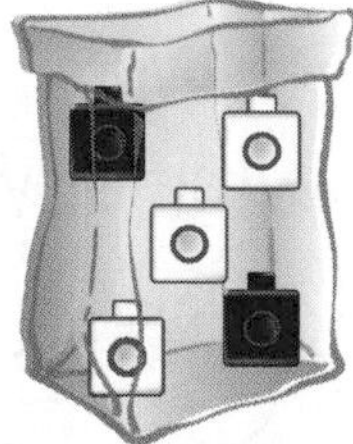

more likely

less likely

25. **Extended Response** Draw a shape and shade $\frac{3}{4}$ of it.

G–1 Class Activity

Name ______________________

▶ Non-Standard Units of Length

1. Find each object. Estimate and then measure the length of each in small and large paper clips.

Object	Estimated length	Measured length
(hand)	about ______ (small paper clips) about ______ (large paper clips)	about ______ (small paper clips) about ______ (large paper clips)
(desk)	about ______ (small paper clips) about ______ (large paper clips)	about ______ (small paper clips) about ______ (large paper clips)

2. Are the measurement numbers larger with small or large paper clips? Explain.

____

____

3. Sona measured the length of a notebook using small paper clips. The length was 35 small paper clips. She then measured the same length using large paper clips. Was her new measurement more than 35 large paper clips? Explain.

____

____

G–1

Class Activity

Name ______________________________

Vocabulary
mass
capacity

▶ Non-Standard Units of Mass

4. List objects you might use as non-standard units of **mass**.

____

____

____

____

____

____

____

____

▶ Non-Standard Units of Capacity

5. List objects you might use as non-standard units of **capacity**.

____

____

____

____

____

____

____

____

Dear Family,

Your child is beginning another unit on measurement.

Children will first investigate measuring using non-standard units. They will measure length in units such as paper clips and mass in units such as pennies, using a handmade balance scale. Children will arrange containers in order of increasing capacity and test the order by transferring water from one container to another. They will also discuss ideas for measuring volume and time using non-standard units.

Children will continue to measure length in customary units. They will make their own inch ruler and yardstick to measure in inches, feet, and yards. They will also make conversions between customary units using these relationships:

1 foot = 12 inches
1 yard = 3 feet
1 yard = 36 inches

These are examples of the types of conversion they will do for homework in Lesson 2.

1 ft = __12__ in. 3 ft = __36__ in. 2 yd = __6__ ft

In the last lesson of this unit, children will have an opportunity to measure length, mass, weight, capacity, time, and temperature using standard units.

To help bridge your child's classroom learning with home, ask your child to estimate and measure objects that he or she uses in everyday activities. For example, you might ask, "How much do you think this pot holds?" and have your child measure its capacity in cups.

If you have any questions or comments, please call or write to me.

Sincerely,
Your child's teacher

Estimada familia:

Su niño empieza otra unidad sobre las medidas.

Los niños empezarán a medir con unidades no. Medirán la longitud usando sujetapapeles y la masa usando unidades tales como monedas de un centavo con una balanza que ellos harán. Los niños ordenarán recipientes según su capacidad y comprobarán el orden pasando agua de un recipiente a otro. También comentarán ideas para medir el volumen y el tiempo usando unidades no usuales.

Más adelante, los niños medirán la longitud en unidades del sistema usual. Harán su propia regla de pulgadas y su propia regla de 1 yarda para medir en pulgadas, pies y yardas. También harán conversiones entre estas unidades utilizando las siguientes relaciones de pulgadas:

1 pie = 12 pulgadas
1 yarda = 3 pies
1 yarda = 36 pulgadas

Estos son ejemplos de los tipos de conversiones que harán como tarea para la Lección 2.

1 pie = <u>12</u> pulg   3 pies = <u>36</u> pulg

2 yd = <u>6</u> pies

En la última lección de esta unidad los niños tendrán la oportunidad de medir la longitud, la masa, el peso, la capacidad, el tiempo y la temperatura usando unidades usuales de medida.

Para ayudar a su niño a hacer la conexión entre el aprendizaje en la escuela y la casa, pídale que estime y mida objetos que se usan en las actividades diarias. Por ejemplo, podría preguntarle, "¿Cuánto crees que cabe en esta olla?" y pedirle que mida su capacidad usando una taza.

Si tiene alguna duda o comentario, por favor comuníquese conmigo.

Atentamente,
El maestro de su niño

Name

▶ Make an Inch Ruler

Directions:

Step 1: Cut along the dashed lines.

Step 2: Place the sections in the correct order.

Step 3: Tape or glue together the sections at the tab.

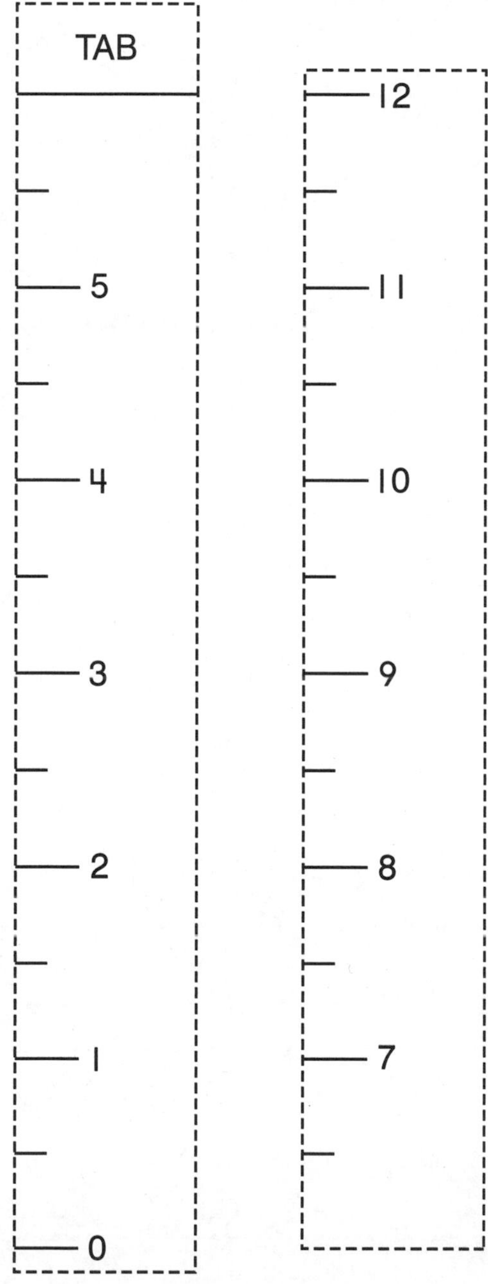

Name ____________________

Vocabulary
inch (in.)

▶ Measure to the Nearest Inch

To measure to the nearest **inch (in.)**, place the zero mark on your ruler at the left end of the object. Find the inch mark that is closest to the right end of the object.

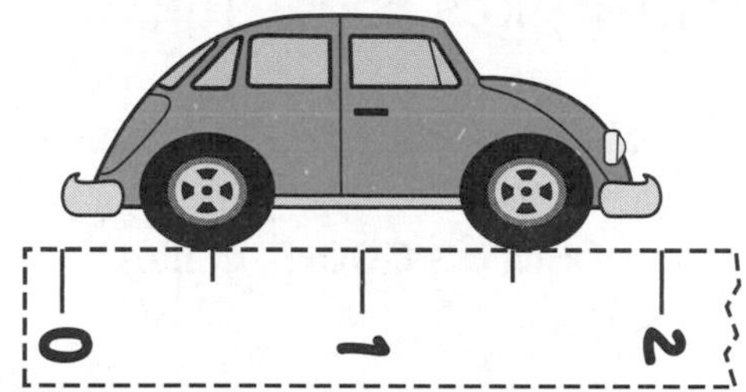

To the nearest inch, the length of this toy car is 2 inches.

Measure the length of each object to the nearest inch.

1. 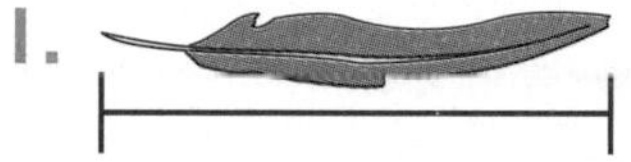 ____________________

2. 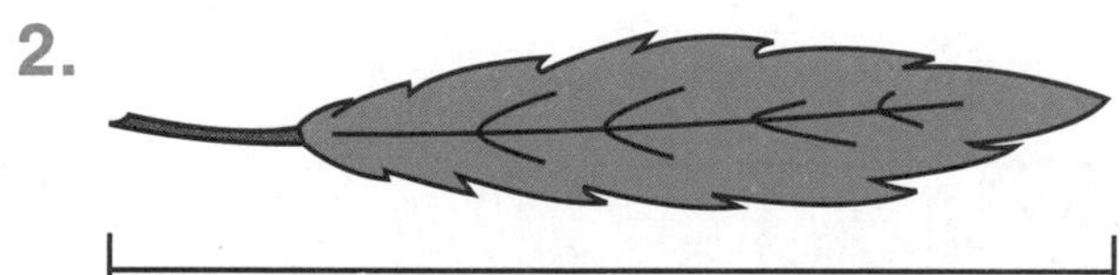 ____________________

3.  ____________________

4. Draw a horizontal line that is 2 in. long.

5. Draw a horizontal line that is 6 in. long.

G–2

Class Activity

Name ______________________________

▶ Estimate and Measure in Inches

6. Describe a part of your hand that measures about 2 in.

____

7. Describe a part of your hand that measures about 1 in.

____

8. Describe a part of your hand that measures about 6 in.

____

Estimate and measure the length of each line segment.

9. ______________________________

Estimated length: ____________

Measured length: ____________

10. ____

Estimated length: ____________

Measured length: ____________

11. Find four classroom objects that you can measure in inches. Estimate and then measure the length of each object to the nearest inch. Complete the table.

Object	Estimated length (in.)	Measured length (in.)

Name ____________________

▶ Make a Yardstick

Directions:

Step 1: Cut along the dashed lines.

Step 2: Place the sections in the correct order.

Step 3: Tape or glue together the sections at the tab.

TAB	TAB	TAB	TAB	TAB	36
5	11	17	23	29	35
4	10	16	22	28	34
3	9	15	21	27	33
2	8	14	20	26	32
1	7	13	19	25	31
0					

G–2 Name ______

Class Activity

Vocabulary
foot (ft)
yard (yd)

▶ Measure in Feet and Yards

Find each length to the nearest **foot (ft).**

12. width of your desk

______

13. length from your knee to your ankle

______

Find each length to the nearest **yard (yd).**

14. height of the classroom door

______

15. length of a bookshelf

______

Measure each length to the nearest foot and to the nearest yard.

16. width of the classroom door

______ ft

______ yd

17. length of the classroom board

______ ft

______ yd

18. What do you notice about the numbers when you measure in yards instead of feet?

______

▶ Select a Unit

Tell the unit you would use to measure the length of each object. Write *inch, foot,* or *yard.*

19. 

______

20. 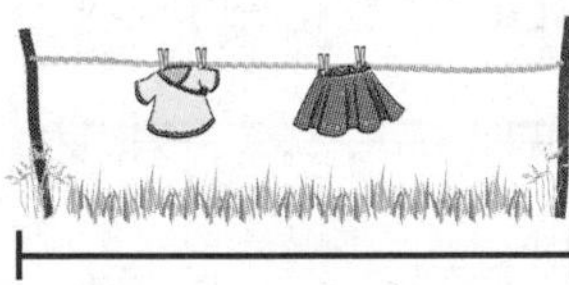

______

21. 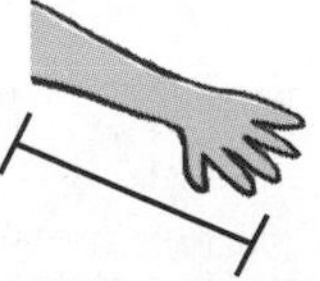

______

22. 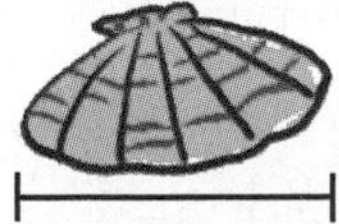

______

G–2

Class Activity

Name ___

▶ Change Units

Customary Units of Length
1 ft = 12 in.
1 yd = 3 ft
1 yd = 36 in.

Complete each table.

23.

Feet	1	2	3	4	5	6
Inches	12	24				

24.

Yards	1	2	3	4	5	6
Feet	3	6				

25.

Yards	1	2	3	4	5	6
Inches	36	72				

26. Fill in the correct number.

2 ft = ______ in. 1 yd = ______ ft 24 in. = ______ ft

4 yd = ______ ft 36 in. = ______ ft 5 ft = ______ in.

Name ______________________

Measure the length of each object to the nearest inch.

1. ________

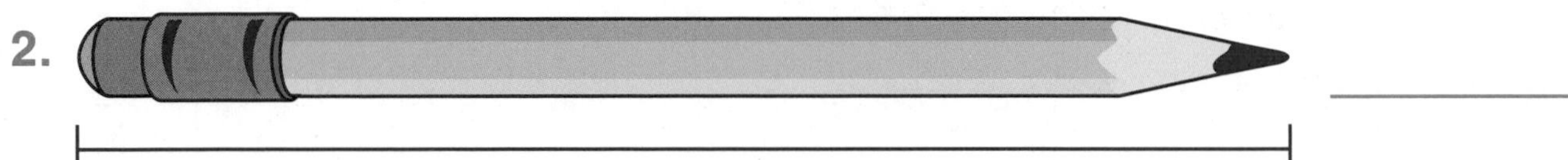

2. ________

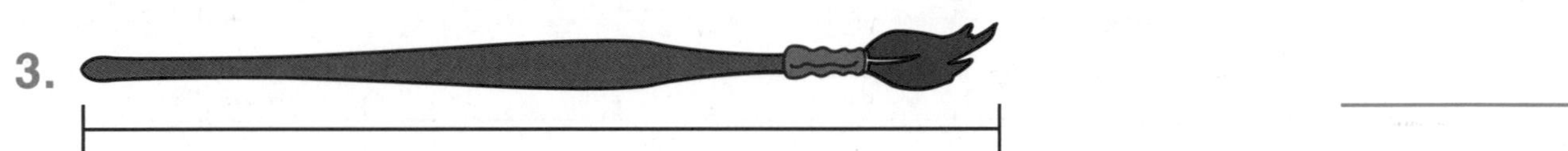

3. ________

Fill in the correct number.

4. 1 yd = ______ in.

5. 1 ft = ______ in.

6. 1 yd = ______ ft

7. 24 in. = ______ ft

8. 9 ft = ______ yd

9. 72 in. = ______ yd

Name ______________________________

10. Extended Response If you measured the length of the classroom board in inches and in yards, which measure would have a larger number? Explain.

____

____

____

____

____

____

Glossary

A

add

●●●● ●●
4 + 2 = 6

addend

5 + 6 = 11
↑ ↑
addends

Adding Up Method (for Subtraction)

144 − 68 76	68 + 2 = 70 70 + 30 = 100 100 + 44 = 144 76

after

98, 99

99 is after 98.

A.M.

The hours between midnight and noon.

angle

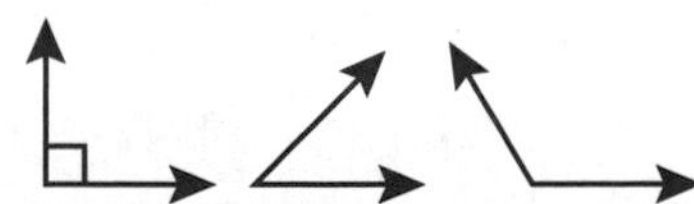

These are angles.

area

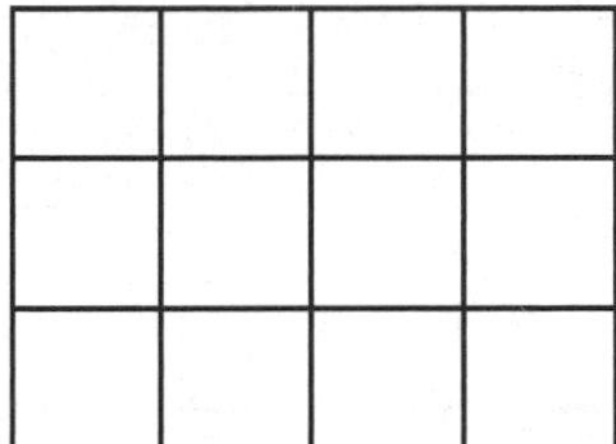

Area = 12 square units

You can find the area of a figure by covering it with square units and counting them.

array

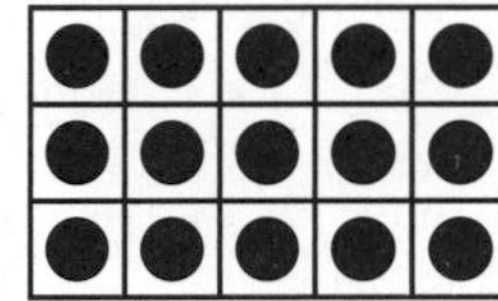

This picture shows a 3 × 5 array.

B

bar graph

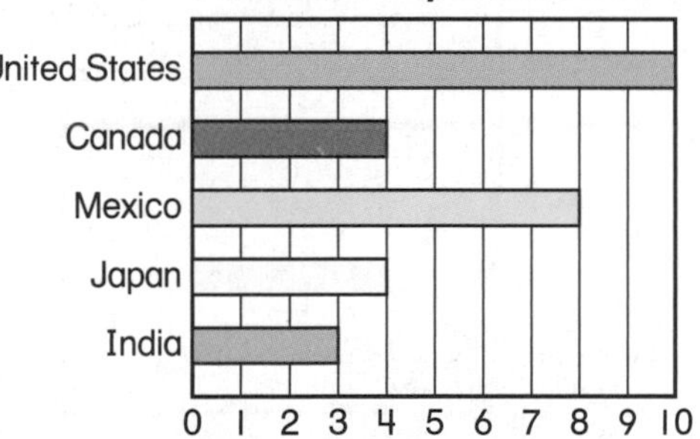

horizontal bar graph

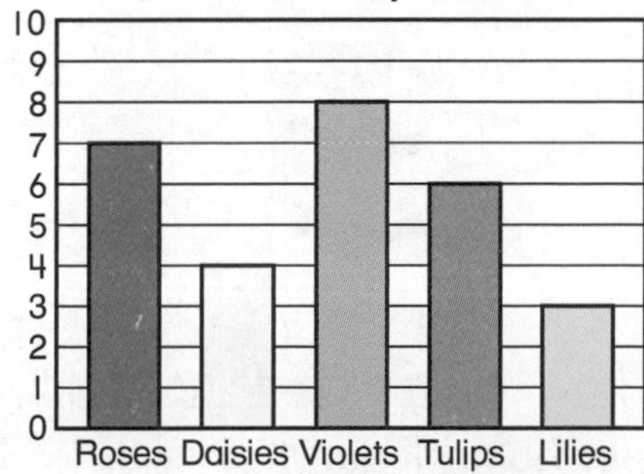

vertical bar graph

before

31, 32

31 is before 32.

between

81, 82, 83

82 is between 81 and 83.

break-apart

You can break apart a larger number to get two smaller amounts called break-aparts.

10

6 4

break-aparts of 10

C

calendar

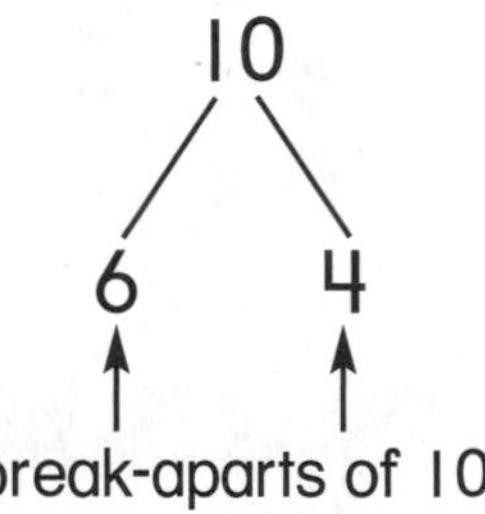

March

February

January

Sun	Mon	Tues	Wed	Thurs	Fri	Sat
1	2	3	4	5	6	7
8	9	10	11	12	13	14
15	16	17	18	19	20	21
22	23	24	25	26	27	28
29	30	31				

capacity

Capacity is how much a container holds. This container holds 1 quart of milk.

cent

front back

1 cent or 1¢ or $0.01

centimeter (cm)

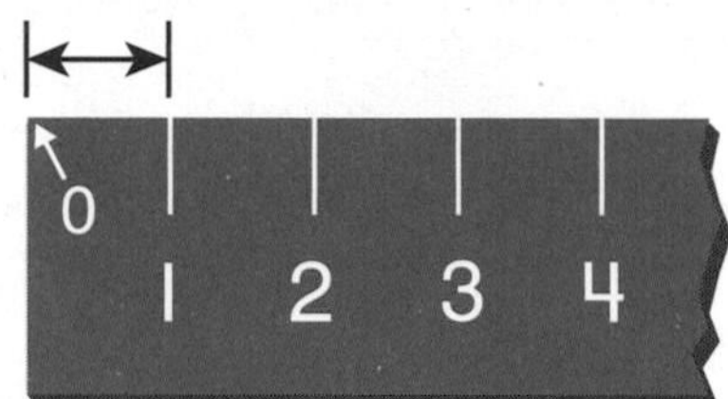

certain

You are certain to choose a black button from the jar.

change minus problem

Sarah had 12 books.
Then she loaned her friend 9 books.
How many books does Sarah have now?

12 − 9 = 3

had loaned now

Any number may be unknown.

change plus problem

Alvin had 9 toy cars.
Then he got 3 more.
How many toy cars does he have now?

9 + 3 = 12

had got now

Any number may be unknown.

circle graph

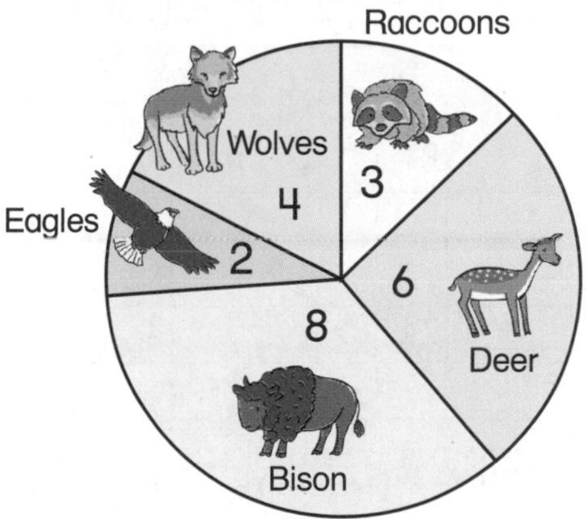

clock

analog clock

digital clock

collection problem

Jason put 8 large plates and 4 small plates on the table. How many plates are on the table altogether?

8 + 4 = 12

large small altogether

comparison problem

Joe has 6 roses. Sasha has 9 roses.
How many more roses does Sasha have than Joe?

6	?
9	

J S

6 + ☐ = 9

9 − 6 = 3

S J

cone

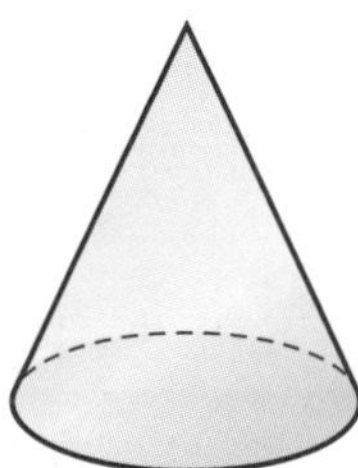

congruent

These are congruent figures.

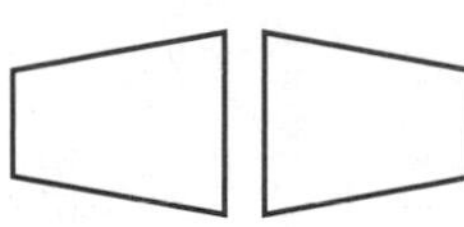

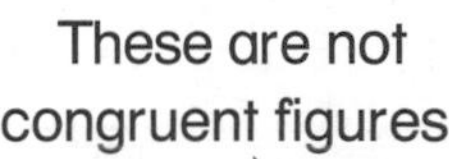
These are not congruent figures.

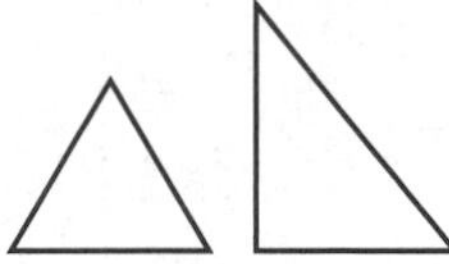

Congruent figures have the same size and shape.

count all

5 + 3 = ☐

1 2 3 4 5 | 6 7 8
● ● ● ● ● | ● ● ●

5 + 3 = 8

count by/count-bys

I can count by 2s.

2, 4, 6, 8, 10, 12, 14, 16, 18, and 20 are 2s count-bys.

count on

5 + 3 = 8

5 + 3 = 8

8 − 5 = 3

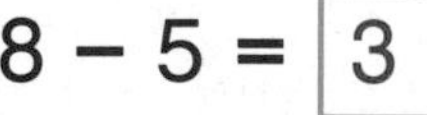

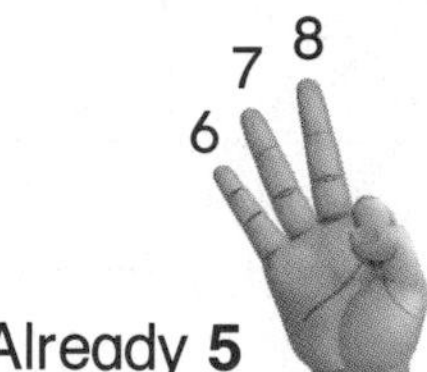

cube

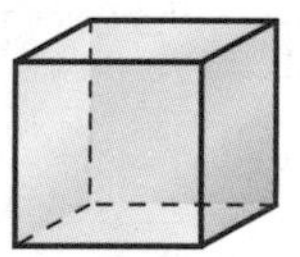

cylinder

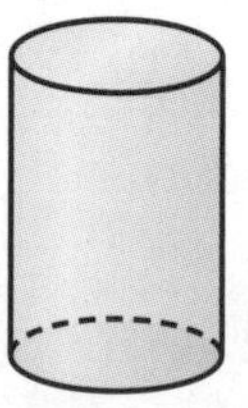

D

data

	Hamsters	Mice
Kendra	5	8
Scott	2	9
Ida	7	3

← data

The data in the table show how many hamsters and how many mice each child has.

day

November

Sun	Mon	Tues	Wed	Thurs	Fri	Sat
	1	2	3	4	5	6
7	8	9	10	11	12	13
14	15	16	17	18	19	20
21	22	23	24	25	26	27
28	39	30				

November has 30 days. Each day has 24 hours.

decade numbers

10, 20, 30, 40, 50, 60, 70, 80, 90

decade partners

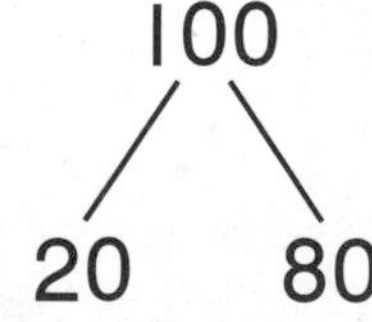

20 and 80 are decade partners of 100.

decimal point

$4.25

↑ decimal point

decimeter (dm)

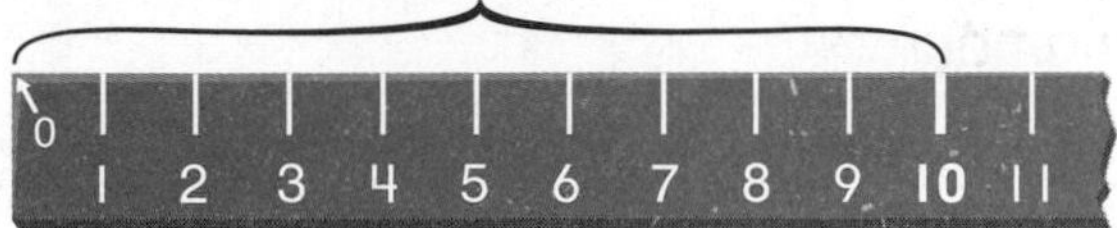

10 centimeters = 1 decimeter
(not drawn to scale)

denominator

$\frac{3}{4}$ ← denominator

The number of equal parts into which the 1 whole is divided.

diagonal

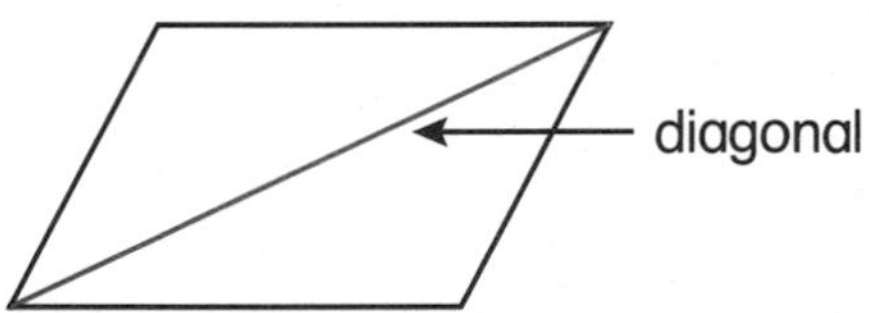

difference

11 − 3 = 8

$$\begin{array}{r} 11 \\ -\ 3 \\ \hline 8 \end{array}$$

difference → 8

digits

0, 1, 2, 3, 4, 5, 6, 7, 8, 9

dime

front

back

10 cents or 10¢ or $0.10

dollar

100 cents or

100¢ or $1.00

front

back

dollar sign

$4.25
↑
dollar sign

doubles

Both addends (or partners) are the same.

4 + 4 = 8

doubles minus 1

7 + 7 = 14, so

7 + 6 = 13, 1 less than 14.

doubles plus 1

6 + 6 = 12, so

6 + 7 = 13, 1 more than 12.

E

edge

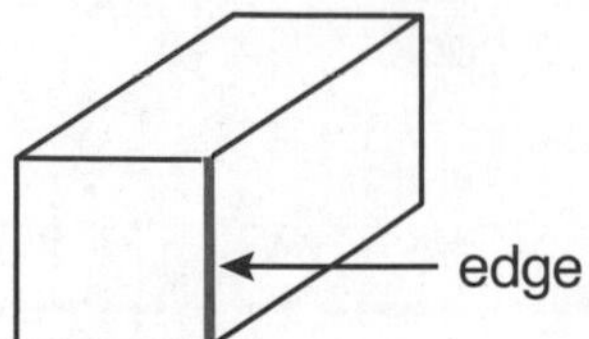

equal shares

Maria

Rachel     

Maria and Rachel have equal shares of pennies.

equal to

$5 + 3 = 8$

5 plus 3 is equal to 8.

equation

$4 + 3 = 7$ $7 = 4 + 3$

$9 - 5 = 4$ $4 + 5 = 8 + 1$

An equation must have an = sign.

equation chain

$3 + 4 = 5 + 2 = 8 - 1 = 7$

estimate

An estimate is a number that is close to an exact amount.

$$\begin{array}{r} 28 \\ +\ 23 \\ \hline \end{array} \;\longrightarrow\; \begin{array}{r} 30 \\ +\ 20 \\ \hline 50 \end{array}$$

You can estimate a sum.

about 10

You can estimate the number of objects in a set.

even number

A number is even if you can make groups of 2 and have none left over.

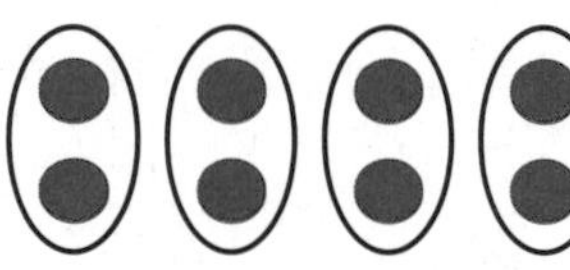

8 is an even number.

exact change

I will pay with 4 dimes and 3 pennies. That is the exact change. I won't get any money back.

Expanded Method (for Addition)

$$\begin{array}{rcrcr} 78 & = & 70 & + & 8 \\ +\ 57 & = & 50 & + & 7 \\ \hline & & 120 & + & 15 = 135 \end{array}$$

Expanded Method (for Subtraction)

$$\begin{array}{rcccc} & & 50 & + & 14 \\ 64 & = & \cancel{60} & + & \cancel{4} \\ -\,28 & = & 20 & + & 8 \\ \hline & & 30 & + & 6 = 36 \end{array}$$

expanded number

283 = 200 + 80 + 3

face

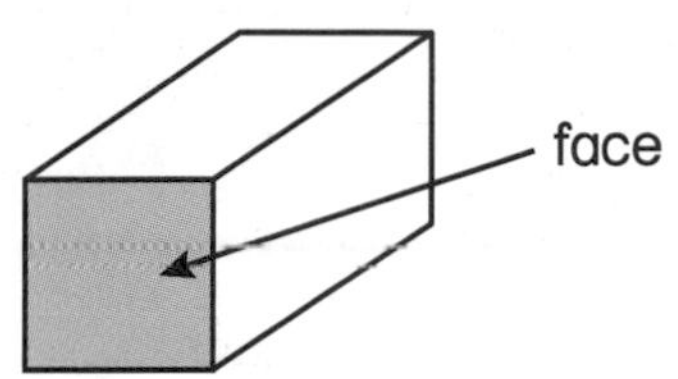

fair shares

fewer

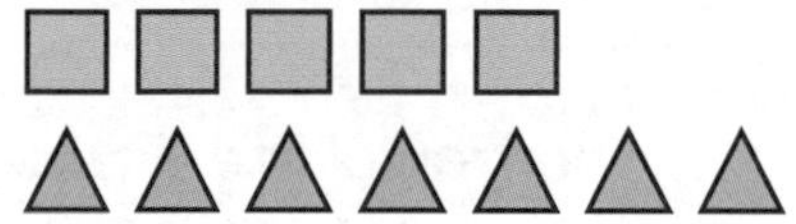

There are fewer □ than △.

flip

You can **flip** a figure over a **horizontal line**.

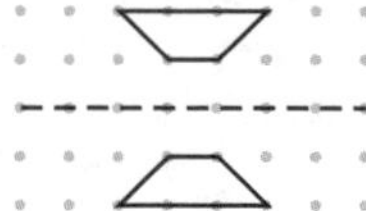

You can **flip** a figure over a **vertical line**.

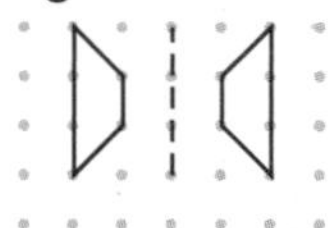

foot (ft)

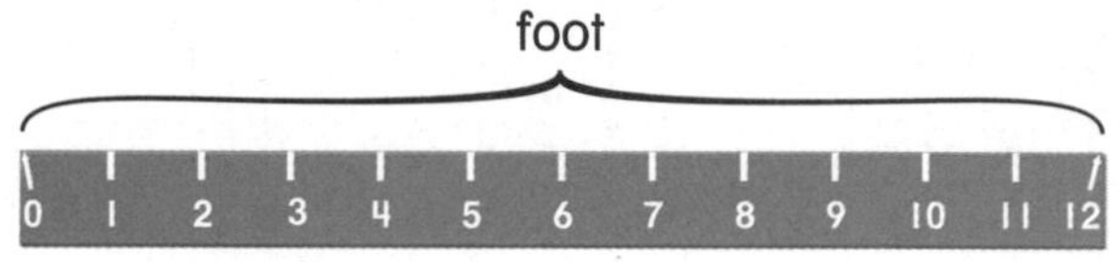

12 inches = 1 foot
(not drawn to scale)

fourth

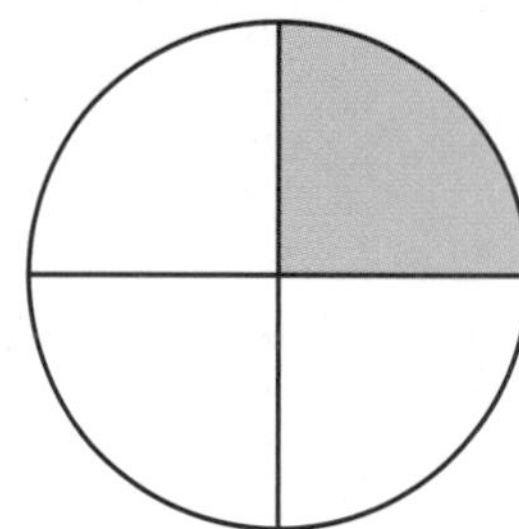

$\frac{1}{4}$ (one fourth) of the circle is shaded.

fraction

$\frac{3}{4}$

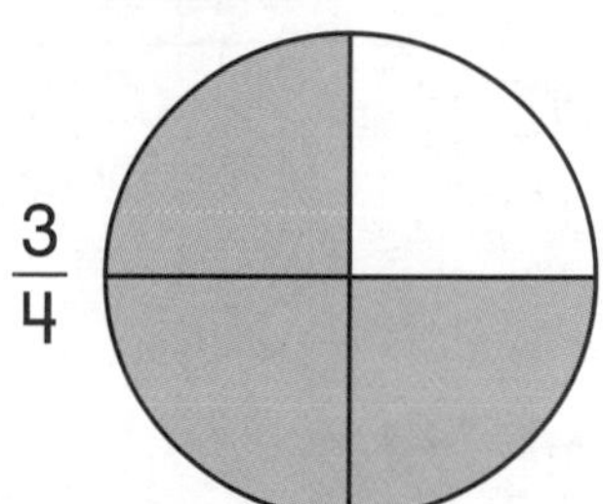

The fraction $\frac{3}{4}$ shows that 3 of 4 equal parts are shaded.

$\frac{3}{4} = \frac{1}{4} + \frac{1}{4} + \frac{1}{4}$

front-end estimation

$$\begin{array}{r} \textcircled{3}4 \\ +\textcircled{1}5 \\ \hline \end{array} \longrightarrow \begin{array}{r} 30 \\ +\ 10 \\ \hline 40 \end{array}$$

function table

Add 3.	
0	3
1	4
2	5
3	6

G

greater than

||| oooo || ooooo

$34 > 25$

34 is greater than 25.

greatest

25   41   63

63 is the greatest number.

group name

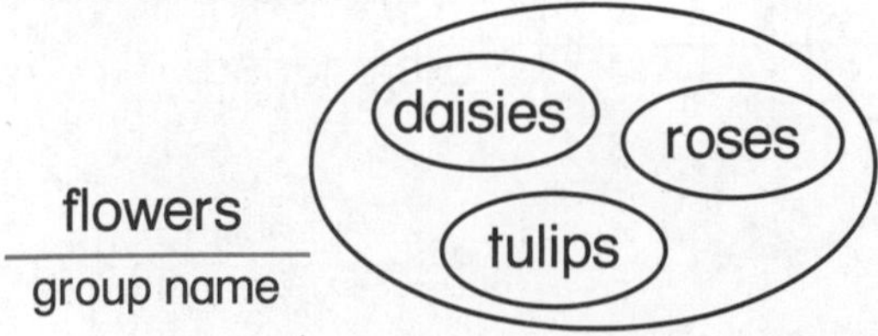

H

half

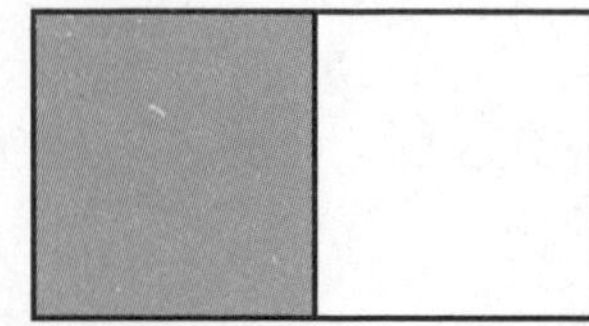

$\frac{1}{2}$ (one half) of the rectangle is shaded.

half-hour

30 minutes = 1 half-hour

hidden information

Heather bought a dozen eggs. She used 7 of them to make breakfast. How many eggs does she have left?

$12 - 7 = \boxed{5}$

The hidden information is that a dozen means 12.

horizontal

$4 + 5 = 9$ ⟷

horizontal form   horizontal line

hour

60 minutes = 1 hour

hour hand

hundreds

3 hundreds

347 has 3 hundreds.

hundreds

I

impossible

It is impossible to choose a white button from this jar.

inch (in.)

1 inch

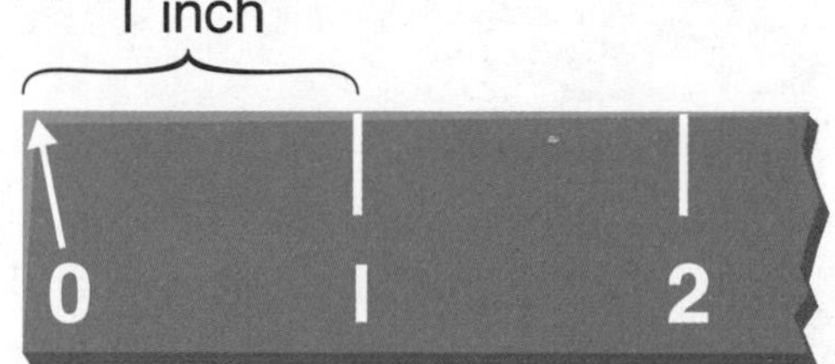

K

key

Apples Bought

Red	
Green	
Yellow	

Key: Each stands for 2 apples.

L

least

14   7   63

7 is the least number.

length

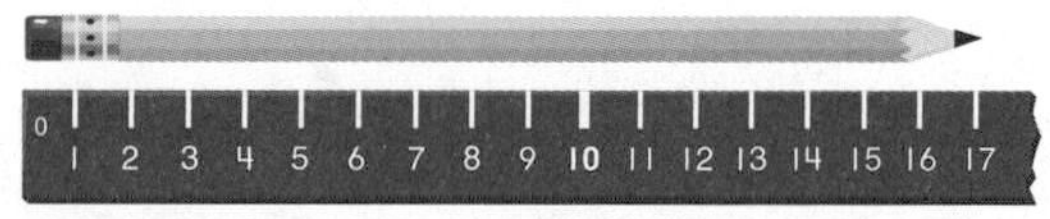

The length of the pencil is about 17 cm.

less likely

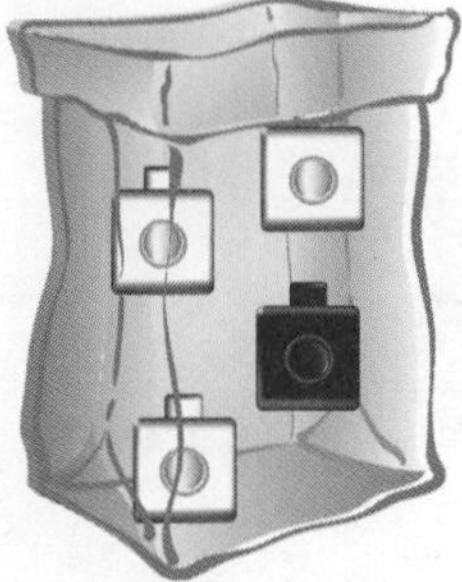

It is less likely that I will choose a black cube than a white cube if I choose a cube without looking.

less than

45 < 46

45 is less than 46.

line

line of symmetry

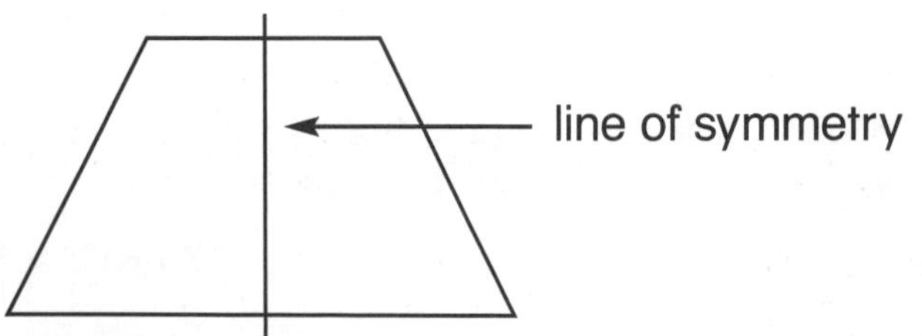

line segment

M

Make a Ten

8 + 6 = ☐

8 •• | ••••

10 + 4 = 14,

so 8 + 6 = 14

make change

Sellers make change when they give back money when a buyer pays too much.

mass

The mass of this bag of salt is 3 kg.

matching drawing

○○○ fewer

○○○○○○○ more

Math Mountain

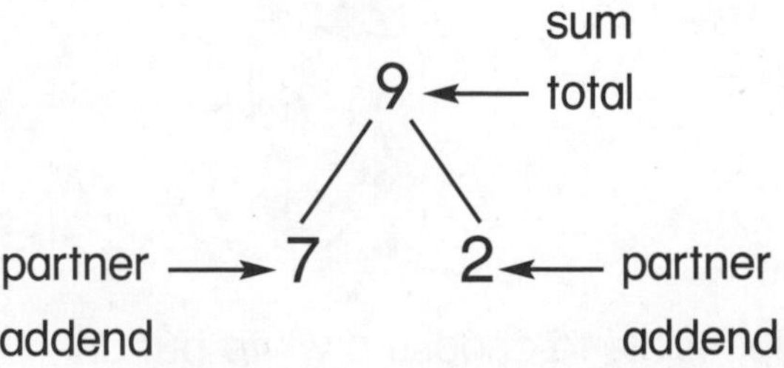

measure

You measure to find the length, weight, mass, capacity, volume, or temperature of an object. You find how many units.

meter(m)

100 centimeters = 1 meter
(not drawn to scale)

midpoint

midpoint

The point exactly halfway between the ends of a line segment is the midpoint.

minus

8 − 3 = 5

$$\begin{array}{r} 8 \\ -\ 3 \\ \hline 5 \end{array}$$

8 minus 3 equals 5.

minute

60 seconds = 1 minute

minute hand

minute hand: points to the minutes

money string

\$1.00 = 25¢ + 25¢ + 25¢ + 10¢ + 10¢ + 5¢

month

June						
Sun	Mon	Tues	Wed	Thurs	Fri	Sat
				1	2	3
4	5	6	7	8	9	10
11	12	13	14	15	16	17
18	19	20	21	22	23	24
25	26	27	28	29	30	

June is the sixth month. There are twelve months in a year.

more

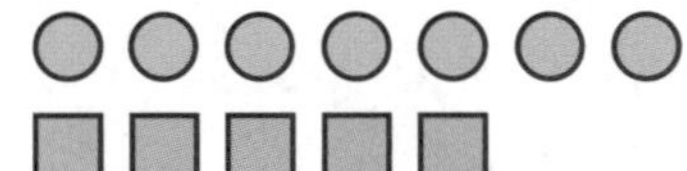

There are more ◯ than ▢.

more likely

It is more likely that I will choose a black button than a white button if I choose a button without looking.

multiply

$3 \times 5 = 15$

5 + 5 + 5
3 fives

mystery addition

$28 + \square = 43$

$43 = \square + 28$

Find the unknown addend.

N

New Groups Above Method

```
  1
  56
+ 28
----
  84
```

6 + 8 = 14
The 1 new ten in 14 goes up to the tens place.

New Groups Below Method

```
  56
+ 28
  1
----
  84
```

6 + 8 = 14
The 1 new ten in 14 goes below in the tens place.

nickel

front

back

5 cents or 5¢ or $0.05

non-standard unit

The length of the pencil is 5 paper clips.

A paper clip is a non-standard unit of length. An inch and a centimeter are standard units of length.

not equal to

$6 + 4 \neq 8$

6 + 4 is not equal to 8.

number line

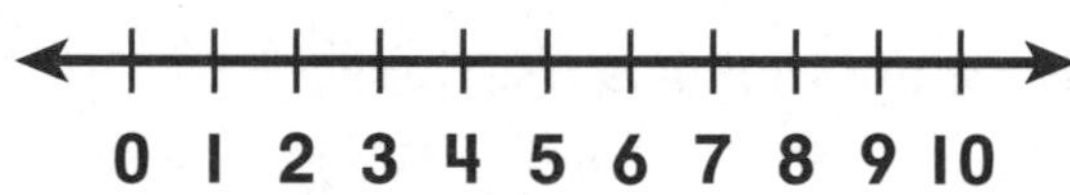

This is a number line.

number path

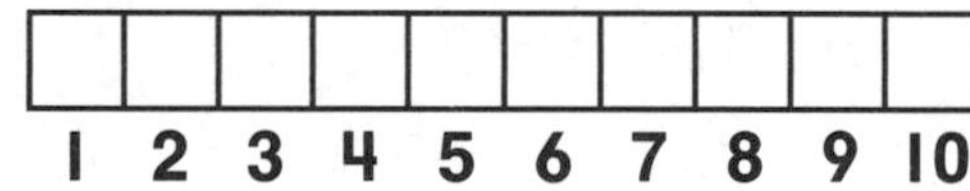

This is a number path.

numerator

$\frac{3}{4}$ ← numerator

$\frac{3}{4} = \frac{1}{4} + \frac{1}{4} + \frac{1}{4}$

The numerator tells how many unit fractions.

O

odd number

A number is odd if you can make groups of 2 and have one left over.

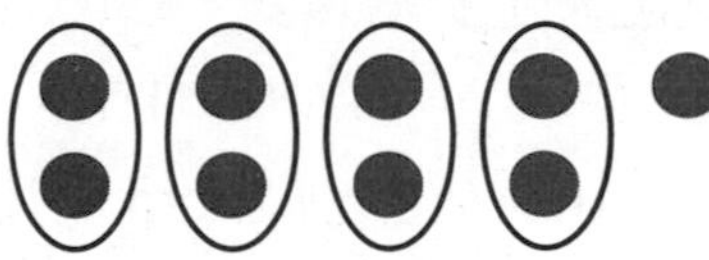

9 is an odd number.

ones

347 has 7 ones.

opposite sides

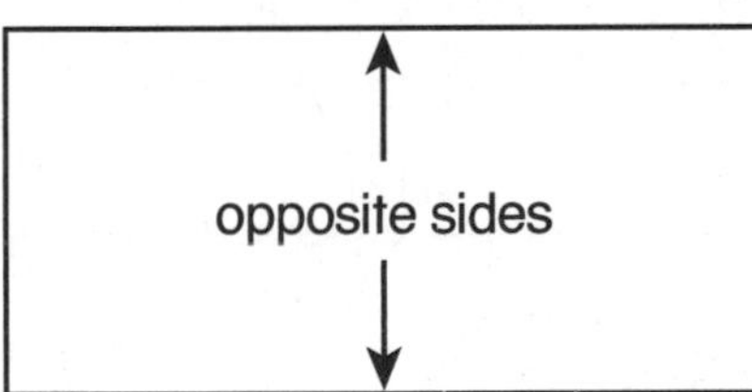

order

The numbers 2, 5, and 6 are in order from least to greatest.

ordinal number

Ordinal numbers name positions.

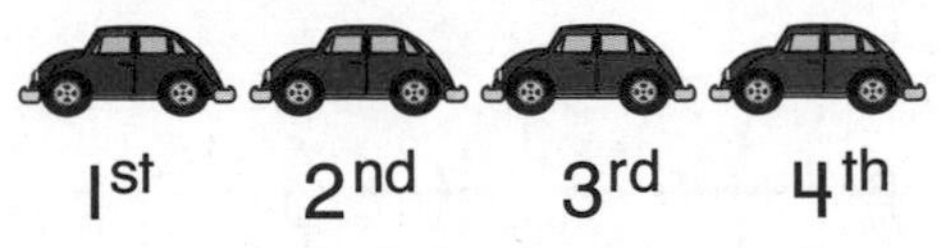

first second third fourth

P

parallel

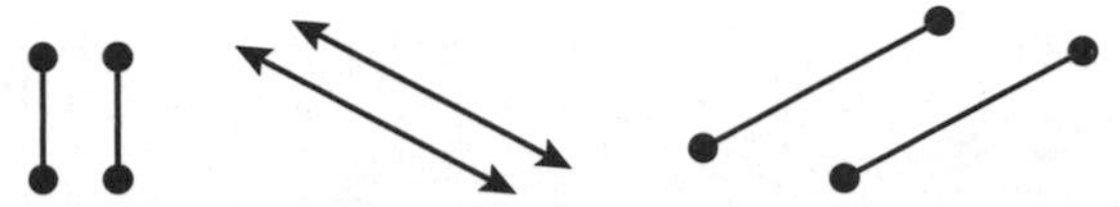

Lines or line segments that are always the same distance apart.

parallelogram

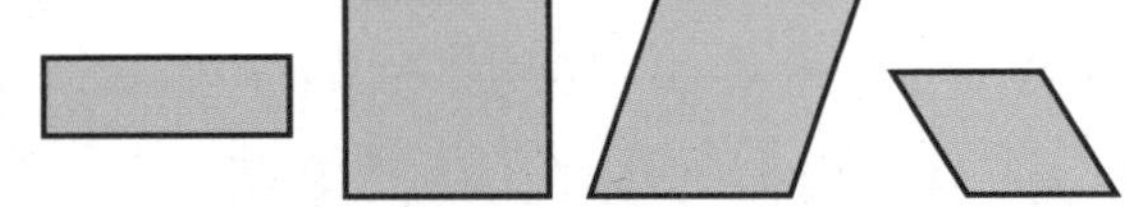

A parallelogram has 2 pairs of parallel sides.

Partner House

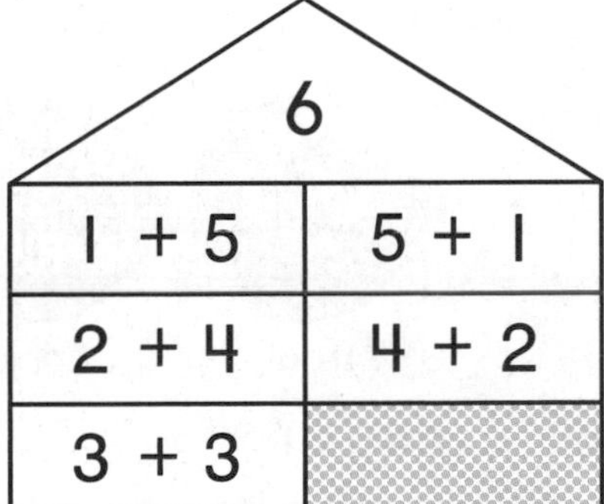

partner lengths

partner lengths of 4 cm

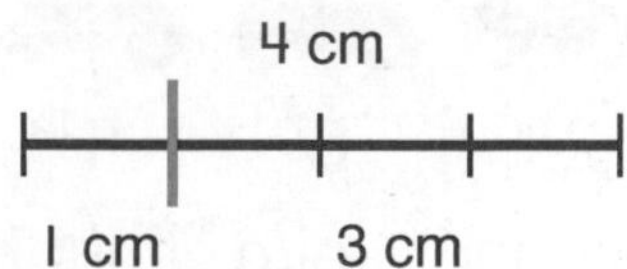

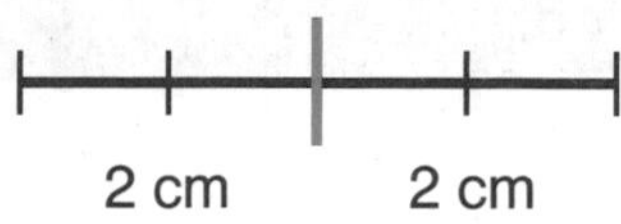

partners

9 + 6 = 15

↑ ↑

partners

addends

pattern

2, 4, 6, 8, 10, 12

These are patterns.

penny

front

back

1 cent or 1¢ or $0.01

perimeter

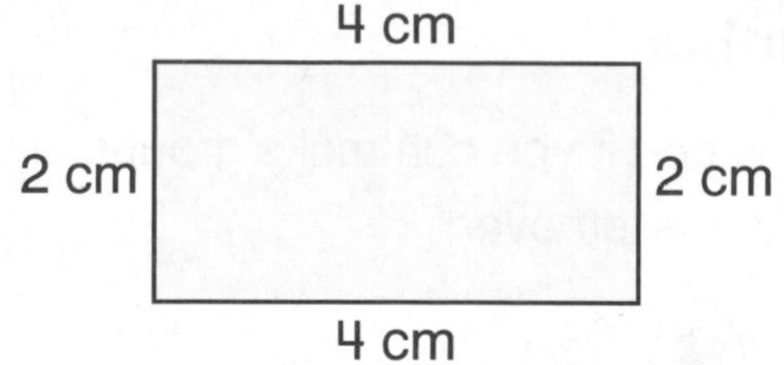

perimeter = 2 cm + 4 cm + 2 cm + 4 cm = 12 cm

Perimeter is the total length of the sides.

pictograph

Apples Bought

Red	🍎 🍎 🍎 🍎
Green	🍎 🍎
Yellow	🍎 🍎

Key: Each 🍎 stands for 2 apples.

picture graph

Flowers	✿ ✿ ✿ ✿ ✿ ✿ ✿
Vases	⚱ ⚱ ⚱ ⚱ ⚱ ⚱ ⚱ ⚱ ⚱

pie graph

Animals at Grasslands Nature Park

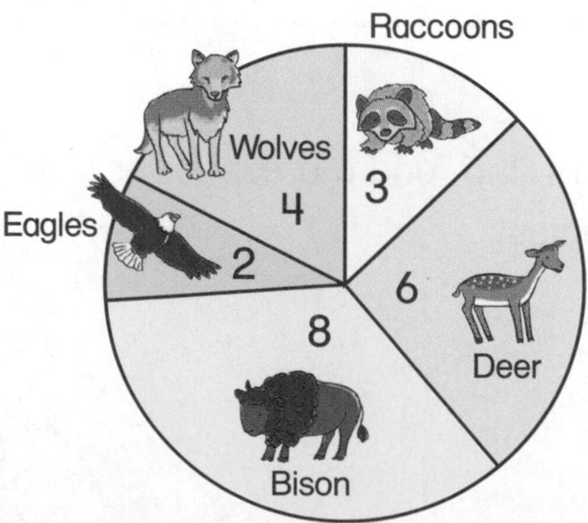

same as a circle graph

plus

3 + 2 = 5

3 plus 2 equals 5.

$$\begin{array}{r} 3 \\ +\ 2 \\ \hline 5 \end{array}$$

P.M.

The hours between noon and midnight.

polygons

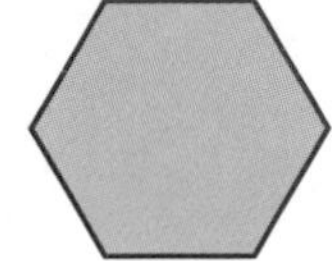

Polygons have sides that are line segments.

possible

It is possible to choose a white button.
It is possible to choose a black button.

predict

I think it will rain tomorrow.

I predict that it will rain tomorrow.

probability

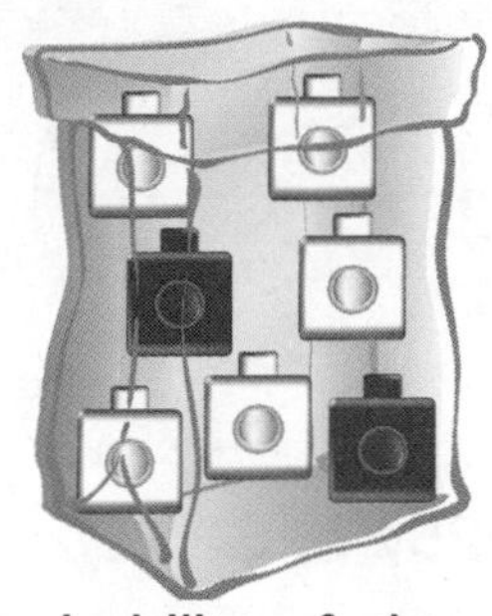

- What is the probability of choosing a white cube?
- It is likely.

Proof Drawing

Proof Drawing

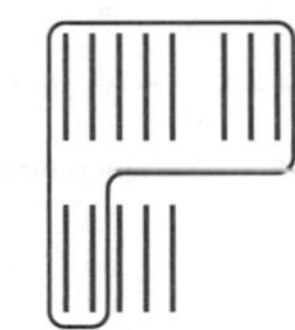
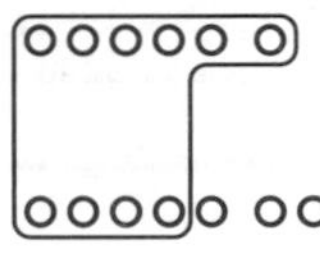

86 + 57 = 143

pyramids

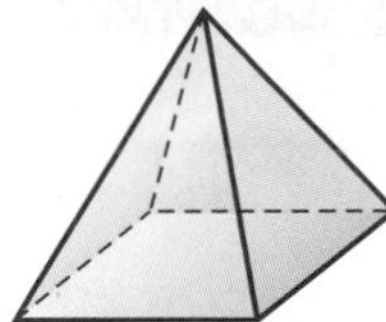
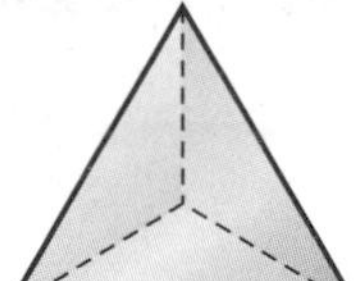

Q

quadrilateral

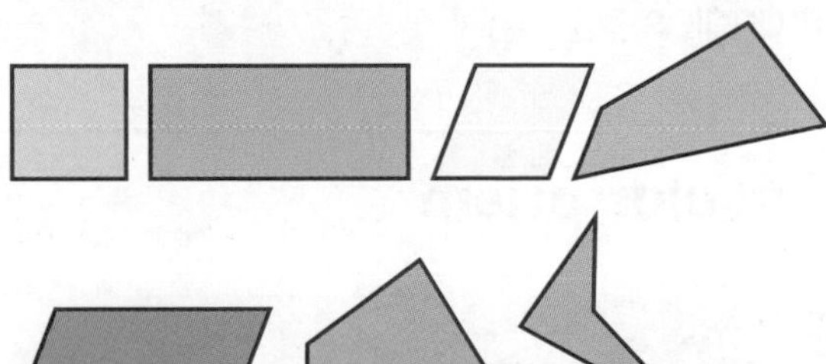

A quadrilateral has 4 sides.

quarter

front back

25 cents or 25¢ or $0.25

Quick Hundreds

347

Quick Hundreds

Quick Tens

162

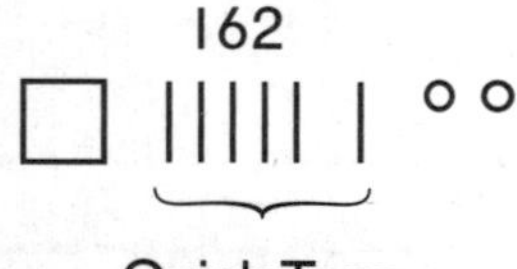

Quick Tens

R

rectangle

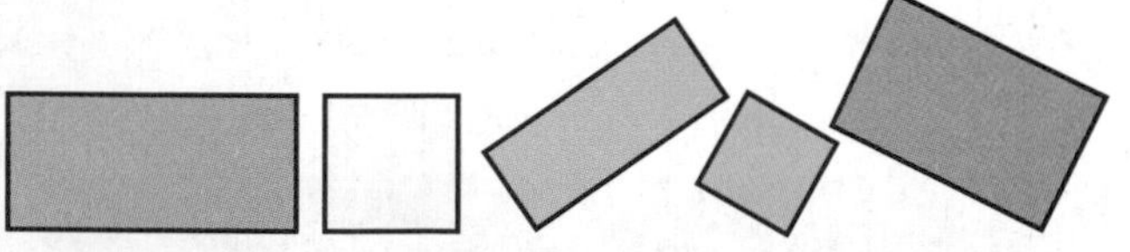

A rectangle has 4 sides and 4 right angles.

rectangular prism

regular polygons

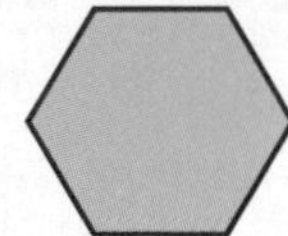

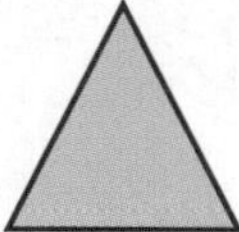

A regular polygon has all sides and all angles equal.

right angle

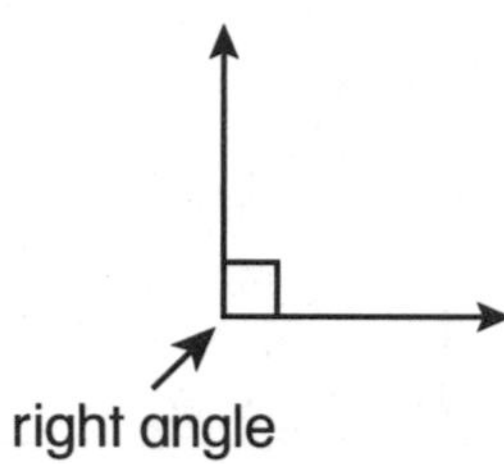

right angle

rotation

You can turn or rotate a figure around a point.

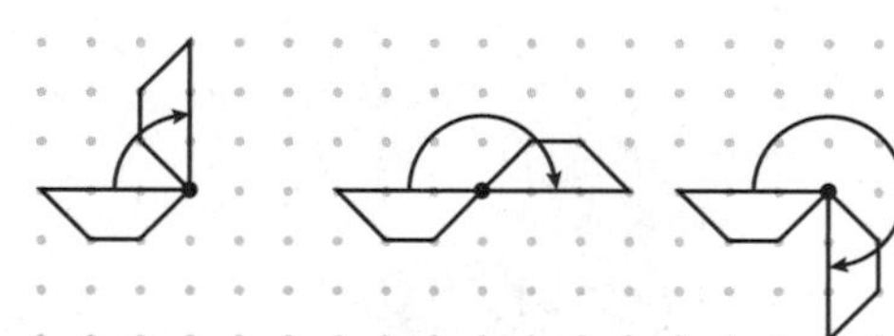

round

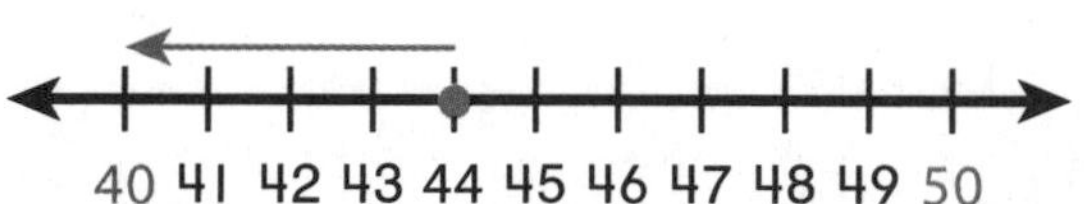

44 is closer to 40 than 50.

44 rounds to 40.

ruler

A ruler is used to measure length.

S

scale

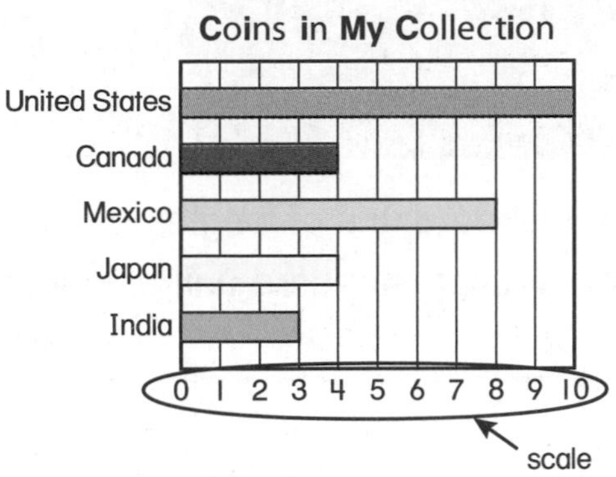

The numbers along the side or the bottom of a graph.

sequence

Sequences follow a pattern.

2, 4, 6, . . .

9, 8, 7, . . .

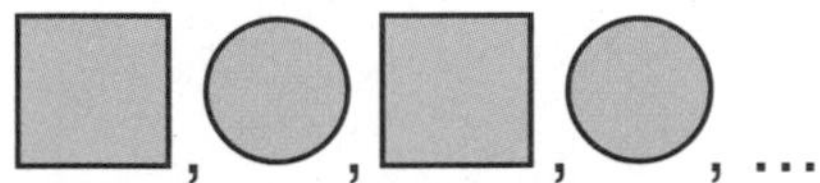

Show All Totals Method

$$\begin{array}{r} 25 \\ +\ 48 \\ \hline 60 \\ 13 \\ \hline 73 \end{array} \qquad \begin{array}{r} 724 \\ +\ 158 \\ \hline 12 \\ 70 \\ 800 \\ \hline 882 \end{array}$$

similar

These figures are similar. These figures are similar. These figures are not similar.

Similar figures always have the same shape and sometimes have the same size.

situation equation

A baker baked 100 loaves of bread. He sold some loaves. There are 73 loaves left. How many loaves of bread did he sell?

100 − □ = 73

situation equation

skip count

skip count by 2s: 2, 4, 6, 8, . . .

skip count by 5s: 5, 10, 15, 20, . . .

slide

You can slide a figure right or left along a straight line.

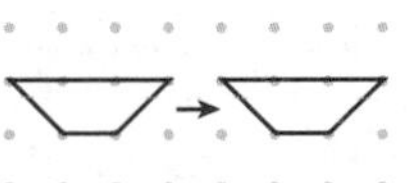

You can slide a figure up or down along a straight line.

solution equation

A baker baked 100 loaves of bread. He sold some loaves. There are 73 loaves left. How many loaves of bread did he sell?

$$\underbrace{100 - 73 = \square}_{\text{solution equation}}$$

standard unit

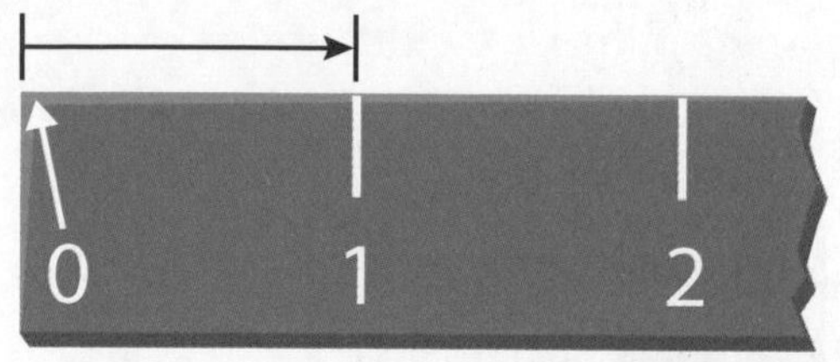

An inch is a standard unit of length.
A paper clip is a non-standard unit of length.

sphere

subtract

●●●●● ●●●

8 − 5 = 3

square

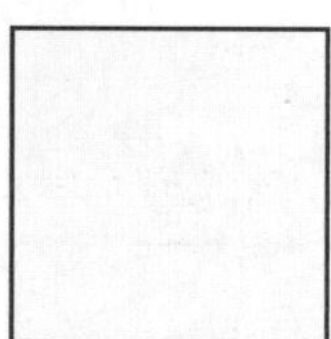

A square has 4 equal sides and 4 right angles.

sum

4 + 3 = 7

$$\begin{array}{r} 4 \\ +\ 3 \\ \hline 7 \end{array}$$

sum → 7

square centimeter

Each side measures 1 centimeter.

1 square centimeter

survey

To collect data by asking people questions.

square unit

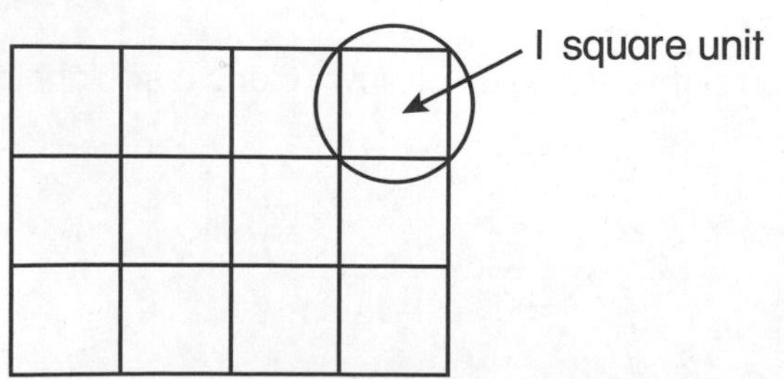

The area of this rectangle is 12 square units.

switch the partners

Show partners in a different order.

6 + 4 = 10 (partners: 6, 4)

4 + 6 = 10 (partners: 4, 6)

symmetry

A figure has symmetry if it can be folded along a line so that the two halves match exactly.

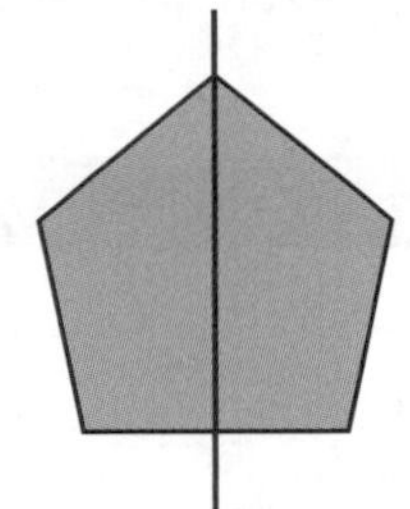

T

table

	Hamsters	Mice
Kendra	5	8
Scott	2	9
Ida	7	3

tally chart

Favorite Color	Tally Marks	Number of Students
red	||||	4
blue	~~||||~~ |	6
yellow	~~||||~~ ||	7

teen number

any number from 11 to 19

11 12 13 14 15 16 17 18 19

temperature

A thermometer measures the temperature.

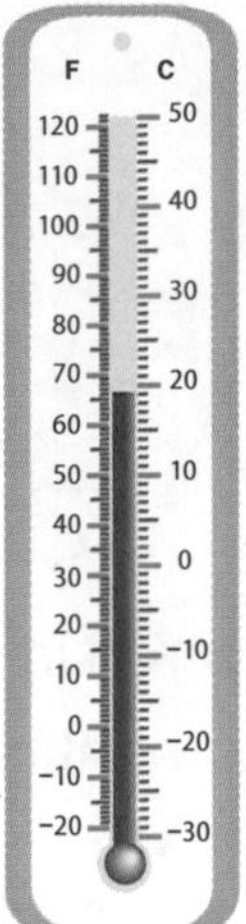

tens

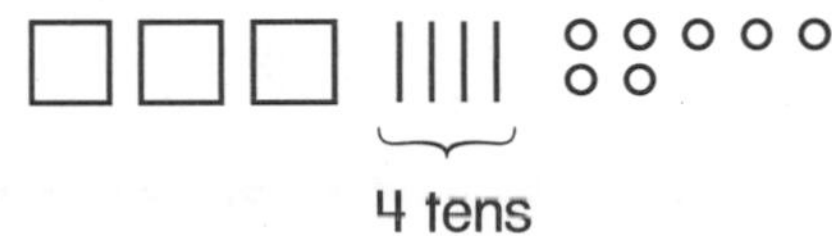

4 tens

347 has 4 tens.

tens

third

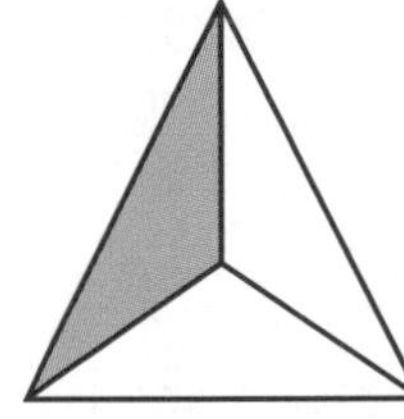

$\frac{1}{3}$ (one third) of the triangle is shaded.

1 of 3 equal parts.

thousand

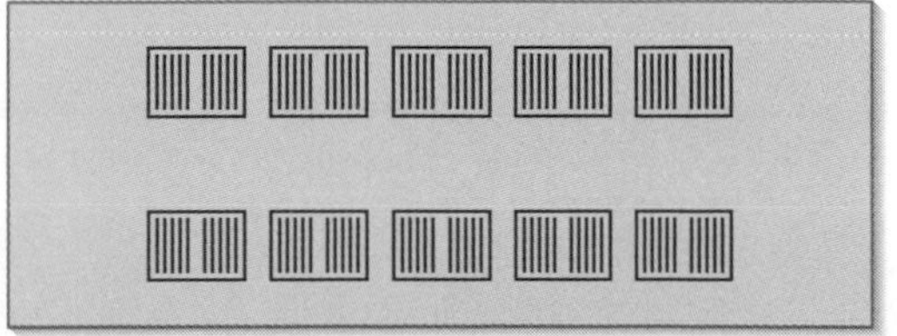

1,000 = ten hundreds

time

January						
Sun	Mon	Tues	Wed	Thurs	Fri	Sat
1	2	3	4	5	6	7
8	9	10	11	12	13	14
15	16	17	18	19	20	21
22	23	24	25	26	27	28
29	30	31				

Time is measured in hours, minutes, seconds, days, weeks, months, and years.

total

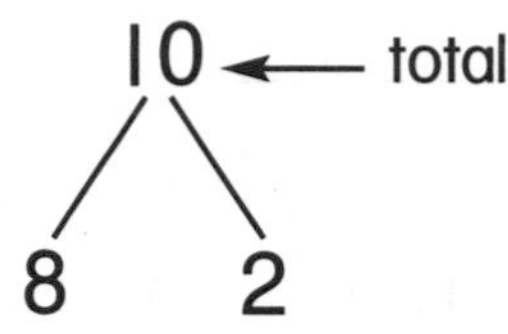

triangle

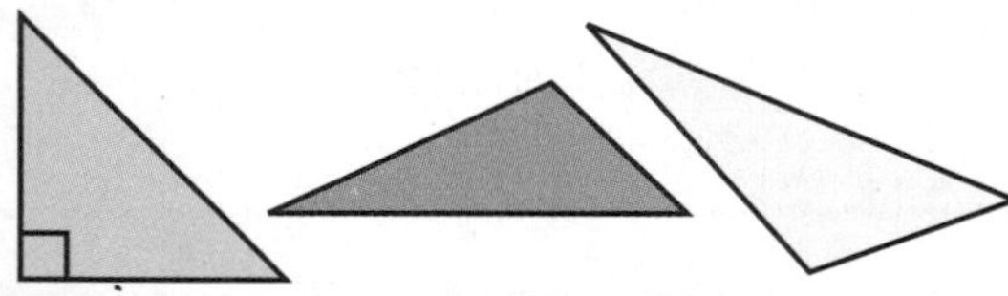

A triangle has 3 sides.

turn

You can **turn** or **rotate** a figure around a point.

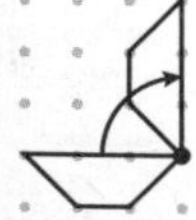

twice

Jeremy 

Michael 

Jeremy has twice as many books as Michael.

U

ungroup

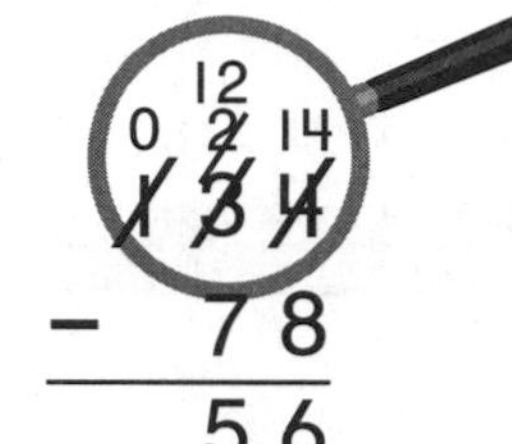

$$\begin{array}{r} 134 \\ -\ 78 \\ \hline 56 \end{array}$$

Ungroup when you need more ones or tens to subtract.

Ungroup First Method

$$\begin{array}{r} 64 \\ -\ 28 \\ \hline \end{array}$$

↑ yes ↑ no

1. Check to see if there are enough tens and ones to subtract.

$$\begin{array}{r} \scriptstyle 5\ 14 \\ \not{6}\,\not{4} \\ -\ 28 \\ \hline \end{array}$$

2. You can get more ones by taking from the tens and putting them in the ones place.

$$\begin{array}{r} \scriptstyle 5\ 14 \\ \not{6}\,\not{4} \\ -\ 28 \\ \hline 36 \end{array}$$

3. Subtract from either right to left or left to right.

unknown

$3 + \square = 9$ — ↑ unknown partner

$3 + 6 = \square$ — ↑ unknown total

V

Venn diagram

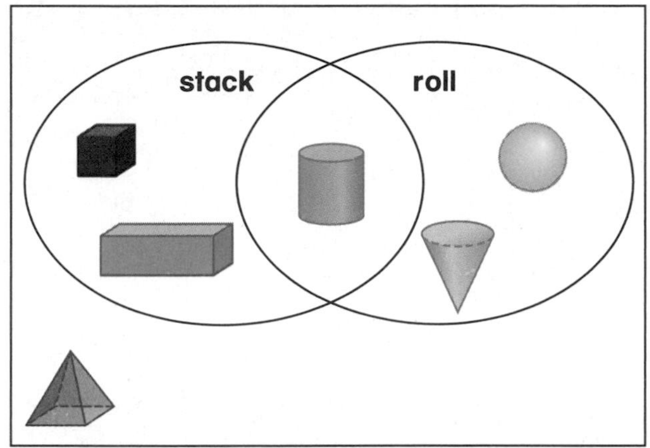

vertex

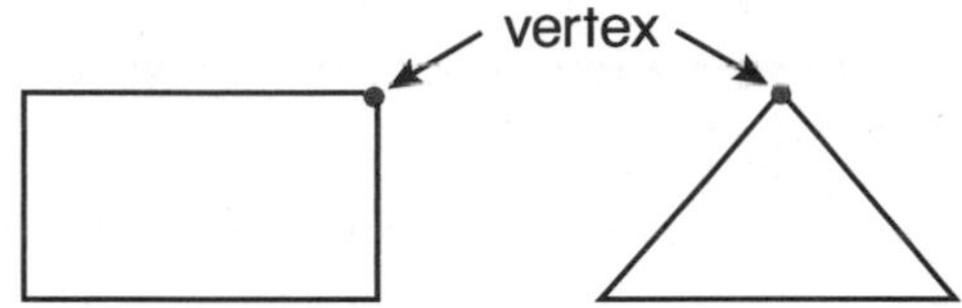

vertical

$$\begin{array}{r} 4 \\ +\,3 \\ \hline 7 \end{array}$$

vertical form — vertical line

view

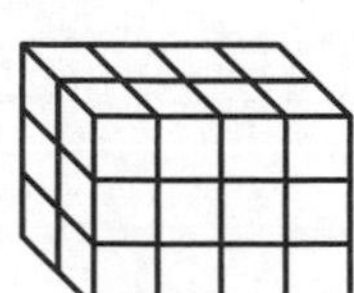

This is the side view of the rectangular prism above.

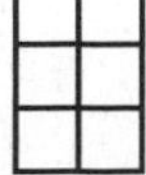

volume

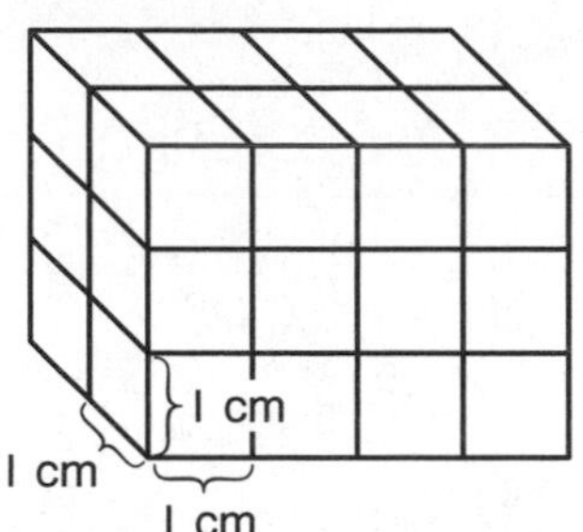

The volume of this rectangular prism is 24 cubic centimeters.

W

weight

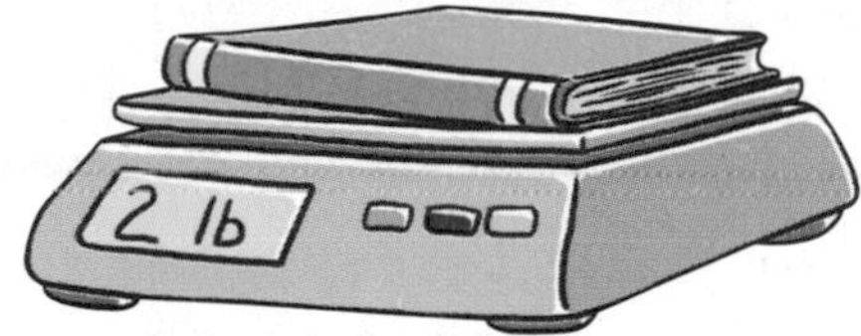

The weight of this book is 2 pounds.

width

width or length
length width

word name

12

twelve ← word name

Y

yard (yd)

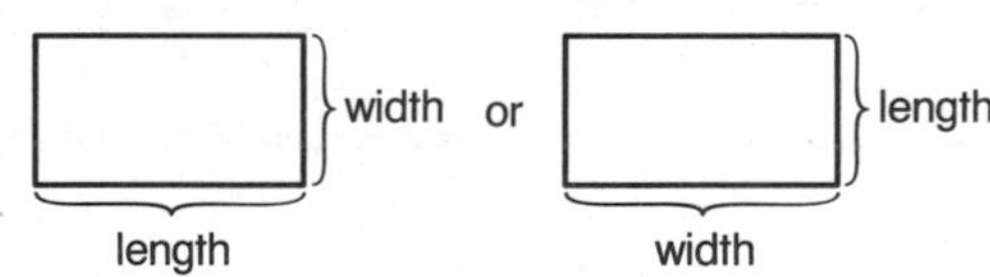

3 feet = 1 yard (not drawn to scale)